Them Damned Pictures

Them Damned Pictures

Explorations in American Political Cartoon Art

by Roger A. Fischer

ARCHON BOOKS

1996

First published 1996 as an Archon Book,
an imprint of The Shoe String Press, Inc.,
North Haven, Connecticut 06473.

Library of Congress Cataloging-in-Publication Data

Fischer, Roger A., 1939–
Them damned pictures : explorations in
American political cartoon art /
Roger A. Fischer.
p. cm.
Includes bibliographical references.
ISBN 0-208-02298-8 (acid-free paper)
1. Caricatures and cartoons—
Political aspects—United States.
2. United States—Politics and government—
19th century—Caricatures and cartoons.
3. United States—Politics and government—
20th century—Caricatures and cartoons.
4. American wit and humor, Pictorial.
I. Title.
NC1425.F57   1995
(741.5)0973—dc20   95-8892

The paper in this publication meets the
minimum requirements of
American National Standard for Information Sciences—
Permanence of Paper for
Printed Library Materials,
ANSI Z39.48—1984.⊗

Book design by Abigail Johnston
Printed in the United States of America

To

Dorothy Jane Fischer

and

Roger A. Fischer, Sr.

[1913–1993]

In memoriam

Contents

Acknowledgments

My labors in finally bringing this volume to fruition were eased by a sabbatical leave during the 1993–94 academic year, for which I thank the University of Minnesota. For support above and beyond the call, I owe debts to my University of Minnesota–Duluth colleagues Craig Grau, Beth Kwapick, Alexis Pogorelskin, Neil Storch, and to my incomparable wife, Susan. Fellow Lincolnologist Frank J. Williams generously supplied me with copies of many recent Lincoln cartoons, as did two anonymous readers who reviewed chapter 8 for journal publication. My colleague Eve Browning Cole saved me embarrassment by calling to my attention that the term *nasty* was already centuries old in the English vernacular when Thomas Nast savaged Boss Tweed, Horace Greeley, and the Irish Catholics. I am indebted to my son Brian for the blurred eyesight and spinal fatigue he incurred while filming for me a slide inventory of Gilded Age political cartoons, a bare fraction of which are reprinted here with his credit. To Sandy Northrop, producer of a pilot PBS documentary film on the history of American political cartooning, I owe many thanks for a boundless creative curiosity that caused me to rethink many mindless platitudes and sharpen my own focus accordingly.

I am indebted to Doug Marlette, the consistently creative if under-appreciated Steve Sack, and other friends in the profession of the "ungentlemanly art" for many insights and kindnesses. My obligation to Draper Hill, *Detroit News* cartoonist and our greatest living expert on Thomas Nast, is an immense one. His willingness to share insights, information,

and sources on a work yet unpublished has epitomized the Webster defi-
nitions of *colleague* and *friend*. Richard S. West, whose knowledge of
American editorial cartooning extends far beyond his special province of
Joseph Keppler, has been uncommonly supportive and helpful. Stephen
J. Whitfield, Max Richter Professor of American Studies at Brandeis Uni-
versity and a good friend of thirty years, served as a cogent guide to
Gilded Age ethnic prejudice.

To Steve I also owe many thanks for introducing me to James
Thorpe III, president of The Shoe String Press. Authors rarely thank their
editors or publishers, usually with good reason. For Jim, however, an
exception must be made. For his enthusiasm for the power of ideas, generosity with his time and incisive intellect, and patience through long
delays while I exorcised demons personal and professional, I owe him
much. Jim's untimely death in 1994 compounds my regret over my delays. I shall miss him. To his partner and widow Diantha, I owe my
thanks for bringing the volume to fruition, and in so doing, exemplifying
the ideal of grace under fire.

No son has been blessed with a finer set of parents. My mother,
Dorothy Jane Fischer, worked for years, sometimes through the blur of
cataract surgeries, to supply me with cutouts of the *Minneapolis Star &
Tribune* cartoons of Steve Sack and syndicated artists. My debts to this
wondrous woman neither begin nor end with her skill with a pair of
scissors. My father, Roger A. Fischer, Sr., died before this volume was
readied for press. I still cannot express in words my debt to him. To both,
I dedicate this volume.

Introduction

Fifteen years ago it was my pleasure to host Doug Marlette, at the time drawing for the *Charlotte Observer*, at a campus forum at the University of Minnesota–Duluth. After the lecture, a young woman asked Doug whether or not his art had ever attained social significance. He paused reflectively, then deadpanned, "Yes. I ended the Vietnam War." Hearty laughter greeted this self-deprecation.

As I have worked through the essays that follow, I have come to appreciate a deeper irony than Doug intended, for had such a boast been proffered by a Thomas Nast or a Joseph Keppler a century ago, it might well have been taken seriously. This change has little to do with genius. I believe that a larger number of gifted cartoonists are now doing better work more consistently than at any time in our history, including that golden age in editorial cartooning dominated by Nast, Keppler, and Bernhard Gillam. They simply get much less respect for their labors. It would be difficult, if not impossible, to imagine disciples in the tens of thousands awaiting in avid anticipation the thump on the doorstep of *Newsday* or the *Los Angeles Times* or the *Dayton Daily News* for their daily dose of Marlette, Paul Conrad, or Mike Peters. An occasional politician might in anger elevate a nettlesome cartoonist to the stature of an enemy of the republic, but Richard Nixon's talk of his "Herblock image" and an "enemies' list" that targeted Conrad revealed much less of Block and Conrad and their art than it did of his own paranoia. Marlette's

Duluth audience knew full well that he had not ended the Vietnam War—Walter Cronkite had!

A century ago there were no Walter Cronkites, no Larry Kings; print journalism suffered no rivals. Despite its dominance, it was still a raw medium, infused with an ebullient, no-holds-barred partisanship that feared factual commentary as a formula for electoral disaster. As Thomas Leonard and others have reminded us, the visual image was still a novelty and graphic symbolism still one of the most potent of political weapons. Thus Nast, Keppler, Gillam, and their contemporaries enjoyed a twofold advantage over their modern-day successors: a media monopoly and free rein for their powers of invention. No modern cartoonist could create from whole cloth an ogre to rival Nast's Tweed. As I argue in my concluding chapter, the key difference is that despite their inspired savaging of Nixon, neither Herblock nor Conrad, nor Marlette, Peters, Pat Oliphant or the whole collective creative output of the cartoonists of the day, defined for Americans the essential Richard Nixon. Nixon defined Nixon.

A century ago, however, as I have tried to detail in my first five chapters, Nast was able to create in Tweed a compelling visual symbol of universal political corruption and urban decadence. Poor Tweed undoubtedly deserved better, as did Nast himself a decade later when the tables were turned and he was caricatured repeatedly as a little monkey scrounging in spittoons for artistic inspiration. During the 1890s the artists of *Puck* and *Judge* were able to create and sustain a mythic archetype of Kansas Populist William Peffer as a demented rustic Rasputin, not because his character or actions warranted such caricature, but because he so strongly looked the part and because an absence of conflicting information allowed such liberties. Similarly, when the cartoonists of the day turned their talents to ethnic caricature for little five-dollar black-and-white filler cartoons for *Puck, Judge, Life, Harper's Weekly,* and other publications, reality became a refugee and the stereotypical bigotry of vaudeville, minstrelsy, and WASP folk wisdom reigned supreme. During a period of burgeoning heterogeneity and diminishing economic opportunity, the damage to traditional American toleration was in all likelihood considerable. The golden age of American political cartooning—the heyday of Nast, Keppler, and Gillam—was one in which ethical integrity warred against partisan and cultural hyperbole and lost, time and time again. Jeff MacNelly's terse dictum that "Many cartoonists would be hired assassins if they couldn't draw" seems far more true of graphic satire a century ago than today.

Although a minority of cartoonists who have written of their craft have sought to sanctify it as a holy quest for truth and justice, the majority of artists have been candid on the lack of linkage between genius and fairness. Academic scholars, with few exceptions—chief among them Leonard, Leo Hershkowitz, and Charles Press—have been traditionally less critical and, at worst, have lauded leading political cartoonists for caricatures embodying higher truths than words can convey. Also with few exceptions, historians of the genre and of American politics in general have been remiss in failing to explore the esential purpose for which cartoons have been drawn, apart from artistic commentary. In most instances they have been created in large part to earn paychecks from employers eager to reap both partisan advantage and revenue derived from friendly patrons and advertisers. I recognize a danger inherent in playing devil's advocate on this theme, for exaggeration and incongruity are the mother's milk of the medium. As P.G. Wodehouse once reminded us in comparing analyses of humor to dissecting a frog: although much is learned, the frog invariably dies. Yet I would argue that there are critical differences between a playful incongruity of graphic exaggeration and downright dishonesty, and between unfettered artistic expression and the more restrictive realm of political economy.

Much more helpful in understanding the medium have been several published analyses of the visual symbolism by which an effective artist establishes rapport with an audience, but even here lacunae exist. The contemporary cartoonist exploits almost unconsciously such mother lodes of popular culture as current motion pictures, television shows, animated cartoons, and the comic strips to pillory political figures or movements. A century ago the prevailing cultural referents would have come from Scripture, Aesop, the classics, or Shakespeare, a theme I explore in chapter 6. Similarly, Uncle Sam, Old Glory, and the successive representations of Miss Liberty have provided cartoonists with symbols universally viewed as those of the American nation, but with the exception of Uncle Sam, the development of these symbols into national icons has not been detailed adequately. My explorations of the evolution of the Statue of Liberty and the posthumous Abraham Lincoln into American symbols in chapters 7 and 8 and of Boss Tweed and Richard Nixon as generic symbols of sleaze in chapter 9 are intended to shed some light on this phenomenon. Throughout, my intent has been to raise questions in need of further scrutiny rather than to provide definitive answers.

I

"Them Damned Pictures"

"Stop them damned pictures," Boss Tweed of Tammany is said to have urged his lieutenants after viewing Thomas Nast's cartoon "Who Stole the People's Money?" [I–1], explaining, "I don't care so much what the papers say about me. My constituents can't read. But, damn it, they can see pictures!"

The story of William "Marcy" Tweed and his bête noir Tom Nast is known to most students of American history, and familiar to every afficionado of the history of American political cartooning. After lightening the pockets of Gotham's grafters and taxpayers of a sum that grew in the telling to $200 million or more, Tweed had taunted critics, "So long as I count the votes, what are you going to do about it?" What Nast did about it, of course, was to produce for *Harper's Weekly* a succession of deadly cartoons pillorying the Tammany kingpin and cohorts Peter "Brains" Sweeny, Richard "Slippery Dick" Connolly, and Mayor A. Oakley Hall. Spurning a Tammany bribe of $500,000 (equivalent to a century's salary) to take a European sabbatical, he tripled *Harper's* circulation with such gems as "The Brains" [I–2] and "Too Thin" [I–3]. He crowned these endeavors with the chilling 1871 election-eve portrayal of a ferocious tiger mauling the fair maiden of republican virtue, "The Tammany Tiger Loose—What Are You Going to Do About It?" [I–4]. The Tweed Ring was dethroned and two years later the Boss himself was sporting prison stripes. He later escaped and sailed to Spain, where a customs clerk identified him from Nast's recent cartoon "Tweedledee and Tildendum" [I–5] and apprehended him. In his bags, it was said, was a complete set of Nast's cartoons of him.[1]

Albert Bigelow Paine's reverent 1904 biography of Nast made this saga its textual centerpiece, and every subsequent volume or essay on

[I–I] Thomas Nast, "Who Stole the People's Money?," Harper's Weekly, August 19, 1871.

Nast, nearly every general volume on political cartooning, and many scholarly studies of Gilded Age political history and urban life pay homage to it. Stephen Hess and Milton Kaplan began their sprightly 1968 volume, *The Ungentlemanly Art*, with Tweed's "Stop them damned pictures," followed by the tale of his undoing by the sustained power of Nast's cartoons. This confrontation is credited by consensus with establishing once and forever a fledgling craft, cartooning, as an enduring presence in American political culture. In its telling is exemplified those salient themes dear to the collective scholarship of the medium, such as it is—the power of the giants of the genre to fuse creative caricature, clever situational transpositions, and honest indignation to arouse the populace and alter for the better the course of human events: the ethical imperative which lifts transitory journalism into transcending art. The pen is indeed mightier than the sword, the picture verily worth ten thousand words. In the jargon of contemporary political historians, the

THE "BRAINS"

THAT ACHIEVED THE TAMMANY VICTORY AT THE ROCHESTER DEMOCRATIC CONVENTION.

[I–2] Thomas Nast, "The Brains," Harper's Weekly, October 21, 1871.

[I–3] Thomas Nast, "Too Thin!," Harper's Weekly, September 30, 1871.

"WE KNOW NOTHING ABOUT THE STOLEN VOUCHERS." "TOO THIN!" "WE ARE INNOCENT."

Opposite: [I–4] Thomas Nast, "The Tammany Tiger Loose," Harper's Weekly, November 11, 1871.

THE TAMMANY TIGER LOOSE.—"What are you going to do about it?"

[I–5] Thomas Nast, "Tweedledee and Tildendum," Harper's Weekly, October 7, 1876.

undoing of Boss Tweed by Thomas Nast stands as a "defining moment"—perhaps *the* defining moment—in the history of American political cartooning. According to Thomas C. Leonard, it marked no less than the genesis of "visual thinking about political power" in American journalism.[2]

As familiar to its students as the fable of young George Washington and the cherry tree was to generations of schoolboy readers of Parson Weems and *McGuffey's Reader*, the tale of Tweed and Nast shares another bond with that of little George, his hatchet, and the doomed sapling. Both legends are based upon compelling myth crafted by outright invention and then embellished by exaggeration.

Tweed, to be sure, was no figment of Nast's imagination. As a state senator, grand sachem of Tammany Hall, and New York City controller, he exercised considerable power over the government and politics of the metropolis during the boom years following Appomattox. Several homes, two motor yachts, a lavish lifestyle, grand donations to the needy, and the marriage of a daughter in a manner befitting an eastern potentate attest to an income substantially greater than the sum of its legitimate parts. An immense, blunt man utterly lacking in self-protective savvy, he served superbly as the personification for Nast and others of what became known as the "Tweed Ring." His transgressions were in no way unique, for the oiling of political machines through kickbacks and "boodle" was more the rule than the exception in American cities of the period; but New York in the midst of a postwar boom in public projects did offer uncommon opportunities. Tweed spent his final years in prison, minus his months as a fugitive, and it was indeed a Nast cartoon by which he was identified in Spain. Toward the end, it was observed, the old Tammany sachem grew more and more to resemble in appearance Nast's caricatures of him.[3]

Many other facets of the saga are simply too good to be true. Strictly speaking, New York was not governed from 1865 to 1871 by a ring of any sort, let alone a "Tweed Ring," but by a rather ordinary political coalition. Connolly, Sweeny, and Hall were neither lieutenants nor intimates of the more plebeian Tweed. A modest share of the monies purportedly gleaned from the coffers and boodlers of New York by Tweed would have made his four-million-dollar bail a matter of petty cash. Instead, he died in prison a pauper. His alleged decree to "stop them damned pictures," which surfaced in an 1875 exposé by Charles Wingate, has never been attributed or authenticated, and seems unlikely at best. A rumor of unknown origin and equally improbable is the existence of a full set of Nast's Tammany cartoons in Tweed's bags when he was arrested in Spain. A *Harper's* profile of Nast in August 1871 made a fleeting reference to a Tammany bribe attempt, but the source of the details, and verbatim dialogue featured in Paine's biography and parroted by subsequent scholars, was almost surely Nast himself more than thirty years after the fact. His 1902 conversations with Paine were the recollections of a proud man so forgotten that he spent his days rebutting references to "the late Thomas Nast."[4]

Nast's major role was to add the impact of visual imagery to the anti-Tammany propaganda of patron Fletcher Harper, *New York Times* editor George Jones, and other avid New York City Republicans who loathed the political culture and style of the Democrats and resented their control of the metropolis. These cartoons played a key role in narrowing the focus from a scatter-gun assault on the Empire State Democracy to a nefarious "Tammany Ring" and then simply the "Tweed Ring," promoting improbably but effectively to the starring role of ogre of ogres the vulnerable and superbly cartoonable sachem. Nast then elevated caricature in American cartooning to a genuine art form and a deadly political weapon by his metamorphosis of Tweed's hulking but benign, even dignified, visage [I–6] into the embodiment of unbridled greed and autocratic arrogance waxing fat upon a helpless citizenry. Simultaneously, he exploited brilliantly two conventions used successfully by cartoonists ever since: a blending of symbolism and animalism with the Tammany tiger, and the running gag rich in sustained irony of his omnipresent "gang of four"—a loutish Tweed, Hibernian plug-uglies "Brains" Sweeny and "Slippery Dick" Connolly, and soulful little owl-eyed "Mare Haul."

Two of Nast's inventions merit special mention. Tweed's vaunted challenge, "So long as I control the votes, what are you going to do about it?"—an idiotic statement for a man dependent upon the allegiance of the poor but immensely proud and independent Irish-Americans and other New York City ethnics—came to life in a June 10, 1871, cartoon collage. A few weeks later it was refined by Nast in "That's What's the Matter" [I–7] to, "As long as I count the votes, what are you going to do about it?" Nast even bestowed on Tweed the middle name of "Marcy,"

*[I-6] William M. Tweed. Library of Congress
photograph; reprinted with permission.*

[I-7] Thomas Nast, "That's What's the Matter," Harper's Weekly,
October 29, 1871.

after the New York Jacksonian William L. Marcy, the purported author of the dictum, "To the victor belong the spoils." Tweed's parents had christened their second son William *Magear* Tweed to carry on his mother's family name, but because of Nast, for generations the Tammany sachem has been identified as William *Marcy* Tweed in virtually every standard dictionary, biographical compendium, and American history textbook, and by such meticulous scholars as Morton Keller. I committed the same sin of slipshod scholarship, and others, in a 1990 essay that formed the foundation of chapter 9.[5]

The crowning result of Nast's handiwork was a compelling and enduring mythic symbol of big-city political sleaze. As Leo Hershkowitz has observed, Tweed's caricatured "ugly features, small beady eyes, huge banana-like nose, vulturish expression and bloated body are the personification of big-city corruption . . . the essence of urban rot, malodorous, the embodiment of all that is evil and cancerous in American municipal and political life," exemplifying the unnatural decadence of the city (New York especially) to a culture still captivated by the vision of an agrarian Eden.[6] As I suggest in chapter 9, this mythic Tweed evoked passions and prejudices so potent that Nast's creation evolved into only one of two generic symbols of political sleaze in the annals of American editorial cartooning. The other was Richard Nixon.

So in company with Edison's electric light and Bell's telephone, Nast's Boss Tweed stands as one of the epic inventions of Gilded Age America. Like the lightbulb and telephone, Nast's Tweed evolved by trial and error, not happenstance. As Thomas Leonard's cogent study makes clear, Nast crafted some thirty anti-Tammany cartoons over two years before he had an inkling of the machine's alleged criminality. Moreover, he encountered great difficulty creating a central graphic symbol of Tammany evil. At first he aped Tammany tradition by drawing the spoilsmen as Indians in war bonnets and buckskin; then he moved to rendering them as unkempt, Neanderthal Irish hooligans. Patently dishonest, this motif failed because the Irish were still only junior partners in the organization and Connolly and Sweeny were the only Hibernians among the notables. Governor John T. Hoffman was of Finnish stock, Mayor Oakley Hall an old-line Yankee, and Tweed Scottish by ancestry. Simultaneously, city parks commissioner and chamberlain Sweeny replaced Hoffman as ringleader. Nast annointed him "Peter the Great, Chief of the Tammany Tribe," whipping his Irish underlings, with his "loyal lieutenant" Tweed at his side. Finally, in the third year of Nast's endeavors, that lieutenant became "Boss Tweed" and took center stage, not because of any factual revelations of wrongdoing but because, as Leonard has noted, the hulking, high-living Tweed was "the easiest man in government to portray as a menace."[7]

If poor Tweed was victimized by physiognomy and a lack of guile, he also suffered from terrible timing. As a perceptive new study by Mark Summers argues, the years spanning Tweed's ascendance to Nast's ogre and his final, pathetic failure to trade testimony for a parole were characterized by public hysteria over political corruption and by the opportunistic efforts of an increasingly independent press to use lurid, often fabricated exposés of such chicanery to attract new readers. In the vanguard of this new journalism were such press lords as George Jones of the *New York Times* and Nast's boss George W. Curtis of *Harper's Weekly*, deploying a new breed of investigative reporter to "fabricate descriptions, invent scandals, or publish long interviews that no lips ever emitted."[8] One need not hold Tweed or such other miscreants as Oakes Ames and "Silver Spoons" Ben Butler as pure as Caesar's wife or Mother Theresa to note the chronology of their careers as singularly unfortunate.

This element of opportunism, plus Nast's invention, artistic sleight-of-hand, and downright political demagoguery, does more to establish his vendetta against Boss Tweed as the "defining moment" of American political cartooning than do all the pious paeans to truth, justice, and the American way proffered by the artist's myriad admirers. First, his systematic destruction of the Tammany kingpin pioneered many artistic and conceptual conventions used for more than a century by exemplars of the "ungentlemanly art." His caricature of Tweed represents as well as any yet created the ability of a cartoonist to "mythologize the world by physiognomizing it," as art historian E. H. Gombrich described the phenomenon.[9] His invention of the Tammany tiger, purportedly inspired by the emblem of Tweed's volunteer fire brigade, did much to establish a venerable cartooning tradition of animal symbolism. His exploitation of the running gag to develop the cumulative impact of sustained ridicule did likewise. He brought this device to fruition a year later in his repeated mocking of Horace Greeley's preachy omniscience, with a series of "What I Know About . . ." volumes protruding from Greeley's pocket

[I–8] Details from Thomas Nast, "Diogenes Has Found the Honest Man," Harper's Weekly, *August 3, 1872, and " 'What Are You Going to Do About It,' If 'Old Honesty' Lets Him Loose Again,"* Harper's Weekly, *August 31, 1872.*

and his obscure running mate, B. Gratz Brown, reduced to a succession of tags hanging from Greeley's frock coat [I–8]. In two years, Nast did more to define the craft of cartooning and demonstrate its potential for political expression than had all his forebears since the cave artists of prehistoric times.

What Thomas Leonard dubbed the dawn of "visual thinking" in American journalism represented to Gerald W. Johnson a "dividing line, the Height of Land, between the old dispensation and the new" in establishing editorial cartooning as a facet of American journalism. Unlike predecessors who created engraved or lithographed prints to sell one by one, Johnson noted that Nast's ongoing participation in collective editorial policy "made him essentially a journalist. His skill, indeed, made him an artist and a fine one, but it was his secondary, not his primary status."[10] It is true that by 1871 Nast enjoyed the stature to assure a measure of freedom from editorial dictatorship and that his minor disagreements with editor G.W. Curtis became a regular feature of life at *Harper's*, but Johnson's point is useful. When of a mind, Nast contributed the power of his art to an overall *Harper's* editorial effort, not to a purely personal expression of his opinions. Moreover, because he was the first celebrated American artist to draw for a mass-circulation weekly sold mainly by subscription, Nast was the first to be afforded the luxury of a continuing audience for which to develop sustained themes. Ever since, cartoon artists have continued his struggle for creative freedom from editorial interference. Still, *Chicago Tribune* immortal John McCutcheon best defined the essence of cartooning as journalism when he wrote that a "cartoonist's role is to produce the same thing in drawing as the editorial writer does in writing. The cartoon is a tool in the editorial arsenal. It must not work against a newspaper's single editorial purpose."[11]

Second, Nast's Tammany crusade demonstrated convincingly the most sacred article of faith among editorial cartoonists and their admirers: the power of the medium to punish wrongdoing and facilitate reform. We do not know if Nast's efforts were responsible for the 1871 defeat of Tammany, or if the result would have been the same if Nast had never drawn a single Tweed cartoon or, for that matter, had championed the Boss. We do know, however, that the circulation of *Harper's Weekly* tripled that year and that no innovations in format, editorial policy, or added features were responsible. Because most of this growth took place outside the metropolis, it is possible that Nast's role was not so much exerting influence on the New York electorate as it was elevating a local politico into an enduring symbol of civic venality. That this symbol has been identified through the ages as William *Marcy* Tweed, renowned for his arrogant challenge, "What are you going to do about it?," suggests a power that cannot be measured in vote probabilities alone.

We also know that these Nast cartoons had an enormous impact on at least one New Yorker, Tweed himself. Whether or not he ever declaimed his desire to "stop them damned pictures" or lugged to Spain a set of the cartoons in which he starred, he did author in 1870 a a tax levy to finance public and Catholic parochial schools that contained a bitter attack on "an artist encouraged to send forth in a paper that calls itself a 'Journal of Civilization' pictures vulgar and blasphemous, for the purpose of arousing the prejudices of the community against a wrong which exists only in their imagination."[12] Here, too, Nast and Tweed were trendsetters, for several subsequent targets of cartoonists' satire have responded with lawsuits or legislation to outlaw political cartoons altogether. Richard Nixon as vice president cancelled his *Washington Post* subscription because of Herb Block's cartoons. As a 1960 presidential candidate he softened his attacks on John Kennedy because, he said, "I have to erase the Herblock image first." As president he put *Los Angeles Times* artist Paul Conrad on his infamous "enemies list." So Tweed's tirade over Nast's "pictures vulgar and blasphemous" may have begun a long tradition, unscientific but hardly invalid, of judging the impact of a cartoon by the angry bellow of its victim.[13]

It is impossible to ascertain precisely *how* a cartoon achieves its impact, although Nast's 1871 Tammany cartoons provide some clues. Although the scholarly volumes exult in such lofty pronouncements as "a great cartoon fuses memorable art and idea, each reinforcing the other," leading cartoonists view the phenomenon more simply. *Palm Beach Post* artist Don Wright has stated, "Impact is what makes a cartoon good and, in order to have impact, I'm not sure that you should be all that subtle." Bill Watterson has observed, "The editorial cartoon is a blunt instrument. It has power, but little finesse." In his perceptive analysis of Nast's effectiveness in *The Political Cartoon*, Charles Press stressed the shock value of raw emotional impact:

> The Nast cartoon is great because of the emotional impact of its presentation. It continuously goes beyond the bounds of good taste and conventional manners. Nast is like the man who rings your bell and, when you open the door, runs in shouting insults at you and throwing rocks and mud at you and your wife and on your front-hall walls. Your reaction is that what excites him must be a grievous wrong you somehow unwittingly committed.

As Gerald W. Johnson once noted, a cartoon "shall produce its main effect in the first ten seconds, for ordinarily it will not be given an eleventh second."[14]

Although an implicit premise in much of the literature on cartoon art is that an effective cartoon is one that wins converts through its power of persuasion, many masters of the medium disagree. Pat Oliphant has argued that cartoons do not change minds, but at best precipitate thought and dialogue. According to Watterson, "People do not turn to cartoonists to learn what to think. Rather, they turn to cartoonists to be confronted with an opinion—one that could just as easily be unpalatable as palatable."[15]

From the little we do know about the psychology of political behavior, it is likely that those cartoons most effective as propaganda have tended not to confront and to challenge but rather to reinforce and build on a priori beliefs, values, and prejudices. Andrew Jackson and William Henry Harrison as frontier farmer–warriors and Abraham Lincoln as the "railsplitter of the West" were served superbly by images of rustic virtue and primal vigor conforming so well to the popular mythic ideal of the western wilderness, just as John Quincy Adams in 1828 and Martin Van Buren in 1840 fell victim to outlandish smear campaigns, mainly because as small, balding men of ideas, they epitomized the effete East and Europe. The 1964 LBJ countdown television ads, and Roger Ailes's masterful 1968 Nixon media campaign and 1988 Willie Horton spot, became the stuff of Madison Avenue legend. They were successful not because they inspired the millions to behold Barry Goldwater, Hubert Humphrey, and Michael Dukakis in alarming new lights, but because they built upon existing fears that Goldwater was a reckless war-hawk and that Humphrey and Dukakis were both "soft on crime" and pandering to minority ghetto voters.[16]

This phenomenon helps to explain the extraordinary effectiveness of Nast's Tammany cartoons. He drew many cartoons over his quarter-century with *Harper's* that succeeded primarily on the strength of the shock value of immediate impact, but few of his 1871 efforts did so. His delightful and untypically economical "The Brains" stands as an exception, as does his "Tammany Tiger Loose," lauded by Paine in his *Thomas Nast* as "a pictorial projectile so terrific in its power . . . that ring rule and plunder the world over shall never cease to hear the echo of its fall." His transformation of Catholic prelates into grotesque crocodiles in "The American River Ganges" was arguably the most powerful graphic image Nast ever drew. For the most part, however, his 1871 Tammany handiwork attained celebrity and then immortality less for immediate impact than for the creation of a Tweed caricature that uncannily reinforced every salient American Protestant prejudice against the metropolis, its ruling clique, and its unnatural, un-American political culture of urban

machines and ethnic coalitions. These Nast cartoons may well have pro-
voked some sober second thought and prompted a few New Yorkers
to change their votes, but their primary hold on the American political
imagination was not their iconoclasm, but their comforting conformity
to mainstream prejudices older than the republic.

Finally, these 1871 Nast cartoons provide insights into a longstanding quarrel among cartoonists and scholars as to the link between
cartooning greatness and ethical integrity. What Allan Nevins characterized as "a rough fidelity to fact"—with Nast's undoing of Tweed put
forth as a crowning example—is commonly noted as an essential for
greatness. Former *Minneapolis Star & Tribune* artist Scott Long has as-
serted that the editorial cartoon is "the most effective way of telling the
truth." *Richmond News-Leader* cartoonist Bob Gorrell has argued that
the alteration of a viewer's perceptions through falsehoods constitutes a
corruption of the professional canon:

> We, like those we accuse, allow our power and its use to become
> ends in itself, neglecting our proper purpose of enlightening the pub-
> lic in favor of toying with our pictorial armament. Self-proclaimed
> protectors of truth, we become irresponsible dispensers of falsehood.

Others invoke not only truth but a higher artistic truth, above the ethical
parameters of the printed word. To Gerald W. Johnson, because a cartoonist "works with line, not with language, he escapes the bondage of
words and thus has a more direct approach to truth than does the editorial writer." To Charles Press, a successful cartoon "presents an underlying truth—one more true than the facts themselves."[17]

Dissenting artists have argued that truth, or even fairness in seeking
truth, have little or nothing to do with effective cartooning. *Dayton
Daily News* artist Mike Peters once stated, "Cartooning is not a fair art.
You can never treat anyone justly," adding that "most cartoonists like
me—who like to attack—are like loaded guns." *Louisville Courier-Journal* mainstay Hugh Haynie has defined the cartoon as "an offensive
thing," and Bill Mauldin has characterized his calling as "a destructive
art," insisting that the proper function of cartoonists is not to act as
"pontificators, or molders of thought," but rather as gadflies who "circle
and stab, circle and stab." Jules Feiffer has voiced a belief that "outside
of basic intelligence, there is nothing more important to a good political

cartoonist than ill will." Bill Watterson has argued that the cartoonist's role in our political process "is not so much to instruct his audience, or illuminate the Truth, as it is to simply take an honest stand and present it vehemently enough so that it must be confronted." *Chicago Tribune* artist Jeff MacNelly once quipped, "Many cartoonists would be hired assassins if they couldn't draw."[18]

Nast was clearly in the camp of the assassins. It is not that his composite portrayal of Tweed and his cohorts was deliberately dishonest, for it echoed faithfully the extravagant charges leveled by George Jones and other architects of the Tweed legend. On the whole, his Tammany cartoons probably passed, if barely and with a D−, the acid test of integrity posited by Charles Press, that "the aroma of genuine sentiment seems to be floating about in the air somewhere, instead of the more pungent stink of false emotion or false political morality covered with cheap perfume." A few Nast Tammany cartoons in particular, however, reek with this noxious stench: those linking Tweed and Tammany to the protests of New York's Catholics against mandatory Protestant religious indoctrination in the city's public schools. They include one of the most powerful pieces he ever drew, arguably the most vicious cartoon ever created by an American artist, "The American River Ganges" [I–9]. His transformation of bishops' miters into reptilian jaws to turn the clerics into Hibernian crocodiles slithering ashore to devour helpless Protestant children provides an unparalleled example of his genius for caricature and animalism. None of his other Tammany cartoons—surely not "Tammany Tiger Loose," based as it was upon a well-known canvas by Jean-Léon Gérôme—rivals it in macabre impact. Richard Samuel West has observed that "Ganges" still "glows red, like some molten rock, radioactive with a hundred-year-old fire that we can get close to and still feel the heat." It also provides an unparalleled example of ethical bankruptcy transformed into superb cartoon art.[19]

Born and raised Catholic in Bavaria (a fact seemingly missed, or fudged, by every Nast scholar other than Press and Draper Hill), Nast became an avid anti-Catholic. Apologists have proffered as explanations incidents of intolerance in the Landau parish church of his boyhood, the secular tenor of liberal European nationalism, and the Protestant political culture of the Radical Republicanism he married into and embraced with the zeal of a convert. Others have admitted that Nast was a bigot, pure

THE AMERICAN-RIVER GANGES.

and simple. Whatever its root causes, Nast's anti-Catholicism found expression in several cartoons savaging the doctrine of papal infallibility and Vatican repression of secular scientific inquiry. Linked to this bias was a loathing for Irish-Americans that bordered on the pathological and cannot be explained away by the ennobling intellectual tenets of European liberalism or American Radical Republicanism. However, the possibility that he was pandering to the baser prejudices of his employers cannot be dismissed altogether. Avid anti-Catholic xenophobes, James and Fletcher Harper had in 1836, on behalf of a small New York printer, published and disbursed royalties for Maria Monk's *Awful Disclosures*, probably the most reprehensible hate literature ever produced in the United States. In 1844 James had won the New York mayoralty as a "Know-Nothing" nativist and had served as a founding father of the militantly xenophobic Order of United Americans. In all probability, it was neither religious zeal nor political purity that infused Nast's cartoons on this theme with such fierce intensity, but rather Tammany's role in Irish-Catholic political empowerment in New York City.[20]

Ironically, James Harper's 1844 campaign had been aided by the vote and volunteer labors of a young Bill Tweed. A quarter-century later, however, this Scottish-American Protestant was particularly vulnerable to nativist wrath. More than any Tammany Catholic, he had emerged as the city's most committed champion of Irish-Catholic interests. During the 1869–70 legislative session in Albany, Senator Tweed had authored and guided to passage a funding bill—including his tirade against Nast's "pictures vulgar and blasphemous"—which provided a sizeable appropriation for New York's Catholic parochial schools. The measure prompted Nast and Fletcher Harper to sound the alarm of a Vatican conspiracy to destroy the American public schools in its diabolical quest for world domination. Nast's focus shifted from general Vatican-bashing to the more principled theme of the separation of church and state, featuring ecclesiastical leaders and their Hibernian minions in the American church and Tammany wantonly assaulting the hallowed ramparts of the First Amendment [I–10]. In "The American River Ganges," Nast blended

Opposite: [I–9] Thomas Nast, "The American River Ganges," Harper's Weekly, September 30, 1871.

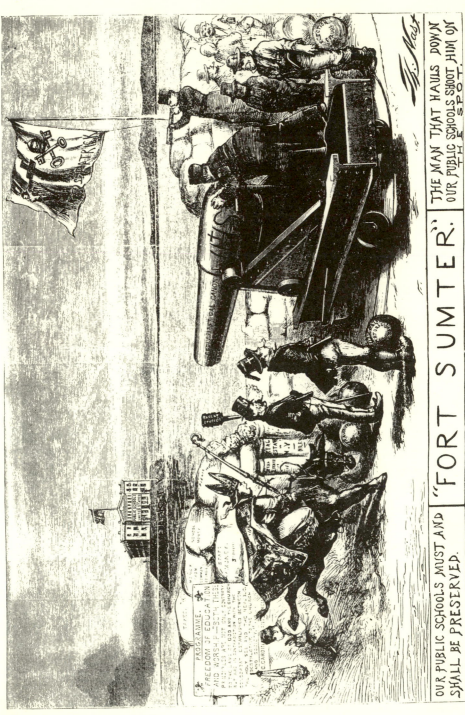

"FORT SUMTER."

OUR PUBLIC SCHOOLS MUST AND SHALL BE PRESERVED.

THE MAN THAT HAULS DOWN OUR PUBLIC SCHOOLS SHOOT HIM ON THE SPOT.

neatly his two ruling passions of 1871, featuring Tammany Hall in the background and Tweed and his cohorts leering from a bluff as the crocodile clerics slither ashore to feast upon praying cherubs and a plucky young teacher armed only with the Holy Bible.

Papal infallibility and authoritarianism, and public aid to private schools, are clearly topics on which Nast and other dissenters from Catholic dogma cannot be faulted for impassioned protests. But when he shifted to the theme of separation of church and state, Nast entered the domain of sheer demagoguery. For a generation a devoutly Protestant agency, the Public School Society, had controlled city public schools and their curricula, subjecting Catholic students to daily religious instruction featuring readings from the King James Bible, the singing of Protestant hymns and recitation of Protestant prayers, and textbook references to "deceitful Catholics" and to Rome as an agency of murder and torture. Led by Bishop John Hughes, the Catholics mounted a campaign in 1840 to purge religious instruction from the curricula and to replace the Public School Society with a secular agency to accomplish the separation of church and state.

A secular board was established by state law in 1842, but it was packed with nativist Protestant militants who decreed the King James Bible a nonsectarian textbook! In 1852 a Protestant teacher in Oswego, New York, became a hero for beating a Catholic boy severely for refusing to read from it, and until the Civil War this offense led to routine expulsion from city schools. Faced with no plausible alternative, Catholics began establishing parochial schools that immigrant families could scarcely afford, and sought tax monies to fund them, as they already paid taxes for public schools they could not use.[21] To portray this initiative in "Ganges" as a Vatican–Tammany plot to subvert the Constitution and destroy American public schools speaks volumes about the freedom of art from the shackles of ethics.

The same could be said of the only other Nast cartoon known to have used his powerful device of the Hibernian prelate transformed into a predatory crocodile [I–11]. Pairing this beast with a "Mormon

Opposite: [I–10] Thomas Nast, "Fort Sumter," Harper's Weekly, September 19, 1870.

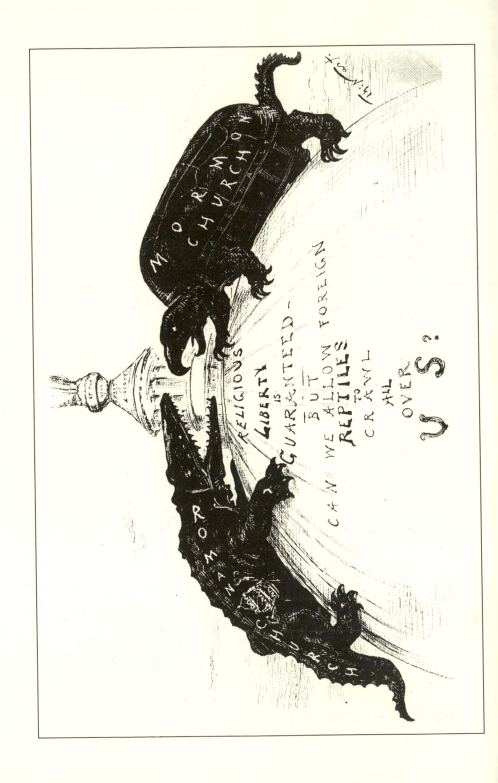

Church" snapping turtle crawling up the Capitol dome made for fine artistic counterpoint. Nast's inclusion of Mormons as "foreign reptiles," however, defied common sense as well as elementary fairness, for of all major American religious denominations during the period, only the Church of Jesus Christ of Latter-Day Saints could boast a uniquely New World pedigree.[22] Again, Nast attempted to stake out the civic high ground with the Capitol dome and a rhetorical nod to First Amendment guarantees of religious liberty, but the message of "Religious Liberty Is Guaranteed" is clear: "foreign" heresies such as Mormonism and Catholicism were beyond the pale of safeguards fashioned by the framers of the Bill of Rights. Probably drawn during the early 1890s, while such nativist organizations as the American Protective Association were reviving the worst excesses of "Know-Nothing" xenophobia, this cartoon is not known to have been published.[23]

Printable or not, this convocation of reptiles embodied the salient characteristics of the memorable Nast cartoons drawn at the peak of his power: vivid, inventive artistic imagery (the turtle's "Tabernacle" shell in particular); reinforcement at both the surface and deeper mythic levels of pervasive prejudices and majority values; and (perhaps most telling), a mean intensity rooted in malevolence to produce an immediate impact. Thomas Nast was not a nice man; had the adjective "nasty" not been six centuries old already, it might have been coined to characterize him and his artwork. He was, however, an intuitive genius whose tantrums against Tammany and Rome essentially defined the profession of political cartooning for the Kepplers, Herblocks, Mauldins, and Oliphants who followed.

Opposite: [I–11] Thomas Nast, "Religious Liberty Is Guaranteed . . . ," original drawing on scratchboard, Library of Congress archives.

II

Mugwump's
Monkey

Despite the extraordinary political celebrity achieved by Thomas Nast and, on occasion, by cartoonists after Nast, almost never have any of them been exploited as characters in the cartoons of rival artists. This protocol of politeness is difficult to reconcile with a profession mandating a modicum of meanness, an insensitivity toward targets, and a healthy ego—a calling notorious for petty jealousies and intense rivalries among its greatest talents.[1] During the heyday of Nast and Joseph Keppler of *Puck*, an era of intensely partisan personal journalism, such powerful publishers and editors as Charles A. Dana, James Gordon Bennett, Whitelaw Reid, Joseph Pulitzer, and *Harper's* George W. Curtis were pilloried in cartoons as commonly as presidents and party leaders, but rarely were cartoonists so treated by their peers. A major exception occurred in 1884, however, when the mighty Nast was caricatured in a long series of uncommonly venomous cartoons in the Republican humor weekly *The Judge* and in other GOP publications as a result of his defection from Republican party ranks to support Democrat Grover Cleveland over James G. Blaine for the presidency.

To be sure, Nast provided a tempting target for rival artists. His acerbic personality earned him few friends within the cartooning fraternity. Although a willingness, often unto glee, to lampoon a target unmercifully and often unfairly had become a hallmark of the profession, it was Nast who had elevated graphic assassination to an art, and Nast who continued to straddle the thin line between commentary and downright defamation. His celebrity fed jealousies. During the Civil War, Lincoln had anointed Nast the Union's premier recruiting sergeant; of his own 1868 presidential victory, Ulysses Grant had said, "Two things elected me, the sword of Sheridan and the pencil of Thomas Nast." At the peak of his popularity, *Harper's* paid Nast a president's salary simply not to take his work elsewhere, and from his art and lecture tours he earned in a year what rival cartoonists dreamed of pocketing over a career. Public men ambitious for success showered flattery and lavish dinners upon Nast to elicit his blessing or blunt his wrath, establishing him as the only American editorial cartoonist in the history of the profession to reign as a major political powerbroker in his own right. Such uncommon celebrity made him, his distinct style, and his ideological passion uniquely prime for parody.[2]

Before 1884, however, such gibes were rare, often as not rather good-natured, and limited almost exclusively to the pages of Joseph Keppler's *Puck*. Nast starred as a *Harper's Weekly* chicken in *Puck*'s "A Stir in the Roost," the front cover of the journal's March 14, 1877, English-language edition; represented *Harper's* in Keppler's January 1, 1879, cast-of-dozens "*Puck*'s New Years Reception;" and appeared cavorting in the surf at Coney Island with Keppler in the August 6, 1879, centerfold "Puck's Picnic." Each was lighthearted and devoid of criticism. The back cover of the June 4, 1879, *Puck* featured James A. Wales's "Puck Sends His Compliments to Mr. Nast Once More!" [II–1], a wry black-and-white parody of Nast's artistic style, affinity for symbolism and strident broadsides ("Yellow Fever Must and Shall Be Put Down"), and interminible captions resembling "a chapter from the Patent-Office reports" in his less disciplined, more formulaic cartoons. Wales, who knew and apparently disliked Nast from a stint as an underling at *Harper's*, struck again on September 29, 1880, with "Shirking the Feat" [II–2], which portrayed Nast on a *Harper's* rocking horse refusing to leap through a "Credit Mobilier Jim Garfield" hoop held up by GOP national chairman Marshall Jewell. A gentle satire, the piece was inspired by Nast's disdain for 1880 Republican candidate James A. Garfield, implicated in a minor way in the 1873 Credit Mobilier scandal, and his refusal to draw for *Harper's* cartoons that exalted Garfield and demeaned his Democratic rival (and Nast friend), Winfield Scott Hancock.[3]

The Viennese Keppler shared with the Bavarian Nast a cultural heritage, kindred views on labor and leftist radicalism and political and religious liberty, and strong antipathies to Tammany, Irish and Irish-American hooliganism, and the ultramontane hierarchy of the Catholic Church both were born into. Their differences in temperament and out-

Our independent artist, finding ideas very scarce this week, has quietly left the last page to be filled by the unfortunate editor, who has been forced to avail himself of one of his esteemed friend Mr. Thomas Nast's patent double-back-action reversible cartoons, suitable to all occasions, and to all weathers.

What is sauce for the *Harper's* is sauce for *Puck*. The reader can select for himself an idea appropriate to the young woman in the picture. Behold the works of the editorial genius. You pays your money and you takes your choice of ideas. This is a genuine Nast caption.

SHIRKING THE FEAT.

NAST:—"I went through that Ring in 1873; but I can't go through it again. I am not that kind of a Jim Nast."

[II-2] James A. Wales, "Shirking the Feat," Puck, September 29, 1880.

look, however, were many and deep. Nast's stark, black-and-white style and Keppler's penchant for Viennese levity in outrageous, multicolored clutter reflected sharply contrasting views of human nature and political commentary. A reform independent hostile to the very notion of political parties until Cleveland's presidency, Keppler found Nast's rock-ribbed Republicanism and pious reverence for Ulysses Grant unacceptable. While Nast married into old-line Yankee culture and embraced it with the fervor of the prodigal son come home, Keppler remained at heart an Austrian with a genuine interest in European events, empathy for European peoples, and ardent devotion to German opera. Nast, born Catholic in Bavaria and raised Catholic in a German neighborhood in New York

Opposite: [II-1] James A. Wales, "Puck Sends His Compliments to Mr. Nast Once More," Puck, June 4, 1879.

City, converted to the Protestant faith as an adult, and in his art dishonestly portrayed rank-and-file Catholics as subhuman Hibernian slime. Although Keppler shared Nast's loathing for the Vatican and the authoritarianism of the Roman hierarchy, and created some memorable cartoon art in expressing this bias, he remained a Catholic communicant until death, and usually depicted the rank-and-file with an element of empathy and human dignity.[4]

Keppler almost certainly resented Nast's celebrity, especially at the outset of his career. He found it necessary at first to ape to a degree bordering on outright plagiarism Nast's caricatures of such luminaries as Boss Tweed, Ben Butler, Roscoe Conkling, Carl Schurz, James G. Blaine, and Samuel Tilden—including the theft of such Nast creations as Blaine cast as a magnet and Tilden as a mummy. That he did so was surely due less to a paucity of his own ideas than to a need to assure audience recognition, so pervasive was the dominance of Nast's imagery. Moreover, Nast's xenophobic portrayals of the Old World and immigrant peoples (other than the Irish) might well have inspired the resentment of the Viennese Keppler and other foreign-born artists and publishers who dominated the medium.

Indicative of a strong personal dislike of Nast among the fraternity was a March 10, 1880, *Puck* commentary by H.C. Bunner on Nast's "Give the Natives a Chance, Mr. Carl," a pro-Indian cartoon featuring an oafish German-American among a trio of implied inferiors already "civilized by the ballot." This clearly outraged Keppler, his German-born partner, Adolph Schwartzmann, and the German-American Bunner. In rebuke, *Puck* mocked Nast's wood-block art as the handiwork of a hatchet, snow shovel, or machine, and then lampooned the "Bavarian cartoon-builder" for positing the premise that "the German was an uncivilized barbarian until he dropped his first American vote in the box presided over by a Tammany heeler or a Ku-Klux desperado."[5]

Nast did not emerge as a prime cartoon caricature, however, until he shifted allegiances in 1884 to join ranks with Keppler (and presumably with Tammany heelers and Ku-Klux desperados as well) in championing Cleveland over Blaine. Never has an artist's decision to endorse or condemn a candidate inspired such a controversy, for by 1884 Nast had enjoyed for more than a decade the status of a prime political celebrity, and he was linked universally in the public mind to the Republican party he had endowed with its elephant symbol. In 1864 and 1868, Nast had drawn acid-penned "bloody shirt" indictments of the Democrats on behalf of Lincoln and Grant; in 1872 he lampooned Horace Greeley more brilliantly (and cruelly) than any presidential candidate has ever been caricatured; and in 1876 he promoted the cause of Republican standard-bearer Rutherford B. Hayes with many creative efforts. Even in 1880, when the Democrats had run his personal friend Hancock against the Republican Garfield, a man he regarded as lacking in stature and ethical probity, Nast had come to the aid of his party with a series of hard-hitting cartoons contrasting Civil War Republican patriotism with Democratic perfidy. Confronted with a similar dilemma four years later, however, Nast sacrificed party loyalty to personal conscience.

The problem was Republican nominee James Gillespie Blaine, the charismatic but careless senator from Maine. Blaine's notoriously lax personal finances lent credibility to the brilliant series of *Puck* cartoons depicting him as the Tattooed Man, and prompted Carl Schurz to claim that he had "wallowed in spoils like a rhinocerous in an African pool." Factional Republican rival Roscoe Conkling also balked at taking the stump on Blaine's behalf, claiming that he had "abandoned the practice of criminal law long ago." Historian H. Wayne Morgan has noted that "men went insane over him in pairs, one for and one against,"[6] and in 1884 both Nast and his *Harper's Weekly* editor, George W. Curtis, in agreement for once, came down squarely in the latter camp.

For Curtis, opposition to Blaine was rooted in an enthusiasm for civil service reform; he was a leader of the genteel, patrician reformers known derisively as "mugwumps" for their tendency to straddle the partisan fence with "mug" on one side and "wump" on the other. For Nast, it appears to have been a simpler, more visceral reaction to a man he viewed as morally unfit to serve as president. He had on past occasions pilloried the Maine senator for anti-Chinese demagoguery and for his personal conduct, most notably in an imaginative May 8, 1880, caricature of Blaine as a figural magnet [II–3] attracting sleaze like iron filings: the imagery of xenophobia, the Credit Mobilier and Mulligan Letters scandals, and (improbably for Nast) the support of Grant Republicans and the politics of the "bloody shirt."[7]

In 1884 neither Nast nor Curtis hid their aversion to Blaine, but conventional wisdom held that both would fall into line (or at least sulk

[II–3] Thomas Nast, "The 'Magnetic' Blaine; or, A Very Heavy 'Load'-stone for the Republican Party to Carry," Harper's Weekly, May 8, 1880.

in silence) once the Republican slate had been selected. On June 14, 1884, however, a week after Blaine's nomination in Chicago, *Harper's Weekly* featured both a Curtis editorial endorsing Cleveland and Thomas Hendricks, and the Nast cartoon "Too Heavy to Carry" [II–4], depicting a GOP elephant buckling under the weight of a magnet labeled "Magnetic Blaine." To remove any doubt as to his leanings or his intent, Nast drew for the June 21 *Harper's* the vitriolic "Death Before Dishonor," a double-page portrayal of a Free Republican Virginius preparing to slay his fair Republican party daughter rather than surrender her to the evil Appius Claudius Blaine. However overblown as commentary and hackneyed and derivative as art, the cartoon shocked a political culture rooted in party regularity.[8]

Cartoons responding to Nast's apostasy began to appear as soon as the technology permitted. On June 24 the pro-Cleveland *New York Daily Graphic* ran a front-page Miranda cartoon, "The New Salvation Army," gently chiding Cleveland's new mugwump allies by featuring many of them, including "Glory Tom" Nast and Curtis, with angel wings, on the road to the "new political Jerusalem." But as might have been expected,

TOO HEAVY TO CARRY

[II–4] *Thomas Nast, "Too Heavy to Carry,"* Harper's Weekly, *June 14, 1884.*

the vast bulk of Nast caricatures during the duration of the campaign were drawn not by new political bedfellows but rather by old Republican allies alienated by his reformist apostasy. In the vanguard was the color-illustrated humor weekly *The Judge*, rock-ribbed Republican, evangelically pro-Blaine, and published by old Nast nemesis James A. Wales. On the June 28 *Judge* front cover appeared the opening salvo, a Grant Hamilton cartoon [II–5] lampooning Curtis as an organ-grinder, Nast as his artistic monkey drawing "Too Heavy to Carry," and Uncle Sam complaining of "that whining music" and "that Nasty monkey." A week later *Judge* struck twice. Hamilton's front cover cartoon, "The Republican Pharisees," cast Curtis, Schurz, and Henry Ward Beecher as holier-than-thou hypocrites and Nast once again as Curtis's pet monkey. Frank Beard's centerfold, "The Bugaboo" [II–6], portrayed Curtis, Schurz, and *New York Times* editor George Jones stuffing libelous copy into an Independent Republican scarecrow and Nast in human form on a stepladder drawing "Death Before Dishonor."[9]

[II–5] Grant Hamilton, *untitled,* Judge, *June 28, 1884. Photograph by Brian Campbell Fischer.*

[II–6] Frank Beard, "The Bugaboo," Judge, July 5, 1884. Photograph by Brian Campbell Fischer.

*[II–7] Thomas Nast. Reprinted courtesy of the Morristown-Morris
Township (NJ) Public Library.*

In taking the unusual step of making a fellow cartoonist a key character in their creations, Miranda, Hamilton, Beard, and others who
would follow suit before the 1884 presidential campaign ran its course,
did enjoy two signal advantages. Nast's features were rather well known
to the general public and uncommonly amenable to caricature. Speaking
tours and other public appearances had given broad circulation to photo-
graphs and illustrations of him, and Nast had already appeared in cartoons drawn by other artists as well as a sizable number of his own
efforts at self-promotion in the guise of gentle self-deprecation. Fond of
featuring himself in whimsical cartoons when acid commentary on the
great evils of the day did not supercede, Nast probably drew himself
more frequently than he did any other public figure. Such exhibitions of
egotism may well have served unwittingly as inspirations for hostile rivals, for his diminutive torso, pointed chin, handlebar mustache, and dis-

tinctive goatee [II-7] lent themselves superbly to creative, malicious caricatures of him as a monkey or, for that matter, a malevolent dwarf, bat, rat, or ferret.[10]

If Nast found himself a victim of his prominence and his physiognomy, he found himself to an even greater extent a prisoner of his own crusading past. In many of his memorable portrayals of political evil—especially his attacks on Greeley and Tweed—opposition cartoonists found rich material to parody. A good example was Beard's July 12, 1884, *Judge* centerfold, "Anything to Beat Blaine" [IX-3], wryly subtitled "Let Us Clasp Hands Over the Bloody Chasm"—a Greeley plea for sectional reconciliation lampooned again and again by Nast in 1872. With Curtis clasping the hand of current Tammany sachem John Kelly across a ditch and a simian Nast doing likewise with his own ghostly caricature of Tweed (who in turn forgives his old nemesis now that both are anti-Republican), Beard's effort represents brilliant political satire in every respect except artistic execution. Another successful parody on Nast's 1872 work was Louis Dalrymple's "A Nast Cartoon (Slightly Changed)" in the August 30, 1884, *Judge* [II-8], featuring Nast and Curtis supplanting the original Greeley and Charles Sumner [II-9] coaxing a black Republican to embrace Tammany and the Ku Klux Klan over the bodies of his murdered wife and child. An outstanding Walter cartoon, "Comparisons Are Odious," in the October 11, 1884, *Wasp* (San Francisco), portraying Blaine throttling figural vultures Beecher, Curtis, Schurz, and Nast, aped Nast's 1876 "Another Carrion Bird Strangled," a defense of Rutherford B. Hayes against defamatory accusations by Democratic editors.[11]

Despite such imaginative parodies of Nast's artistic style and ideological intensity, the most frequent anti-Nast cartoon convention throughout the 1884 campaign and for more than a year afterward was Hamilton's portrayal of him as the pet monkey of organ-grinder Curtis. This theme was reiterated in the Barkhaus centerfold "Ready for the Fray" in the July 26, 1884, *Wasp*, and in nearly two dozen Hamilton and Beard color cartoons in *Judge* lithographed during the campaign, its aftermath, and the first ten months of the Cleveland presidency. This inspiration too was dredged from Nast's renowned legacy of Democrat-trashing. In his June 8, 1872, cartoon, "The New Organization on its 'New Departure'—Any Thing to Get Votes" [II-10], Nast had portrayed

A NAST CARTOON. (Slightly changed.)

[II–8] Louis Dalrymple, "A Nast Cartoon (Slightly Changed)," Judge, August 30, 1884.

[II–9] Thomas Nast, "It is Only a Truce to Regain Power ('Playing Possum')," Harper's Weekly, August 24, 1872.

THE NEW ORGAN- (we beg the "Tribune's" pardon) -IZATION ON ITS "NEW DEPARTURE."—ANY THING TO GET VOTES.

"The brain, the heart, the soul, of the present Democratic Party is the rebel element at the South, with its Northern allies and sympathizers.
It is rebel to the core to-day."—*New York Tribune* (old tune), February, 1871.

Thomas Nast, "*The New Organ-ization on Its 'New Departure,'*"
Harper's Weekly, *June 8, 1872.*

New York Tribune editor and Liberal Republican apostate Whitelaw Reid as an organ-grinder serenading August Belmont, Tweed, and other Democratic chieftains, with a monkey sporting Greeley's parson's hat, frock coat, Gratz Brown tag, and ubiquitous "What I Know About . . ." volume. A month later, in "Anything to Beat Grant!," he repeated the theme. Not among Nast's more inspired 1872 efforts, the cartoons did provide his 1884 adversaries with another avenue for mimicry.[12]

Usually a tiny detail in large cartoons featuring the four primary mugwump apostates—Curtis, Beecher, Schurz, and Jones—Nast as a mugwump's monkey gradually evolved into a running gag worthy of the master himself. Riding in a wooden tub in Beard's "The Tidal Wave Candidate," on a crippled Democratic camel in Hamilton's "It's the Last Straw that Breaks the Camel's Back," in a sinking Cleveland hot-air balloon in the unsigned "Caught in a Blizzard," or foraging through "Nastiness" spittoons in Hamilton's centerfolds "The Angel of Light" and " 'Joy' in the Independent Camp," Nast as monkey with tail wrapped around a porte-crayon or quill pen added to the humor. Even after Beard and Hamilton stopped drawing Curtis as an organ-grinder and began portraying him in drag as the corseted scold "Nancy" Curtis, Nast lived on as his monkey. By election time the gag had become so well established that it could be sustained merely by featuring as an incidental detail a monkey's tail wrapped around a porte-crayon or quill pen floating in debris.[13]

Wickedly clever from its inception, the image of Nast as a mugwump's monkey evolved into one of the more effective caricatures in the annals of American political cartoon art. Like the Beard, Walter, and Dalrymple parodies of Nast's earlier work savaging Cleveland's Democratic forebears, this satiric device owed its inspiration to Nast's previous artistry. It also owed its satirical greatness to Nast's own pioneering endeavors. It built upon the essence of true caricature, a physical resemblance suffused with qualities of soul and character, that Nast had used brilliantly in 1871 to transform the hapless Boss Tweed from an oversized yet dignified Tammany hack into a hulking ogre oozing arrogant sleaze from every invented feature, from his small, porcine eyes to his bulging belly to the immense, garish diamond on his lapel. Since then, Nast had refined this art to the detriment of many victims, notably the elderly, physically frail Samuel Tilden, whose rumored political comeback in 1880 inspired a merciless Nast to transform him into a dessicated, disentombed mummy of Democratic allegations of 1876–77 Republican electoral fraud. Nast as mugwump's monkey also exemplified the art of cartoon animalism brought to creative fruition by his transformation of Catholic bishops into devouring crocodiles. Just as the slithering reptiles epitomized Nast's horrific vision of the Vatican threat to the public schools, portraying Nast as the simian sidekick of organ-grinder Curtis capitalized nicely on Nast's small stature and facial features, and conveyed superbly the furtiveness and subservience of the artist whom his detractors regarded as an apostate lackey of the mugwump presslords.

Adding to the element of ridicule was the size and peripheral positioning of the Nast monkey in these compositions, as if to sustain the specious insignificance of the artist and his work. This, too, had been a satiric device raised to the level of genius by Nast in his wry reduction of the obscure B. Gratz Brown in 1872 to a miniscule name tag hanging from Greeley's frock coat. After the running gag of Nast-as-monkey had been established, the device gradually diminished to the ancillary detail viewers needed to search for. This tactic conveyed clearly the impression that the artist was at worst a minor annoyance and that the true giants of betrayal were presslords Jones and Curtis, German-American kingpin and editor Schurz, and the renowned Plymouth Congregational preacher–philanderer Beecher. The gimmick was brought to its pinnacle of political satire in two Hamilton cartoons, "The Angel of Light" and " 'Joy' in the Independent Camp," in which Nast as a monkey scrounging for inspiration in overturned spittoons was reduced to a lower left corner detail so miniscule that many viewers had to study the cartoons carefully to find him.

Even after the contest had run its course, the renegade mugwumps remained favored foils of Hamilton and Beard, and Nast as mugwump's monkey was a favored accent piece. In Hamilton's November 22 centerfold, "Mother, Is the Battle Over?," Nast was drawn cavorting on the eaves of Cleveland headquarters as Curtis emerged from the cellar, Beecher crawled out of a sewer, and Schurz and Jones lay in a pile of trash. Hamilton's December 6 front cover, "The Castaways," featured Nast floating in a tube near Beecher, Schurz, and a corseted Curtis marooned on the rock of Reform. "Cleveland's Cabinet," a December 13 Hamilton centerfold, depicted a simian Nast in the mail pouch of Curtis, postmaster general in a fancied Cleveland cabinet with such cohorts as John Bull, Roscoe Conkling, and Jefferson Davis! Beard's January 17, 1885, "Repulsed, 1861—Victorious, 1885" portrayed Nast with the three mugwumps bowing down to Confederate veterans. Hamilton's inaugural centerfold, "Cold Comfort," on March 7, 1885, featured just Nast's tail and pen protruding from a snowbank as Jones, Beecher, Schurz, and a corseted Curtis stood ostracized in a wintry blizzard. More than a year after the election, Beard drew Curtis as organ-grinder and Nast as his monkey in his November 28, 1885, centerfold, "Unappreciated," but with Beard's January 2, 1886, centerfold, "Ring Out the Old, Ring in the New," the celebrated running gag of Nast as mugwump's monkey finally ran its course.[14]

It is difficult to ascribe much importance to Nast's stint as a caricature. Given the *Judge* circulation in New York through newsstand sales and subscriptions, it could be argued that these cartoons could have created a president, if only Blaine had carried the Empire State instead of falling short by a bare 1,100 votes. Such claims have been put forth for *Puck*'s simultaneous series depicting Blaine as the tattooed man of myriad scandals, for Nast's own rather crabbed 1884 efforts, and, more persuasively for a Blaine supporter's arrogant "Rum, Romanism and Rebellion" assessment of the Democratic party, a slur that infuriated Irish New Yorkers previously unfriendly to Cleveland and inspired huge Democratic majorities in Irish wards. Indeed, in an electorate the size of New York, the swing of 1,100 votes could be attributed to vagaries of weather, barometric pressure, or mass biorhythms, and undoubtedly were accounted for, many times over, by stuffed ballot boxes and missionary mathematics by Tammany wardheelers in the metropolis and their Republican counterparts in outstate constituencies. Such allegations on behalf of these *Judge* cartoons would be even sillier than those proffered for *Puck*'s Tattooed Man sequence or Nast's 1884 work. At least the *Puck* artists and Nast attacked Republican candidate Blaine. In foolishly focusing upon a trio of editors, a clergyman, and a cartoonist instead of the opposition ticket, the *Judge* cartoons only served to magnify the ethical fragility of Blaine's candidacy, despite the superiority of their sustained graphic satire.

This flawed focus may account for the complete silence in Nast biographies and scholarly surveys of American political cartoon art on this stellar sequence of caricatures, unlike the accolades given the artistically inferior Tattooed Man series, Joseph Keppler's wry 1889–92 work portraying Benjamin Harrison as a shrinking midget who finally disappeared into his grandfather's top hat, or Hamilton's incisive 1896 sequence of William Jennings Bryan as a free-silver fool. Nast as the mugwump's monkey began no trends in American political cartooning. In more than a century since 1884, no subsequent editorial cartoonist has ever again been singled out by his fellow artists for such mockery. The sequence wrecked no epic friendships, for the prickly Nast was something of a loner within his fraternity. It neither made nor broke cartooning careers, although Hamilton's work in 1884 did help begin to engender for him a reputation worthy of his talents. This hoisting of Nast on his own petard does represent one of the crowning ironies in the annals of American political cartoon art, however: that in this last great presidential campaign in which he played a major role in the cartooning mainstream, Nast did so in large part as a thoroughly "nasty" little caricature in the drawings of other men.

III

Rustic
Rasputin

Exaggeration and distortion are staples of all humor, of course, and especially essential to graphic satire. Yet to be both effective and honest, they must be rooted in some semblance of factual reality, akin to what Huckleberry Finn termed "stretchers" in attesting that Mark Twain had "told the truth, mainly" in narrating his adventures. To cast Jesse Helms as a bespectacled big bad wolf set to devour the Little Red Riding Hood of expanded affirmative-action guarantees for women and racial minorities would be a legitimate exercise in graphic exaggeration. To place Jesse Jackson or Ted Kennedy in this role would be both dishonest and silly. Yet a century ago, the targets of cartoonists were routinely subjected to graphic distortion based on factual error.

Unlike the distortions of character and motivation visited upon Tweed, New York Catholics, and the apostate Nast, this cavalier attitude toward factual authenticity probably owed less to the personal nastiness of the artists or the role of editorial cartooning in the Gilded Age journalism of partisan hyperbole than it did to simple political illiteracy among cartoonists. Many of them had come from Europe as adults and never fully mastered the idiom and culture of American politics; Friedrich Graetz of *Puck* never even learned the language. Even American-born artists drifted into the trade because they could draw, not because they were driven by a keen political curiosity. One result was a blithe indifference to such factual trivia as party membership, positions on the salient issues of the day, and White House aspirations.[1]

An example of this phenomenon is the treatment accorded Kansas Populist William Alfred Peffer. Odd man out in a two-party chamber, Peffer left no great legacy of note from his 1891–97 stint in the U.S. Senate, save perhaps a wealth of speeches in the *Congressional Record*

46

distinguished mainly by their interminable length and plethora of statis-
tics. Even within the Populist movement he became something of a peripheral player after 1891, removed by half a continent from the political
fray in Kansas and at odds with his party's drift toward fusion with the
Democrats and single-issue silver politics.

Yet through much of the 1890s Peffer experienced the dubious distinction of extraordinary prominence in one facet of political celebrity—
color cartoon art. During his years in office, as Peter Argersinger has
noted, Peffer served as "the political cartoonists' symbol of the People's
party more consistently than either the donkey or the elephant served the
major parties."[2] He surely achieved more prominence as a caricature
than he did as a statesman. On sixty or more occasions during the eight
years following his election to the Senate in January, 1891, Peffer's caricature served a succession of *Puck* and *Judge* artists as the ubiquitous
symbol of the Populist presence in American politics.

The agrarian upheaval that brought Peffer to the Senate and national prominence marked something of a milestone for the rival cartoon
weeklies, bringing the Republican *Judge* and the nominally independent
but predictably pro-Cleveland *Puck* into a rare convergence of political
ideology. At the same time, it served to rekindle the creative fires of artists
gone stale on an unending fare of cartoons devoted to the problems and
personalities of the 1880s. Until 1890, *Puck* and *Judge* had rarely agreed
on anything of substance. Beneath broad but superficial differences over
party preference and policy positions, however, lurked in both editorial
suites an abiding conservatism on fundamental social, economic, and political values. Confronted with such perceived threats to the status quo
as trade union activism, an 1886 bid by Henry George to bring the single
tax to Gracie Mansion, or international manifestations of anarchism or
communism, both *Puck* and *Judge* had routinely put aside Viennese levity for lurid demagoguery.[3] When 1890 election returns from Kansas and
other Great Plains constituencies signaled a serious challenge to politics
as usual, *Puck* and *Judge* rallied to the cause of such verities as a two-
party system and the sanctity of private property and the gold dollar.
Populism became the bogeyman of New York color cartoon art, and Peffer of Kansas its bewhiskered visual image.

His debut came in Frederick Burr Opper's April 8, 1891, *Puck* centerfold, "Spring Nonsense," a sequence of farcical sketches with rhymes,

There is an old chap, quite a brisk cuss,
Whose opinions are somewhat
                          promiskous ;
In the Senate he'll sit,
And he'll need all his wit,
Or the wind there will blow through
                          his whiskers.

[III–1] Detail from Frederick B. Opper, "Spring Nonsense," Puck, April 8, 1891.

including one of senator-elect Peffer [III–1] at his desk reading the rules of debate and sporting "clodhopper" boots and a beard that trails across the floor. This portrayal of Peffer as a comic-relief rustic primitive endowed with more facial hair than brains pioneered a basic formula for Peffer caricature that resisted major modification in all but one respect throughout his years in public life. The one essential deviation was endowing his small and rather intense eyes with a demonic quality, exemplified by Bernhard Gillam's October 28, 1893, *Judge* centerfold, "Gulliver Bound Down by the Democratic Lilliputians," and Louis Dalrymple's July 8, 1891, *Puck* centerfold, "The Grangers' Dream of Cheap Money" [III–2], more appropriate for fellow Kansan John Brown of Ossawatomie than Bill Peffer of Topeka. On several occasions, especially in the more creative Peffer caricatures, he was thus portrayed as something of a rustic Rasputin, apostle of agrarian dementia. In others, however, he was drawn with vapid eyes to create the effect of a simple-minded, innocuous, altogether inconsequential hayseed visionary. The drollery of the Peffer caricature was embellished in many cases by such creative touches as adorning the grossly exaggerated beard with a bow, tying it into a Hindu knot [III–3], or braiding it in the style of ancient Egypt, or by giving him a shabby carpetbag full of "wild ideas" and "Populist dreams" [III–4], skewed spectacles, or a motley assortment of bedraggled hats.[4]

THE GRANGERS' DREAM OF CHEAP MONEY.

[III–2] Louis Dalrymple, "The Grangers' Dream of Free Money," Puck, July 8, 1891.

[III–3 Detail from C.J. Taylor, "Appropriate Costumes for the
Presidential Carnival of 1892," Puck, December 30, 1891.

In poking fun at Peffer's prairie provincialism with such devices as
whiskers, "clodhopper" boots, and shabby old hats, cartoon artists were
exploiting a hackneyed stereotype crafted in countless black-and-white
cartoons in Puck, Judge, Harper's, and other publications lampooning
farmers for a primarily urban clientele. In one respect, however, they
were required to exercise some care, for the revered national symbol of

THE AMUSING POLITICAL HAYSEED — His intellect is very ordinary; but his whiskers are the wonder of the country.

[III–4] Detail from C.J. Taylor, "Old Jokes in New Political Clothes," Puck, January 30, 1895.

Uncle Sam was also portrayed invariably in the cartoons of the day as a bearded agrarian decked out in boots and a white hat! Without exception, *Puck* and *Judge* artists featuring both Peffer and Uncle Sam in their creations took care to accentuate the contrast between national icon and Populist pariah by drawing Uncle Sam as neat to the point of nattiness and depicting Peffer's beard and hat as uncommonly scruffy.[5]

Despite the many droll variations, the essential Peffer caricature quickly became so universally recognized that he could be drawn in blackface or Indian warpaint, as an elf or fakir or Egyptian pharoah, or even as an ape, a fish, a coyote, a hydra head, or a tree. In most instances his likeness was unnecessarily labeled "Peffer." Accordingly, the Kansan became a prized commodity to artists as an ancillary feature contributing to a cartoon's overall effect without a major expenditure of space or effort. Like Benjamin Butler, Carl Schurz, Joseph Pulitzer, and other contemporaries endowed with truly distinctive physiognomies, Peffer was featured in many more cartoons than his actions or influence warranted, perhaps as a token Populist to give these works partisan balance, but more probably because he caricatured so successfully. He became a fixture in the obligatory holiday and seasonal cartoons with casts of dozens that evolved into a popular tradition during the period.[6]

Before Peffer developed into a cartoon cliché, however, he was for a season a curiosity in his own right. His election to the Senate, and fellow Kansan "Sockless Jerry" Simpson's to the House, prompted F. Victor Gillam's April 25, 1891, *Judge* front cover cartoon, "A Mighty Poor Exchange: From the Sublime to the Ridiculous" [III-5], a lament that giants William McKinley and George Edmunds were giving way to a diminutive duo of Kansas Populists. Bernhard Gillam's June 6, 1891, *Judge* front cover "A Party of Patches" [III-6] made mock of a Cincinnati summit of splinter-party reform groups chaired by Peffer in May by featuring Terence V. Powderly, Ben Butler, Simpson, and Peffer himself riding a "platform of lunacy" held aloft by a balloon made up mainly of patches representing the Alliancemen, Knights of Labor, Grangers, greenbackers, and other participants. Dalrymple's "Grangers' Dream of Cheap Money" ridiculed Peffer's penchant for paper money by drawing the federal treasury as a windmill driven by the bellows of a maniacal Peffer spewing wagonloads of greenbacks, while a merchant demonstrates the inflationary effect by charging a ton of greenbacks for a ton of coal. Populist forays against the major parties led by Peffer and Simpson in 1891 were satirized as a barnyard battle to salt an Alliance turkey in Bernhard Gillam's April 11, 1891, *Judge* centerfold "Too Old a Bird to be Caught That Way"; as a scalping party menacing John Sherman in Dalrymple's August 19, 1891, *Puck* front cover effort "After His Scalp"; and as a Democratic cart impeded by an Alliance rock in Victor Gillam's October 3, 1891, *Judge* centerfold "The Poor Donkey Has Too Many Drivers."[7]

Other 1891 Peffer cartoons, however, were less rooted in reality. Bernhard Gillam's August 8, 1891, *Judge* centerfold, "Most Ripe," starred Peffer with Arthur P. Gorman, President Cleveland, David Hill, Russell Alger, Shelby Cullom, and James Campbell, all in blackface, salivating over a "U.S. Presidency 1892" watermelon in Uncle Sam's garden. It was the first of a succession of cartoons presenting Peffer as a candidate

[III–5] F. Victor Gillam, "A Mighty Poor Exchange," Judge, April 25, 1891.

[III–6] *Bernhard Gillam, "A Party of Patches," Judge, June 6, 1891.*

for the presidency in 1892 and again in 1896. Although the Kansan had exhibited no symptoms of White House fever, the theme was echoed in C.J. Taylor's December 30, 1891, *Puck* centerfold, "Appropriate Costumes for the Presidential Carnival of 1892," with "Faker Peffer" as a gaunt, half-naked Hindu, the one Populist in the piece. Victor Gillam's "President Harrison Speaks for Good Money" and "The Foolish Appeals of the Political Tramps," *Judge* centerfolds on September 5 and 19, 1891, respectively, set a precedent for casting Peffer as a fervent disciple of the free and unlimited coinage of silver at a time when his enthusiasm for this panacea was decidedly less avid than that of such mainstream figures as John J. Ingalls, the rock-ribbed Kansas Republican he had replaced in the Senate![8]

Such cartoons were prophetic of future trends in Peffer's use as a cartoon convention. After 1891, apart from pro forma appearances in holiday extravaganzas and an occasional situational vignette, he was used almost exclusively in *Puck* and *Judge* cartoons as a presidential possibility, a leader of the free silver forces, or both. In 1892, for example, he was cast as a potential candidate in three cartoons before Arkell and Keppler bowed to the inevitability that the Populist party would nominate James B. Weaver instead. In Victor Gillam's "The Political Bichloride of Gold" and "Judge's Political Dime Museum," featured in *Judge* on January 2 and April 9 respectively, Peffer saw duty as a "free money drunk" partial to "presidential mania rum," and a freak-show Lilliputian; and in Opper's May 18 *Puck* centerfold, "Would-Be Models for the Great Painting 'Our Next President,'" as a bedraggled bumpkin in a stovepipe hat, bib overalls, and clodhoppers lining up to audition for artist Uncle Sam. His only other appearance that year was as one of at least forty brownies in a New Year's Eve *Judge* centerfold.[9]

After a seven-month hiatus, Peffer again appeared as a centerfold brownie in a July 29, 1893, *Judge* salute to the World's Fair. A week later Cleveland, responding to business hysteria over the deepening economic slump, summoned Congress into special session to repeal the 1890 Sherman Silver Purchase Act, precipitating an acrimonious Senate filibuster that lasted through October and dominated political cartooning into the new year. A dozen color cartoons pilloried Peffer as a silver obstructionist for his longwinded speeches against repeal, although he played a peripheral role in the fray. His speeches, not especially lengthy or rambling for Pefferian oratory, tended to damn silver with the faintest of praise as a Band-aid measure for westerners in dire need of economic tourniquets and transfusions. Nevertheless, both humor weeklies viewed any role in the filibuster as fiscal treason, and *Puck* considered it a betrayal of a heroic president as well. *Puck* cartoons tended to scorn such silver Republicans as William Stewart of Nevada and Henry M. Teller of Colorado, while *Judge* artists worked in any Democrat they could, especially those with Tammany ties or free-trade tendencies. The Populist Peffer was fair game for both publications.

It began with Victor Gillam's portrayal of Peffer as a "silver rum" Democratic sot in his August 12 *Judge* cartoon, "Cleveland's Cure and the Democratic Incurables." Two weeks later he appeared with a broom at the beach fending off a tidal wave of "public sentiment on the silver question" in Grant Hamilton's *Judge* centerfold "The Old Story—Trying to Sweep Back the Ocean." In his August 30 *Puck* back cover, "Awaiting the News from Washington" [III–7], Joseph Keppler, Jr., drew Missouri Democrat George Vest and Peffer filibustering while a businessman dozed through ticker-tape reports of foreclosures, bankruptcies and Senate paralysis. Victor Gillam echoed this theme in his September 9 *Judge* cartoon, "The Senatorial Firemen Talk While the Fire Burns," featuring Peffer and fellow obstructionists as firefighters debating while an investment house, bank, and factory perish in flames. Peffer starred in two cartoons as a bandit attacking the locomotive of repeal, armed in one with a bellows to symbolize his legendary long-windedness. In Bernhard Gillam's "Gulliver Bound Down by the Democratic Lilliputians," he was cast again as a Democrat, this time a manic midget delivering "Peffer Silver Lunacy speeches" atop an "Industrial Prosperity" Uncle Sam bound by "tariff tinkering" and "free silver" bindings. He was subsequently ejected from a Senate window in Keppler's "Throw 'Em Out" and drawn as an ape in Keppler, Jr.'s, "Through the Jungle"; as a pagan worshipping a smashed silver idol in Samuel Ehrhart's "One After the Other—Let the Good Work Go On"; and as a cheerleader for jackasses and dogs accosting Cleveland in Dalrymple's "The National Honor and Credit in Good Hands"—all *Puck* centerfolds on November 1, November 22, December 20, and January 31, respectively.[10]

During the next year, Peffer was lampooned in several cartoons with varying themes. Taylor's February 7, 1894, *Puck* centerfold, "The

AWAITING THE NEWS FROM WASHINGTON.

[III–7] Joseph Keppler, Jr., "Awaiting the News from Washington,"
Puck, *August 30, 1893.*

'Peanut' Hagenbeck and his 'Senatorial Courtesy' Animal Show," cast him as an ape in David B. Hill's circus in company with several senators who opposed Cleveland's tariff initiative. In Victor Gillam's November 10, 1894, *Judge* centerfold, "An Unjust Distribution of an Iniquitous Tax," he was savaged as an architect of the tariff's most controversial feature, a federal income tax. In truth, Peffer had played no role of consequence in the tariff struggle, favoring the income tax but cool to its cosmetic rate revisions. Taylor's "Dante's Inferno Up to Date," the August 22, 1894, *Puck* centerfold, cast Peffer among the obstructionists in the fifty-third Congress as doomed sinners being led by Uncle Sam as Dante and "Vergilius Maro Puck" through the smoke of "political purgatory" into the flames of perdition. Opper's February 14 "Puck's Valentines for 1894" [III–8] included a sketch of Peffer and fellow Kansan Mary Elizabeth Lease with a verse poking fun at his intellect and windiness and urging him to resign. F.M. Hutchins's October 10, 1894, *Puck* front cover "Peffer's Populistic Boom" [III–9], showed him clinging to a ruptured "Populism" hot-air balloon as it descends over Washington. The inspiration for this fascinating cartoon was not made manifest by written commentary, although it seems improbable that Hutchins could have foreseen the Populist showing in the pending elections or Peffer's increasing isolation in a party drifting inexorably toward single-issue silver politics and fusion with the Democrats.[11]

Beginning with Victor Gillam's "The National Dog Show," a *Judge* centerfold of February 23, 1895, that cast Peffer with "Silver Dick" Bland and senators Jones and Wolcott as a "prize litter of silver puppies" among the canine corps of presidential aspirants, Peffer cartooning reverted to his familiar role as a White House candidate and free-silver evangelist. During the next several months he was drawn among the White House contenders as a "curious and rare orchid (crank species)" in Victor Gillam's April 20 *Judge* cartoon, "Judge's Easter Flower Show"; as a fish of the "Populist skate" species in Bernhard Gillam's March 30 *Judge* effort, "In the Political Swim"; as a befuddled bicyclist in Taylor's June 12 *Puck* piece, "Presidential Aspirants Take to the Wheel"; and as the one Populist examined by the press corps with magnifying glasses in Dalrymple's November 20 *Puck* centerfold, "The Press View at the Candidate Show." As a free-silver zealot foiled by Cleveland's heroic leadership, he was one of a pack of coyotes harrassing the

[III–8] *Detail from Frederick B. Opper, "Puck's Valentines for 1894," Puck, February 14, 1894.*

[III–9] F. M. Hutchins, "Peffer's Populistic Boom," Puck, October 10, 1894.

president's national stagecoach in J.S. Pughe's March 13, 1895, *Puck* centerfold, "The 'Ki-Yis' Can't Rattle Him"; and one head of a "Free Silver Craze" hydra held at bay by Cleveland's "sound money policy" broadsword in Dalrymple's June 19, 1895, *Puck* centerfold "It Cannot Pass While He Is There." In Dalrymple's July 3, 1895, *Puck* centerfold "Fizz! Boom!! Ah!!!," he was featured as "the Windy Man from Kansas" in a silver carnival and Independence Day fireworks exhibit.[12]

After the Populists became junior partners in the Democratic campaign for William Jennings Bryan and free silver in the summer of 1896, Peffer was essentially ignored in a vitriolic *Judge* campaign against Bryan. Perhaps this reflected his rather muted role in the campaign, but more probably it was because, as a Populist, he had no place in what was portrayed as a Democratic party phenomenon. He appeared often in anti-Bryan *Puck* cartoons, however, as part of a Bryan silver entourage in which Democrats were routinely outnumbered by such renegade Republicans as Stewart and Teller, noted radicals Eugene Debs and John Peter Altgeld, and Populists Peffer, Simpson, Lease, Jacob Coxey, and Tom Watson. This was an obvious effort to portray the Bryan insurgency as treason against the revered tradition of Thomas Jefferson, Cleveland, and *Puck* itself. Opper's August 12 cartoon, "The Silver-Tongued Ventriloquist and his Dummies," cast Peffer as a dummy. Taylor's centerfold "A Down-Hill Movement" in the same issue portrayed him as one of ten "silver lunatics" rejoicing that their careening runaway cart was gaining speed since they had unhitched the Democratic donkey! Peffer was drawn as a "Popocracy" buccaneer attacking the good ship "National Prosperity" in Taylor's September 23 centerfold, "Political Pirates"; as part of a motley Bryan army along with such disreputables as Coxey, Altgeld, and a broom-wielding Mrs. Lease in the Dalrymple September 30 centerfold, "In Battle Array—And There's Not Much Doubt About the Result"; and as an Indian in the Dalrymple November 4 centerfold, "Last Ghost-Dance of the Free Silver Tribe—Just Before Being Sent to the Salt River Reservation."[13]

Then, with a final appearance as a *Judge* Christmas brownie and in one post-election *Puck* salt-in-the-wounds gloat over the beating suffered by Bryan and bimetallism, Peffer disappeared from cartoon art even before he disappeared from national politics, a casualty of his failure to embrace fusion and silver with sufficient ardor. Two years after Peffer's return to Kansas and private life, however, Eugene Zimmerman resurrected his caricature as a rotting figural "dead Populistic Peffer tree" in his March 11, 1899, *Judge* centerfold "Splitting 'Old Hickory,' " a blithe commentary on the dismembering of the party of Jefferson and Jackson by the Bryan and Cleveland factions, and a reminder of cartoon artists' enduring fascination with Peffer as a study in caricature and the personification of the party he served in the Senate. This centerfold also exemplified another salient characteristic of the Peffer cartoon tradition—a total disregard for fact. By the time it appeared in print, Peffer had already pronounced Populism dead and buried, run unsuccessfully for the governorship of Kansas as the Prohibition party nominee, and was returning to the Republican party of his youth.[14]

Seldom in the annals of editorial cartooning has an American political figure been so systematically misrepresented so often in so many fundamental respects. The artists for *Puck* and *Judge* drew Peffer superbly as an exercise in pure caricature, exaggerating the unrivaled beard and rustic taste in wearing apparel, from hats to boots, that one suspects had been carefully cultivated for an agrarian Kansas constituency. Those who drew him as the "windy man from Kansas," or symbolized his affinity for marathon speeches with bellows or a coiled script as long as his beard, succeeded in transforming a real foible into the realm of creative caricature. In a number of early Peffer cartoons, printed before he took his Senate seat and began to evolve into a known entity, portrayals of him as a lunatic-fringe crackpot or a rustic Rasputin menacing sacred canons of civilization and the marketplace exhibited a modicum of integrity as manifestations of seaboard bewilderment over the odd new phenomenon of prairie Populism. After 1891, however, Peffer cartoons sacrificed integrity and elementary accuracy almost altogether in featuring him again and again as a candidate for the presidency, avid evangelist for the free and unlimited coinage of silver, or both.

No evidence exists to suggest that Peffer harbored any ambitions for the White House in 1892 or in 1896, or that he ever found it necessary to renounce grass-roots groundswells of popular enthusiasm among the Populist party rank and file for such a candidacy. In late 1891 and early 1892, cartoonists may have been misled by his celebrity status and by the muddled presidential picture within his party organization. By the time cartoons suggesting an 1896 Peffer candidacy began to appear in

1895, however, such ambiguity did not exist, for by then it must have been clear to even casual observers of Populist politics that he had become an anachronism in a party drifting steadily toward a single-issue silver ideology and fusion with the anti-Cleveland agrarian Democrats, an agenda that Peffer decried consistently. A peripheral figure within the Populist movement, and even in Kansas so alienated from the party's mainstream that in January 1897 he enjoyed little serious support for a second Senate term, Peffer was credible as a Populist presidential nominee only in the minds of the New York cartoonists. When he was allegedly urged by a delegation of diehard Texans to declare against Bryan on the eve of the 1896 Populist convention in St. Louis, Peffer was said to have turned them down, sadly explaining that he could not carry a single Kansas county against the Nebraska Democrat.[15]

These artists also strayed far from fact in their persistent portrayal of Peffer as a "silver lunatic." An avid greenbacker who denied altogether the metallic basis of money, he looked condescendingly on free silver as a monetary molehill, remarking that "as long as we use metals for money I favor their unlimited use." In this spirit he supported silver initiatives and opposed repeal of the Silver Purchase Act, but he made no secret of his disdain for the idea that free silver could solve the farm crisis or attack the root causes of the economic depression. That, he believed, required the abolition of rents and interest, the nationalization of the money and railroad trusts, the redistribution of land, and the issue of paper money directly to the needy.

In short, Peffer never deviated from his faith in the early Populist agenda and resisted strenuously its subordination to free silver as the single-issue rallying cry of agrarian reform. He also never wavered in his belief that only an autonomous Populist party provided the one hope for meaningful economic reform, and he opposed openly and persistently fusion with a Democratic party he had loathed since boyhood. To the end, Peffer held firm for party autonomy and broadly based platform initiatives. Although he endorsed the Bryan–Watson Populist slate, he devoted most of his efforts to promoting Watson against Bryan's Democratic running mate, Maine banker Arthur Sewall. For cartoonists to depict Peffer as a "silver lunatic" was to echo an accepted misconception; for them to persistently portray him as a Bryan "groupie" was to indulge in sheer fantasy.[16]

The cartoonists also erred fundamentally in portraying Peffer as either a droll dimwit or a rustic Rasputin, for he was clearly neither. If Mary Elizabeth Lease described him in 1914 as "utterly lacking in brilliancy," his speeches and editorials bear witness to mental powers that compared favorably with those of his colleagues, both in Congress and in the Kansas press corps. Writing in 1891 of the new Kansas Populist members of Congress, the *Washington Post* declared that "no set of men ever merited less the ridicule heaped upon them." In 1893, a *Washington Evening Star* reporter, expecting to interview a "political dime museum freak," found instead "a gentleman of a mild and benevolent countenance, of engaging manners, and of a gentle and persuasive voice." In July 1894, *Review of Reviews* observed that Peffer "seems to have won the respect and esteem of his colleagues, and to have convinced them that he represents a high standard of citizenship." "Instead of being a blatant demogogue and Populist fire-eater," eulogized a *Philadephia Press* reporter in response to Peffer's failure to win a second term in January, 1897, "he has turned out to be a very mild-mannered gentleman indeed, who has, of course, the crazy notions of the Populists, but whose presentations of these notions have been made in the prosiest, least sensational manner imaginable." Perhaps Walter T.K. Nugent put it best when he wrote that Peffer's "sedate, logical, fact-crammed, humorless speeches and editorials justify better the description of single-minded and dedicated rather than fanatical."[17]

Peffer's refusal to play the role of the "political dime museum freak" presented cartoonists with the dilemma of a compelling caricature predicated on egregious falsehood. That Keppler, for one, pondered the dichotomy between image and reality early in the game is clear from the July 8, 1891, *Puck*. The issue featured both Dalrymple's "The Grangers' Dream of Cheap Money" [III–2], arguably the most demonic portrait of Peffer in color-cartoon art, and a companion essay observing that "Peffer is already giving signs of weakening in his capacity of political freak." The essay also noted that Peffer had written a magazine article indicating "great anxiety to prove to the East the entire reasonableness of the Mid-Western idea," and reported rumors that "he has had made for him, or has otherwise procured, civilized or semi-civilized clothes."[18] That Peffer continued to appear in cartoon after cartoon as a rustic Rasputin or a droll dimwit long after he evolved into a familiar Senate figure suggests that the men who perpetuated this image were as gifted at the art of ethical compromise as they were lacking in the science of political observation.

Peffer was by no means unique as the object of such distorted press coverage. In 1890, Jerry Simpson, commonly characterized in major party papers as "simian"—although he more closely resembled a Republican banker—told a crowd in Harper, Kansas: "You may be surprised to see me in the form of a man, after the descriptions of a partisan press, but I'm no zoological specimen—not even a monkey or an orangutan." It grew worse in Republican papers after fusion. In his *Weekly Kansas Chief* (Troy) coverage of the St. Louis convention, Sol Miller described male delegates as "men with unkempt and matted hair, men with long beards matted together with filth from their noses, men reeking with lice, men whose feet stank, and the odor from under whose arms would have knocked down a bull." The female delegates were characterized as "brazen women, women with beards, women with voices like a gong, women with scrawny necks and dirty fingernails, women with their stockings out at the heels, women with snaggle teeth, strumpets, rips, and women possessed of devils." *Emporia Gazette* editor William Allen White stooped in his renowned October 1, 1896, editorial "What's the Matter with Kansas?," to describe the immaculately groomed and intellectually impressive Frank Doster as a "shabby, wild-eyed, rattle-brained fanatic."[19] Clearly, then, perpetuating Peffer's cartoon identity as a rustic Rasputin despite his proper, rather prosaic conduct in office was no isolated phenomenon, but one that sustained itself to serve the needs of discrediting the agrarian insurgency through graphic satire.

The dichotomy raises the question of why *Puck* and *Judge* singled Peffer out as the prime Populist caricature in the first place, for compelling options existed. Jacob Coxey, leader of the 1894 march of the dispossessed on Washington, was rarely cartooned until 1896, when he proved useful in *Puck*'s effort to portray Bryan as head of a contingent of crazies. Among the Kansans, such leaders as Frank Doster and Annie L. Diggs lacked requisite national recognition, as did the truly bizarre John "Milkman" Otis. "Sockless Jerry" Simpson, a more fascinating personality and after 1891 more a mainstream movement leader, saw early duty as Peffer's sidekick but never evolved into a cartoon presence in his own right, perhaps because his erudition, Lincolnesque wit, and urbane features and attire belied the rustic Rasputin stereotype.

This cannot be said of the remarkable Mary Elizabeth Lease, who surely provided more raw material for zany caricature than any public figure of her generation. Six feet tall, with an affinity for what William Allen White described as the "most ungodly hats I ever saw a woman wear" and features that moved one Kansas editor to describe her (somewhat unfairly) as a "lantern-jawed, goggle-eyed nightmare," she enhanced her notoriety by inventing a fictitious Irish birthright and a series of apparently imaginary 1892 dalliances with James B. Weaver. On the stump, she personified the "calamity howl" of agrarian angst, defying every last gender-driven stereotype of public probity in urging Kansas farmers to "raise less corn and more hell" and to combat the money cabals of London and international Zionism. Yet the cartoonists squandered this extraordinary opportunity; only a September 30, 1896, Dalrymple portrayal of her as a broom-toting prune-faced harridan in Bryan's army made a minimal effort to exploit her potential for caricature.[20]

That Peffer evolved into the ubiquitous cartoon image of the Populist crusade over such compelling alternates may defy logical analysis, but common sense suggests that his early prominence and uniquely agrarian appearance undoubtedly had much to do with it. As the only senator created by the 1890 upheaval, Peffer held a special place in the public eye, and his starring role as chair of the Cincinnati conclave and frenetic 1891 campaign endeavors added to his celebrity. When he came East that fall to take his seat, the press proclaimed him "the most extensively advertised Senator that ever came to Washington." As Peter Argersinger has noted, Peffer was so intrinsically identified in the public mind with early Populism that "for a time he lent his name to it. Before the People's party movement became designated as Populism it was popularly referred to as Pefferism; and Populists were frequently referred to as Pefferites or Peffercrats."[21] Since the success of a cartoon is determined in large part by an instant recognition of its caricatures and conventions, artists who had done much to establish Peffer as the accepted personification of his party would have entertained an understandable reluctance to confuse their public with a substitute symbol just because he stubbornly re-

[III–10] William A. Peffer. Reprinted courtesy of the Kansas State Historical Society.

fused to play his annointed role of "political museum freak." So, to some extent, Peffer's niche in cartooning was a result of his status as the movement's first celebrity.

It owed much more, however, to a physical appearance that dovetailed uncannily with the graphic image of the rustic prairie provincial developed over a generation of cartoon satire and firmly established in the popular mind. Tall, almost skeletal, elderly, with gaunt features, piercing eyes that evoked passionate purpose if not dementia, and a magnificent beard that flowed nearly to his waist, Peffer embellished nature's gifts by a fondness for floppy country hats and "clodhopper" boots and a disdain for neckties or even shirt collars [III–10]. Put simply, he represented a rare phenomenon in the annals of American cartoon art, a pristine example of natural caricature. O. Gene Clanton has written persuasively that the pervasive Populist image conveyed by the eastern press was that of "a weather-beaten old man" approximating "the missing link in the evolutionary chain," with a "dilapidated hat perched atop a head that was ornamented with a long but mangy-looking beard . . . and a bony frame covered with a tattered set of bib overalls, from which emerged inevitably a pair of oversized boots recognizable as 'clodhoppers.' "22 The uncanny parallel between this generic stereotype and his living likeness suggests that, as Voltaire quipped about God, if Peffer had not existed, the cartoon artists of the day would have had to invent him.

IV

Aliens

Between the color covers and centerfolds lampooning Peffer and other celebrities and ersatz celebrities of Gilded Age politics in the dime illustrated weeklies were crowded pages of filler copy, mainly essays of whimsy, lame one-liners worthy of no more than a groan from the most besotted of vaudeville crowds, and situational black-and-white cartoons of indifferent execution, inspiration, and wit. During political campaigns in which publishers took a special interest, these black-and-white filler cartoons might take aim at opposition candidates or ideologies, but more often they exploited stereotypes and situations that comprised the pro forma running gags of the era: decadent society fops emulating the fashions and fads of London; college louts maiming one another on Ivy League gridirons; wily farmers fleecing vacationing city tenderfoots; emancipated young women demanding the ballot and access to other hallowed male preserves; and uppity servants terrorizing the gentlefolk.

Most frequent of all were filler pieces based on the familiar foibles and character flaws of those alien elements in the population deemed hopelessly beyond the pale of assimilation into an American community of citizens. Rare indeed was a weekly issue of *Puck* or *Judge* without one or more of these filler cartoons poking fun at the stereotypical shortcomings of ethnic immigrants and racial minorities, for the popular humor of the day was raucously, unapologetically elitist in its ethnicity.

The staples of such humor throughout the period were comical black Americans, the shanty Irish, and coarsely conniving Jewish Shylocks. In a medium dominated by their kinsmen, German-Americans were rarely caricatured, and then for such harmless vices as noisy street orchestras. The Chinese seldom served as targets, and American Indians

70

only when western conflict made them newsworthy. Toward the end of the century a few cartoons gently gibed at Italian immigrants, usually portraying nuisance organ-grinders and women with immense bundles of laundry on their heads. But far more often than Cleveland, Blaine, Bryan, Beecher, Ben Butler, or any other headline luminary or scapegoat, Rastus and Chloe, Paddy and Bridget, and Hockheimer and Rebecca were exploited for ridicule in Gilded Age cartoon art.

A few adroit students of ethnic prejudice during the era have paid proper heed to this filler art, but it has been largely ignored by authorities on American editorial cartooning in favor of the lavish color centerfolds and covers that exhibited genius, brought forth a multitude of dimes, excited public commentary, and, it has been argued, helped determine political fortunes. Yet, aesthetic sensibilities and political and commercial import aside, these dreadful ethnic filler pieces accounted for a generous measure of the total output of a generation of editorial cartoonists. They constitute a distinctive genre of American graphic art and deserve more attention than they received when published and for a century since.

Purchased from staff and freelance artists (usually for five dollars apiece), such cartoons were apparently valued by editors primarily for the empty white spaces they would fill, without the slightest regard to overall editorial or political purpose. In many instances these ethnic fillers conveyed sentiments fundamentally at odds with the color cartoons and written editorials. *Puck*, for example, featured many brilliant color cartoons championing the Jews and lampooning the absurdity of their exclusion from places of public accommodation, often accompanied by editorial commentary essentially benign except for an occasional critique of their "chosen people" resistance to melting-pot assimilation. Yet not uncommonly, the same issues contained scurrilous filler cartoons making mock of Shylockian grotesqueries of shekel over soul. *Judge*, typically Republican in its solicitous regard for black GOP voters in the South and ever willing to wave the bloody shirt over racial atrocities it could link to the Democrats, consistently ran the most outrageously white supremacist filler art of any periodical of the time. Similarly, *Judge*—prompted less by any affinity for Hibernia than by a strident Anglophobia that cast John Bull as the evil puppetmaster of the free-trade opposition—often depicted the Irish and Irish-Americans with a modicum of sympathy in color art, while portraying them in filler pieces as besotted primitives resembling a missing link between Homo sapiens and the lower anthropoids.

In a similar vein, this genre of ethnic cartooning also lacked altogether any cultural or historical context. If editorial cartooning and the art of caricature have thrived upon creative exaggeration and droll absurdities in setting or situation, it has been dependent as well on a certain reality of context. Distortion is not fabrication, exaggeration not wholesale invention. Centerfold and cover color cartoons tended to reflect and comment on historical phenomena or cultural trends, whether real or perceived. Filler pieces simply paid no heed. Nor did they evince much recognition of a dynamic state of flux in American ethnicity during the late nineteenth century. Although fundamental changes occurred in American ethnic communities from 1877 to 1900—especially among the Jews—Hockheimer, Paddy, and Rastus endured essentially unchanged as stock cartoon stereotypes from *Puck*'s genesis through century's end. In short, this ethnic filler art represented not so much an outpost of editorial journalism as a sort of visual vaudeville or minstrelry.

The comical black cartoon figures strutting to impress the opposite sex or idling with daydreams of the purloined melon or plump hen made few connections with a struggling people cast from the frying pan of slavery into the fire of sharecropping and the origins of a rendezvous with mean city streets. One bond with reality was that one cartoon in four or five caricatured blacks in an urban milieu, usually parodying games of chance, droll courtship rites, or humbug resorts to the ubiquitous razor to resolve disputes. The genre was grandly racist: caricatures replete with grossly exaggerated lips, huge splayed feet, and kinky hair [IV-1; IV-2]; tortured dialect imitative of minstrelry; and situational satire that sank as low as cartoons of alligators gobbling up little black children with legends such as "Nigger Savings Bank" and "A Splendid 'Opening' for a Southern Youth."[1] In one sense, fortunately, this filler satire was totally alien to a dominant, ugly drift in Gilded Age racist ideology that cast the newly unchained "Savage Sambo" as a manic brute set free to wreak unspeakable depravities on whites, and helpless white womenfolk in particular.[2] At a time when African-Americans were characterized by Thomas Nelson Page, the reigning master of genteel Cavalier romance, as "a vast sluggish mass of uncooled lava" restrained by no law

A SUGGESTION FOR A SOUTHERN SCARECROW.

"HI YAH! YOU BUH'DS, DON' YOU SPILE DEM WATER-MILLIONS!"

[IV–1] E.S. Bisbee, "A Suggestion for a Southern Scarecrow," Puck, *March 21, 1883.*

WOOL-GATHERING.

A SOUTHERN SCENE.

[IV–2] E.S. Bisbee, "Wool-Gathering," Puck, April 28, 1880.

save that of Judge Lynch,[3] droll "darkey" cartoon characters threatening nothing more sacred than white henhouses and watermelon patches provided a benign departure.[4]

The Irish image in American cartooning during the period owed much to a wholesale expropriation of British stereotypes and caricature, especially the art of John Tenniel in *Punch*, key to the transformation of Paddy into a simian terrorist [IV–3] and a major influence on Nast in his vendetta against Irish Catholics and Tammany. With his small cranium, beady eyes, pug nose, and grossly exaggerated baboon mouth and underslung prognathous jaw, Nast's Hibernian has been described by Perry Curtis as "a *lusus naturae* or cross between a professional boxer and an orangutan." Although a *Puck* commentary derided Nast's creation as the "orang-outang Celt, all jaw and no brain," Keppler plagiarized it shamelessly in myriad *Puck* centerfolds and covers decrying Irish fanaticism and a bloodlust that menaced hallowed Anglo-American verities and social institutions. This Tenniel–Nast–Keppler Irish caricature por-

[IV–3] John Tenniel, "The Fenian Guy Fawkes," Punch, December 28, 1867.

trayed a creature congenitally beneath civilization's mudsill and containable only by the sword or hangman's noose, possibly the most frightening cartoon convention drawn before Grant Hamilton's chilling Spanish brute butchering American soldiers and Cuban innocents during the Spanish-American War.[5]

Irish filler cartoons, however, exuded a much more benign and bucolic image, although their link with reality was no less fuzzy. As the sons and daughters of the refugees from Irish famine began the odyssey from pick and shovel and Hell's Kitchen or Seven Points to respectable vocations and lace-curtain brownstones, filler art from 1877 through the century's end blithely perpetuated the stereotype of rustic Old World cottagers with goats grazing on thatched shanty roofs. The dominant caricature of Paddy, as exemplified by the art of *Puck*'s Frederick Burr Opper [IV–4], was perhaps less mentally imposing but much more innocuous. Gone was the bestial menace and the pair of malevolent beady eyes, replaced by the bemused expression of the daydreamer. If this droll creation posed a threat to anyone, it was not to the WASP community. Rather, Paddy's own liver and family fortunes might suffer through his congenital affinity for "the craythur," and to fellow Irish celebrants within the reach of his ubiquitous shillelagh in saloons, at riotously drunken wakes, and in disputes at St. Patrick's Day parades or with "thim schabs" during labor difficulties. Far from being portrayed as a menacing predator, the filler Paddy lived in constant fear of his better half, a beefy Bridget capable of replacing his crumpled hat and shamrock with the family cookpot. In these cartoons the major menace was the tyranny exerted by Irish janitors and housemaids against hapless employers.

The stereotypical Jew in American filler cartoons and caricatures also owed much to European origins, especially in physiognomy, dialect, and a fondness for symbols more appropriate for the Jewish enclaves of Berlin or Vienna than the United States. Before the epic pogroms in Eastern Europe triggered the mass migration that totally redefined the culture, dress, demographics, and theological orientation of the American Jewish community, a largely Germanic, Reform Jewish population was the most geographically dispersed of any ethnic population and exhibited few external traits of cultural distinctiveness. Yet in filler cartoons, Jews existed as a people apart, denizens of New York's Chatham Street and its

PUCK'S GALLERY OF CELEBRITIES.

THE KING OF A-SHANTEE.

[IV–4] Frederick Burr Opper, "The King of A-Shantee," Puck, February 15, 1882.

Shylockian wizards of shoddy. In grotesque, hook-nosed physiognomy, tortured burlesque Yiddish dialect, and unabashed love of lucre [IV–5], the Jew of filler caricature represented the residue of a stereotype as old as the Inquisition. Once set in the popular imagination, this image remained remarkably constant through the 1880s and 1890s, with the major deviations limited to a plethora of "Jewish lightning" arson gags and such ersatz eastern surnames as "Burnupski" during the 1890s. In contrast to the Irish, Jews fared much worse in weekly filler cartoons than in *Puck* centerfolds and editorials, although the filler fare was somewhat less offensive than the rampant Judeophobia of early color art in *Judge* and the cartoons and verbal sallies of the obnoxiously anti-Semitic newcomer *Life*.[6]

What lesson this visual vaudeville has held for humankind has been a subject of lively debate among scholars of prejudice, most of them authorities on American anti-Semitism. The view that it is better to be laughed at than lynched has had numerous proponents, especially among students of Jewish history who have contrasted the nasty but nonlethal American tradition of defamation with that in Europe, which led to the unspeakable horrors of Auschwitz and Buchenwald. In a 1951 essay, Harvard historian Oscar Handlin implied improbably that the Jewish stereotype in American thought and humor was not that of the scheming Shylock until the nativist upsurge in the 1890s, and even then, on the whole, was essentially benign. To Handlin, such caricature was "not meant and not taken" as defamatory anti-Semitism, and "the American stereotype involved no hostility, no negative judgment." Richard Hofstadter ignored caricature in a synthesis that blamed the relatively insignificant Judeophobia of the 1890s mainly on the Populist ferment, ostensibly absolving the New York cartoonist fraternity altogether. In his 1955 magnum opus, *Strangers in the Land*, and in subsequent essays, historian John Higham agreed that virulent Judeophobia began relatively late in the period, attributing it to a broader upsurge in nativist intolerance wrought primarily by socioeconomic tensions. In Higham's opinion, the older image of the Jew in American humor as the conniving mercantile parvenu was relatively innocuous and leavened with "a grain of truth," for "a fair share of them had risen to affluence too rapidly to acquire the discipline of culture."[7]

In a useful 1973 study, Rudolf Glanz also focused on the image of

VULGAR DISPLAY.

ROSENBAUM.— So hellup me ! How Goldstein worships
der almighty tollar ! Shoost look at dot sofa !

[IV–5] F.M. Howarth, "Vulgar Display," Puck, February 21, 1894.

the Jew as parvenu, interpreting this archetype as a distinctly American symbol of an urban, capitalist culture and drawing sharp distinctions between a poisonous European anti-Semitism and a much less defamatory New World genre of satire. Indeed, Glanz became so enamored of comparative American virtue that he concluded with the bizarre assertion that this anti-Semitic satire had somehow served as a force for cultural cohesion. "In Europe, the symbol of the Golden Calf led to Jew-baiting and pogrom," he wrote, but in America "to a wrestling with spiritual forces" that eventually "made possible an equilibrium of social forces in a new world."

Arguing instead that moderate Judeophobia is akin to being mildly pregnant or slightly dead, Michael Dobkowski's uncompromising 1979 volume, *The Tarnished Dream*, tersely indicted a generation of scholars for such Pollyanna interpretations and Third Reich comparisons. To Dobkowski, the American image of the Jew as an unscrupulous, scheming, conniving Shylock was inherently evil on its face, much older in origins, and born not of hayseed Populist dementia or 1890s urban malaise but rather of longstanding New World Christian nativist ideology. In sharp counterpoint to Glanz, Dobkowski argued that the persistence of this malevolent Shylock image in popular and elite culture served mainly to drive "a wedge between Jews and gentiles simply by sharpening negative stereotypes."[8]

This, it would seem, is the crux of the matter. At issue here is not what happened elsewhere or did not happen at all, but rather the logical effects of this ethnic caricature on popular opinion. Dobkowski's point is not limited to Jew and gentile. In *Apes and Angels*, Perry Curtis made precisely the same point in noting that a result of Irish caricature in Britain was an unchallenged belief among the elite that Catholic Celts "could never be properly civilized or Anglicized," that they were "a peculiar 'race' with a temperament quite unsuited to English norms of rational behavior and political maturity."[9]

An exact parallel could be drawn by any rational student of the Yankee mindset during our country's headlong retreat from the egalitarian imperatives of the Civil War and Reconstruction to a national consensus for a separate, manifestly unequal mudsill status for black Americans. Robert Berkhofer has noted that a persistent tendency in the stereotyping of American Indians since Columbus has been to "describe

Indian life in terms of its lack of White ways," to measure them "as a general category against those beliefs, values, or institutions they most cherished in themselves at that time."[10] The point is simple. However benign the intentions or reception of such ethnic caricature, it surely helped to create and reinforce over the course of a generation an indelible impression that the droll darky, the besotted, belligerent Celt, and the aggressively acquisitive Jew were—by dint of congenital shortcomings of intellect, culture, or character—forever barred from membership in the American family.

The alienness of these cartoon stereotypes went deeper than physiognomies barely humanoid and dialects that wrought havoc with the mother tongue, down to that body of myth, core cultural values, and ennobling ideals we traditionalists allude to as the "American character."[11] Indeed, the discerning scholar might explore the dynamics of this concept more easily through the perceived stereotypical shortcomings of Rastus, Paddy, and Hockheimer than through the proclaimed virtues of its model exemplars. The example that comes most readily to mind is that of the Puritan or Yankee work ethic. The sanctity of honest toil, with concomitant material and spiritual rewards in this world and the next, was rooted deep in European Protestant culture before the first colonials slogged ashore at Jamestown and Plymouth, and no article of faith served better the challenge of a sprawling subcontinent awaiting a rendezvous with ax and plow. The dignity of free labor helped create a republic rooted in the autonomous citizen and a political culture whose compelling icons included Andrew Jackson, a "plain Tennessee ploughman;" William Henry Harrison, an American Cincinnatus partial to log cabins and hard cider; and Abraham Lincoln, a "railsplitter of the West." As Eric Foner has argued persuasively, the latter won his mandate to preserve the Union less because slavery exploited blacks than because it encouraged idleness and extravagance in their owners. For a generation or more after Appomattox, this work ethic remained a hallowed American ideal, until it was corrupted into a success ethic by the Industrial Revolution and later in the 1950s by the personality and positive-thought perversions of Norman Vincent Peale and Dale Carnegie.[12]

This work ethic was broadly based, embracing not only artisans and yeoman farmers but everyone whose labor was involved in the production or distribution of goods. Andrew Jackson excluded from the "producing classes" only speculators, bankers, and lawyers; a half-century later, the Knights of Labor barred from its ranks only the latter two professions, plus pimps and gamblers. Although it was often linked to the promise of upward mobility and in colonial times had been endowed with a theological rationale, the work ethic divorced from concomitant rewards functioned simply as a facet of useful citizenship. From the Puritan founders, through Benjamin Franklin's "Poor Richard" and Thomas Jefferson's ideal of a natural American aristocracy on down to Horatio Alger's "Ragged Dick" and "Nelson the Newsboy," the Yankee work ethic was indeed an ethic. A worthy citizen was expected to toil vigorously to produce at fair prices quality goods that met community needs, and profits and wages honestly earned were to be put to productive use through frugality and temperate habits, not squandered on luxury or vice.

The dominant image of black Americans in period filler cartoons was that of the artful idler, thriving through an innate instinct for subverting the work ethic or practicing it selectively in forays against a neighboring henhouse or melon patch or an employer's liquor supply. This figure was not merely alien to the work ethic; it was its blithe antithesis. In an 1885 E.S. Bisbee cartoon in *Judge*, a lounging teenager queried a chum, "You don't 'spec a feller ter sit down and git up again the same day, does yer?" An 1888 *Puck* cartoon featured an "energetic footman" [IV–6] dusting with a feather duster tied to a horse's tail as it busily swishes away flies. An 1892 *Judge* cartoon by Eugene Zimmerman featured a black man whitewashing a fence and explaining to a crony that this was akin to a vacation for one who had "nebber done a stroke ob wuk befo'." In W.A. Rogers's 1893 *Judge* effort "Not Monodynamic," Nicodemus, perched on a barrel and smoking his pipe, explained to a white passerby, "No sah; don't wanter loaf all de time; wanter sleep some." In 1885, *Puck* carried the tale of Uncle Jake's calling to the pulpit: "It's mighty pow'ful work, hoein' co'n in de hot sun on stony groun', boss, an' I war berry tired, an' I leaned back on de hoe an' got ter thinkin,' an' all ob a sudden like, I feel dat de good Lord called 'pon me ter preach de gospel, sah."[13]

Cartoon blacks were anything but shiftless or dimwitted, however, when it came to their illicit pursuit of plump chickens and prize watermelons. In the filler cartoons of the era, this quest was not merely sport,

ONE-HORSE POWER.

OUR ENERGETIC FOOTMAN. — If dem flies wan's ter be ser
mighty busy, dey jes' well might help dis yer coon do hes wu'k!

[IV–6] Artist unknown, "One-Horse Power," Puck, July 18, 1888.

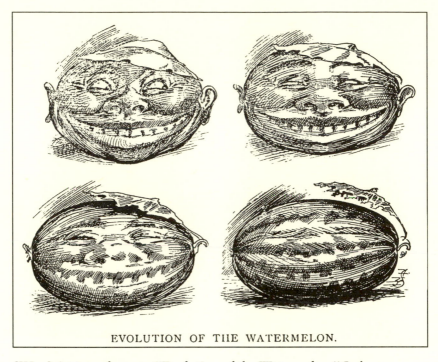

EVOLUTION OF THE WATERMELON.

[IV–7] Artist unknown, "Evolution of the Watermelon," Judge,
September 17, 1892.

it was a Darwinian imperative. The 1892 Judge cartoon "Evolution of
the Watermelon" [IV–7] drolly diagrammed this transformation. An
1894 Syd B. Griffin Judge cartoon portrayed the Jacksons placing their
infant son near a pullet, liquor decanter, and melon to discover "which
fambly he tooks aftah"; when the lad grabbed both chicken and melon,
Jackson exulted, "He am a bohn Jackson." This infatuation tended to
transcend sexual drives and other primal urges, as Zimmerman's splendid 1894 Puck cartoon "Love at First Sight" [IV–8] made clear. As Mose
explained to Abe in another Zimmerman 1894 Puck effort, his impend-
ing marriage to a woman thrice his age was prompted by the dowager
possessing "de fines' watermillion patch in de kentry." Louis Dalrymple's
Aunt Dinah, in his 1889 Puck cartoon "The Melonium Has Come," exulted, "Praise de Lawd! Praise de Lawd!" after Uncle Reuben told her of
his new job, "Doan git no pay. Gwine wuk awn de watermelon dock."
In Zimmerman's 1900 Judge cartoon "A Praiseworthy Talent," a wife

LOVE AT FIRST SIGHT.

[IV–8] Eugene Zimmerman, "Love at First Sight," Judge, September 1, 1894.

"WHERE THERE'S A WILL—"

MR. WOOLBURTON.—"Fo' de Lawd! If dat
fahmah ain't gone an' built er fence more'n
twelve feet high, an' me wid de rheumaticks!

"It jess makes mah heart ache to see dem fowls   "Let's see. Dis 'ere pole looks like it might be
runnin' round loose at dis hour.   ob some use in'r case like dis.

[IV–9] F.M. Howarth, "Where There's a Will—," Puck, March 20, 1895
(continued on p. 87).

castigated her ne'er-do-well spouse as a "low-down, crap-shootin', gin-drinkin' niggah," but when he suggested that she also malign him for chicken theft, she responded, "I ain't singin' none of yo'r praises now, coon; I's showin' yo'r failins'."[14]

Such forays often involved elaborate ruses and ingenuity worthy of a Rube Goldberg. Purloined pullets were carried off inside umbrellas, hats, and, in one 1893 Dalrymple *Puck* cartoon, a stovepipe large enough to accommodate fourteen chickens. Carefully guarded melon patches yielded their bounty to small children feasting from the inside, and to subterranean tunnels that evoked the additional irony of larceny requiring more toil than

"De powah ob inwention was allers somet'm'
wondahful in mah brains.

"Dar! I t'ought dat chick'n could n't resist a
roostin' place; an' she's de bigges'
one in de coop!

"How is dat fo' high?

"De hand ob Providence wuz in dis;
dat's suah!"

honest work. When a hen-house proved too well secured, the intrepid thief prevailed by use of such devices as a fishing rod or a catapult [IV–9]. Often the best-laid plans were foiled, however, by two thieves arriving simultaneously and scaring each other off. When caught red-handed by an angry farmer with a shotgun, the miscreant might respond with a plaintive "Don't shoot, yer might kill yer chickens" or a huffy "Yer jess want ter 'cuse me ob stealin' yer chickens, an' dis chile don't stan' still an' hear himself 'bused no how." In the Bisbee 1884 *Puck* cartoon "Clean-Handed," a thief caught scaling the hen-house fence innocently held up empty hands as he grasped his booty with his bare splayed feet. In an 1891 *Puck* cartoon reminiscent of minstrel repartee, an apprehended thief told a farmer that he had killed the chicken in self-defense. When the farmer protested, "Oh, look here, Mose! A little chicken wouldn't hurt you!," Mose cheerfully agreed, "Ya-as; dat's w'at I thought."[15]

Many cartoons of this genre were cast as morality plays between black preachers, themselves frequent targets for ridicule in filler art, and larcenous members of their congregations. In an 1891 *Puck* Opper cartoon, Reverend Shadbone complained, "I's in trouble, sah; I preached a sermon las' Sunday agin' chicken-stealin', an' de congregation am gwine to try me for heresy." In Samuel Ehrhart's 1894 *Puck* cartoon "Rank Heresy," Brother Silas stopped attending church after the preacher declared that animals lack souls, forcing him to wonder, "How dey gon a git chickens inter hebbin den?" In some cartoons, preachers were themselves the miscreants. An 1889 Griffin *Puck* cartoon portrayed Reverend G. Washington Shortext spotting a wayward chicken, jumping atop the pulpit, and declaring, "De congregatium will keep dere seats. Dat's mah bird!" The most vexing ethical dilemma in these cartoons was not that of sin or salvation, or theft or less arduous honest toil, but rather that suggested by Griffin's droll 1893 *Judge* cartoon "Between Two Loves" [IV-10]—of the melon versus the hen![16]

The cardinal character flaw of the stereotypical Irish caricatured in filler cartoons during the period was neither laziness nor larceny but profligacy. Although the color art in *Puck* and *Judge* sometimes reflected the Irish ascent up the socioeconomic and political ladders, as well as a penchant for terrorism carried over from English humor weeklies, in generic Irish gag cartoons Paddy and Bridget remained fresh famine refugees from the auld sod, hard working but none too bright and slaves to temptation. They were apparently unable to set aside any of their modest earnings for such worthy uses as capital accumulation or a more elevated standard of living. A common theme in these cartoons was that of the tyrannical servant Maggie or Bridget bullying her poor mistress into performing the household drudgery. But the emphasis here was on the maid's Celtic belligerence, not laziness. Similarly, Paddy or Clancy was often portrayed sitting on a barrel or washtub puffing on a clay pipe while a wife or other workers slaved away, but again the point was not laziness per se, but the mindset of the dimwitted dreamer. In one such cartoon featuring two hodcarriers, Dolan asked Clancy why he was loafing instead of working, and Clancy enlightened him, "Oi was t'inkin' what a foine country dhis wud be if Saturday noight kim round as a'fn as Monday marnin'."[17]

Although *Puck* once characterized the Irish as a lazy lot who had

BETWEEN TWO LOVES.

"Kin any one tell a po' culled man what to do in a case like dis?"

[IV–10] Syd B. Griffin, "Between Two Loves," Judge, September 30, 1893. Photograph by Brian Campbell Fischer.

"rarely done any work, even in this free country, to improve their social condition," they were for the most part portrayed in cartoons as a hardworking people, in keeping with the maxim of the day that to perform backbreaking toil was "to work like an Irishman." Sometimes the problem was one of comparative labor values. The 1886 James A. Wales *Puck* cartoon "Ungallant" portrayed O'Brien unable to stir from bed to patch a leaky roof after a hard night "advisin' thim schab car-drivers wid bricks." Zimmerman's 1893 *Judge* effort "It's the Same Man" featured Mike unable to fetch a scuttle of coal for his wife on doctor's orders, but on the docks toting a massive barrel of beer for a free drink. The main problem was that the lure of lace-curtain respectability was overwhelmed by a notorious weakness for the "wee drop," and by a sentimental longing for the auld sod that made the sons and daughters of Erin notorious suckers for every phony scam to raise funds for Irish poor relief or the quest for home rule. Cartoon after cartoon made mock of the Irish affinity for "the craythur," down to a *Puck* parody of Christian iconography by Friedrich Graetz portraying Saint Patrick [IV–11] with staff in one hand and a rye bottle in the other. Other cartoons, notably a *Puck* quartet by Opper, lampooned the avarice of Irish incendiaries and Catholic clergymen, and the consequences to naive immigrants mired in pick-and-shovel or domestic jobs if they could not resist the blarney [IV–12; IV–13].[18]

More frequent by far than filler cartoons featuring the blacks or Irish were those lampooning the Jews, especially in *Puck* during the late 1880s and the 1890s, and in the rancidly Judeophobic *Life* from its genesis in 1883. The stereotypical Semite exhibited less a denial or insufficiency of the Yankee work ethic than an outright perversion of it. Afflicted neither with the affinity for idleness that beset cartoon blacks nor the fondnesses for the "wee drop" and sentimental generosity that burdened the Irish, the cartoon Jew violated the work ethic by a congenital aversion to honest toil and honest dealing, and a mania for the dollar that knew no bounds and suffered no moral restraints. In cartoon after cartoon, the image of the Jew is that of Shakespeare's Shylock, probably the dominant theme in western anti-Semitism since the Middle Ages, transplanted to the New World to prey upon the gullible gentile and one another along New York's Chatham Street.[19]

Never slaves to facts or demographic trends, the cartoonists of the

SAINT PATRICK.

RYE

ST·PATRICK

A Fancy Sketch for the Seventeenth.

[IV–11] Friedrich Graetz, "Saint Patrick," Puck, March 12, 1884.

POOR PAT'S PERSECUTORS.

THE IRISH LEECHES AND THEIR VICTIM.

[IV–12] Frederick Burr Opper, "Poor Pat's Persecutors," Puck, March 7, 1883.

THE SOONER THE BETTER.

Cook.—" Help Ireland, is it? Begorra, the best way to help Ireland wud be for you an' the likes of ye to *die* for Ireland."

[IV–13] Frederick Burr Opper, "The Sooner the Better," Puck, February 6, 1884.

era ignored altogether the Jews who labored as craftsmen or factory workers or who toiled long days for a pittance in sweatshops as garment workers. Thus the cartoon Jews performed no honest labor to create worthy goods or services but rather earned their livings parasitically, as pawnbrokers, moneylenders, or the Chatham Street shopkeepers and street vendors of shoddy goods sold at inflated prices. The major exception was the clothier who produced his own wares, invariably poorly made, ill-fitting garments guaranteed to fade and shrink to indecent-exposure dimensions when laundered and hawked at bogus discount with outlandish pitches and sales gimmicks.

Beginning in 1893, a running theme in *Puck* cartoons was that of "Jewish lightning," or profit-by-arson. In one such cartoon, Burnupski and son Jakey marveled over God's wisdom in guiding the Israelites over the desert with a pillar of fire, "der most addractive ding to our beoples." In another, Isaacstein was given a new safe because the former one had survived so many fires that its manufacturer wanted it as an advertising promotion. Simultaneously experiencing a burglary and a fire, Rosenbaum "came oudt schoost even." Cohenstein trained his dog to bark whenever it saw a fireman. Nicely exploiting this running gag was a vignette of clothier Moses Cohen, insurance policy in pocket, happily watching smoke in the shape of dollar signs rise from his torched store [IV–14] in Grant Hamilton's 1896 *Judge* back cover cartoon, "Judge's Fun With the $ Mark."[20]

As John Higham and other scholars have noted, the stereotypical Jew of the period was the "quintessential parvenu," fond of flaunting the fruits of ill-gotten gains with such ostentatious displays of furs, oversized diamonds, foreign cruises, and pushy forays into gentile seaside spas—vulgarities befitting "a tasteless barbarian rudely elbowing into genteel company." Yet in most filler cartoons, ostentation yielded to epic parsimony. After he gunned down a bird, Griffin's Ikey was told by his father to "go pick der shot oud ohf dot plue-jay, unt we loat up fer anudder." Rescued from drowning, Dalrymple's Steinbach queried bystanders, "Schentlemens, can anyvon schange a kervarter?" so he could reward his rescuer. Frank Beard's little Ikey bought paper flowers for sister Rachel's nuptials [IV–15] so "ve could use dem again ven grandfader dies." Ehrhart's Rosenbaum was so cheap he weighed himself, his corpulent wife, two children, and the family dog together for a single penny. After hear-

What Mr. Cohen saw when his clothing-shop burnt out.

[IV-14] *Center detail from Grant Hamilton, "Judge's Fun with the $ Mark," Judge, February 8, 1896. Photograph by Brian Campbell Fischer.*

A YOUNG FINANCIER.

" Ikey, did you ged dose flowers for Rachel's vedding ?"
" Yes, fader ; unt I got paper vons so as ve could use dem
again ven grandfader dies."

[IV-15] Frank Beard, "A Young Financier," Judge, May 12, 1894.

ing a sobbing Little Ikey confess that he had lost a nickel, J.S. Pughe's
Cohenstein groused to his wife, "Mine crashous, Rebecca, uf I dond't
dink dere musht be Chentile bloodt in your vamily!"[21]

In other cartoons the symbols of the bulbous hooked nose and the
dollar are synonymous. Dollar signs adorned Jewish tombstones, Jews
conversed on streetcars in dollar signs [IV-16], and visualized the holy
symbol in household furnishings [IV-5]. Ehrhart's Loanstein anticipated
a happy hereafter, where "der sthreeds are pafed mit gold!" Opper's
Hocksteins lament after their silver anniversary party that they had not
wed twenty-five years sooner so their "peautiful bresents . . . might haf
peen goldt!" Unable to read huge letters on an eye chart, Howarth's Eise-

ON A MADISON AVE. CAR.

A Pleasant Social Chat on their Way to Business.

[IV–16] F.M. Hutchins, "On a Madison Avenue Car," Puck, *February 8, 1893.*

mann had no difficulty with miniscule dollar and percent symbols "as glear as der noonday sun!" When told by his wife that little Ikey was ill, just lying in his cradle taking no interest in anything, Ehrhart's Cohnstein responded, "Vat! don't dake no interest? Mine Gracious, he must be teadt!" Avarice permeated the generational lore passed down from fathers to sons. When Schwindlebaum asked little Ikey what he would de-

COPYRIGHT, 1895, BY KEPPLER & SCHWARZMANN

A GREAT OPPORTUNITY.

IKEY STEINHEIMER.— Fadder, der doctor says Mr. Sheubinsky has enlargement of der heart.
FATHER STEINHEIMER.— Run ridt avay up to Mr. Sheubinsky's, Ikey, und ask him to lend your fadder dot two hundred tollars vot he did n't haf' last veek!

[IV–17] Joseph Keppler, Jr., "A Great Opportunity," Puck, March 6, 1895.

sire if a good fairy gave him all the money he wanted, Ikey replied, "a leedle more monish, Fadder." Asked how much he loved his father, Dalrymple's little David replied affectionately, "Von hundert per cend, no discound, fasd golors, mit exchanche on Lohndon!" When Aby asked when a fish was on the line, Griffin's Feldheimer advised, "Der line goes down a liddle—Aboud one unt a helluf per cend." To punish the misbehaving little Sol, Howarth's Hockstein threatened to put the lad on the "gounter and make him vatch me vile I scharge der next gustomer only six per cent."[22]

Such cartoons echoed precisely the 1890 condemnation of Jacob Riis: "Money is their God. Life itself is of little value compared with even the leanest bank account." Indeed, this disparity served as the theme of what I believe to be the most obscene anti-Semitic cartoons of the period.

REBECCA—"Oh, Levi, Levi! Liddle Ikey has got killed."
LEVI—"Oh, Moses and Aaron! Oh, oh, oh, mein liddle Ikey!
Vere vas he kilt, Rebecca?"
REBECCA—"On the railroad."
LEVI—"Oh, bless dot poy! he had a goot head on him. He
knew his fader could get damages. He alvays had an eye fer
pizness."

[IV–18] *Eugene Zimmerman, untitled,* Judge, *December 12, 1892.*

In two cartoons, young boys accidentally swallowed silver coins; Cohen responded by marking a coat up a quarter and Ikelstein reassured his wife, "Don'd ged oxcided, Rajel, it vas gounderveid." Told that his friend Sheubensky was seriously ailing with an enlarged heart, Steinheimer [IV–17] ordered son Ikey to run and hit him up for "dot two hundred tollars vot he didn't haf' last veek!" Informing a friend of his wife's death, a weeping Itzig digressed, "Oxgscuse me, Schmool, is dot a real diamond?" A consolation for Widow Isaacs was her husband's acceptance of death, that "dere vas no money in der cloding peesiness nowatays." Howarth's Rubenstein complained bitterly to a friend over the loss of an expensive suit after his son Jacob "goes on dot oxgursion und gets drownt. Dot feefty tollar suit vos entirely ruined." Zimmerman's Levi, disconsolate over the death of his son Ikey [IV–18], was consoled by the thought that he had been killed in a railroad tragedy: "Oh, bless dot poy! He knew his fader could get damages. He alvays had an eye fer pizness."[23]

Parallels can be constructed to negligent black parents who allowed children to serve as gator bait and to E.S. Bisbee's 1882 *Puck* cartoon "Mississippi Martyrs," in which the Widow Muldoon protested from the roof of her shanty on the flooded Mississippi River for a rescuer to ignore her drowning children: "It's plenty of thim I have! Save me pig, for its the only wan."[24] Such graphic grossness serves to underscore the unworthiness of these ethnic untermenschen for inclusion in the American family. The concept, familiar to students of ethnology and the sociology of deviance, reflects a premise suggested by Emile Durkheim that cultures use such aliens to define outer limits of tolerable conduct and identity, and that such deviants, "by marking the outer edges of group life, give the inner structure its special character and thus supply the framework within which the people of the group develop an orderly sense of their own cultural identity."[25] The implication is unequivocal: the millions of white Protestant Americans who plunked down their dimes for copies of *Puck* and *Judge* and then guffawed at these cartoons did so in part as a ritual reassertion that Rastus, Paddy, and Hockheimer would never become anything more than perpetual aliens in their midst.

V

Better Dead Than Red

Even taking into account the most sinister character traits embodied in the caricatures of the Irish, blacks, and Jews in Gilded Age filler art, more chilling by far was the composite portrait of the American Indian. Although the stereotyping of Indians provided many cogent parallels with other maligned minorities in the graphic satire of the era, salient differences seem both more noteworthy and more significant to an understanding of late nineteenth-century ethnic prejudice. Inventories of *Harper's, Puck, Judge, Life*, and other forums for Gilded Age cartooning indicate that Indians were featured less often than even the Italians or the Chinese, and that blacks, Jews, and the Irish were lampooned in thirty to forty filler pieces for every one devoted to Indians. One result was that the cartoon stereotype of the Indian was a far more shallow composite than those of other ethnics. Complexities were avoided, hostile traits magnified, and the element of subtlety necessary to transform bald bias into wry condescension altogether absent.

Moreover, the mythic personification of blacks, the Irish, and Jews in period filler art was closely linked to other genres of Gilded Age popular humor, becoming more or less a visual extension of the world of minstrelry and vaudeville. Neither the Bowery stage nor the dime humor weeklies could have survived commercially had they emulated the shrill ideology of a Hitler Youth primer. Those Americans who laid down their dimes for *Harper's, Puck, Judge,* or an evening of comic opera expected to be entertained, not indoctrinated. As a result, the stereotypical black, Irishman, and Jew evolved into caricatures to make audiences laugh, not lynch. It is not to deny the arguments of Michael Dobkowski and others that such caricatures were inherently cruel, or that they may have caused real harm, to concede that such stereotyping was probably prompted by motives other than malice. Drollery transcended denunciation. Cartoon blacks menaced mainly henhouses and melon patches, the Irish menaced themselves, and scheming Jewish entrepreneurs preyed primarily on Hebraic competitors and hayseed tourists. Apart from the rank anti-Semitism of *Life* and the early *Judge*, this strain of ethnic humor, both verbal and visual, has been characterized by several respected scholars as tending to humanize as well as demean.

In contrast, Indian cartoon satire lacked such leavening links to Gilded Age popular humor. When Indians were portrayed on the popular stage, it was nearly always as foils in Wild West epics, menacing the frontier families with massacre (or virginal young women with worse) until cut down by the bullets of Buffalo Bill or whichever Beadle dime-novel hero was featured in the melodrama. They never achieved status as a penny-opera or cartoon stereotype, with humanizing tendencies and autonomous status as a mythic convention independent from daily events. Inevitably, Indian cartoons were published close on the heels of news reports of federal appropriations for military units or reservation subsidies or of the major confrontations in the western wilderness—with the Sioux from Little Big Horn in 1876 through the 1881 return of Sitting Bull, Chief Joseph in 1877, the Ute in 1879, the Apache during the summers of 1881 through 1886, and the Wounded Knee tragedy in 1890. Thus the cartoon image of the American Indian was not an extension of period popular humor, but of the daily press, a medium not noted for humanizing drollery. Whether depicted as a filthy, besotted idler or a maniacal savage wreaking havoc on helpless settlers, the cartoon Indian mirrored the thrust of Gilded Age popular prejudice more nakedly than any minority stereotype, save maybe those of the Mormon or the Roman Catholic hierarchy.[1]

Although authorities on anti-Indian prejudice have made little use of these cartoons, Gilded Age graphic satire documents with a chilling lack of subtlety the post-Civil War ascendancy of pejorative Indian imagery over the earlier romantic ideal of the "noble savage." As Robert Berkhofer has detailed, during the early decades of the nineteenth century, many whites both here and abroad envisioned Indians as a brave, proud people endowed with "handsomeness of physique and physiognomy" and living lives of "liberty, simplicity, and innocence." This cult of the noble savage enjoyed a vogue among the genteel classes of the American

Northeast, England, and the Continent, and became a popular theme for literati and landscape artists with echoes in early European cartooning. By the Civil War, according to Berkhofer, this ideal was in headlong retreat, as attitudes hardened and Americans began embracing either or both of two competing images: those of the native American as either a bloodthirsty barbarian or a filthy reservation degenerate. Rarely was it acknowledged that any vestige of reality in either stereotype might be a direct result of a governmental policy of encroachment on tribal grounds, and agency reservations that fostered idleness and degeneracy.[2]

In American cartoon art from Appomattox through the century's end, the only vestige of noble-savage idealism was an occasional centerfold or cover cartoon using Indian braves or lovely young maidens as representational figures. When not symbolized by a Quebeçois lumberjack, Canada was sometimes portrayed in *Puck* and *Judge* color art as a fair-featured Indian princess. When Congress conferred statehood on the two Dakotas, Washington, and Montana in 1889, *Puck* paid tribute with C. Jay Taylor's centerfold, "The Debut of the Younger Sisters," portraying the older states as white debutantes in gowns, Montana as a pioneer lass in buckskin, and Washington and North and South Dakota as beautiful, bronzed but thoroughly Caucasoid Indian maidens.[3]

Apart from such sentimental allegory, Indians fared dismally in the medium. Telling were the many Indian cartoons drawn not to comment on Indians but rather to use them as foils to attack enemy politicos or initiatives. With its affinity for ersatz Indian regalia and ritual, Tammany Hall naturally suggested itself for such treatment, but prominent national figures in both parties and the splinter movements of the day were denigrated as well by such portrayals. Thus, in *Puck*, John A. Logan was drawn in 1886 by James A. Wales as a reservation degenerate grunting, "Ugh! Me don't want no Civil-Service Reform"; 1888 candidate Benjamin Harrison and a host of GOP party luminaries were drawn by Taylor as an Indian marauding party waiting in cowardly ambush for the Grover Cleveland locomotive, "Tariff Reform"; and Kansas Populists William Peffer and "Sockless Jerry" Simpson were portrayed by Louis Dalrymple in 1891 as braves sneaking from behind to assassinate John Sherman with "Alliance" daggers. In *Judge*, an octet of Senate Republicans was pilloried by Victor Gillam in 1891 for their apostasy on the "Force Bill" to assure Negro voting rights in the South by portraying them as Indian renegades joining the "Democratic Free-Silver Sioux." Two years later, Tammany satraps Ed Murphy, David Hill, and Richard Croker were drawn by Bernhard Gillam as savages set to ambush Cleveland, cast as Christopher Columbus, over patronage grievances.[4] Other *Puck* and *Judge* color cartoons used Indians, almost always in a pejorative manner, to lampoon such targets as the frontier commands of Oliver Otis Howard and Philip Sheridan; Secretaries of the Interior Carl Schurz and Henry M. Teller for inefficiency or purported profligacy with public monies; or Boston "bleeding hearts" for their misguided charitable impulses.[5]

In this latter category belongs the best-known Indian cartoon of the generation, Nast's 1880 *Harper's* "Give the Natives a Chance, Mr. Carl" [V–1], with a quartet of Indians pondering a glass ballot globe ("the great protector of the age") beneath crude sketches of a freedman, German, and Irishman allegedly "civilized by the ballot." Although the cartoon is often cited as evidence of Nast's championing of the Indian, his primary inspiration was more probably his loathing for fellow German emigré Schurz for his desertion of Ulysses Grant for Horace Greeley in the 1872 campaign. More likely representative of Nast's thoughts on the Indian was his 1881 cartoon "Give the Red Man a Chance" [V–2], portraying a grotesque Indian on a scaffold, noose around his neck and ballot in hand, over the cryptic dictum "Make him a citizen, with all the *privileges* which that implies." Such a belief, prevalent among the genteel reform Republicans of the era, presumed that the best hope for the Indians was abandonment of reservations for assimilation into the larger American community, an impulse responsible for the well-intentioned but catastrophic Dawes Severalty Act of 1887. That Nast probably cast his chips with the noose instead of the ballot was made manifest in several other *Harper's* cartoons he executed during the period portraying Indians as skulking marauders, reservation wretches, clamorous leeches milking the public purse, and, in one instance, a grossly repulsive "polygamous barbarian" squatting in anticipation of the springtime slaughter.[6]

Nast's July 4, 1885 effort "The Usual Summer Eruption" [V–3], inspired by the fifth straight summer of Apache hostilities in the Southwest, was also more typical of the era's Indian cartooning in general. An 1879 Ute uprising in western Colorado came in response to a highhanded decree by White River Agency superintendent Nathan C. Meeker to plow under grazing meadows to force the Ute into domestic agricul-

[V–1] Thomas Nast, *"Give the Natives a Chance, Mr. Carl,"* Harper's
Weekly, *March 13, 1880.*

GIVE THE RED MAN A CHANCE.
Make him a citizen, with all the *privileges* which that implies.

[V–2] Thomas Nast, "Give the Red Man a Chance,"
Harper's Weekly, *September 24, 1881.*

ture. The rebellion prompted a pair of *Puck* cartoons, one protesting an ambush at Mill Creek in which ten soldiers were killed and the other portraying Sitting Bull, in exile in Canada, lamenting, "Oh, if I could only be with the Utes!" Much more prolific were anti-Apache cartoons prompted by 1881–86 hostilities between the military and Geronimo's Chiracahua, rebelling against the confines of reservation life. Three Frederick B. Opper *Puck* filler pieces included his October 1881 "The Red-Handed Prodigal" [V–4], with innocent white pioneer blood dripping from Apache hands; his 1882 "The Irrepressible Injun" with its Apache lament, "Here it is the tenth of May and we haven't taken a scalp yet!"; and his April 1883 "A Tough Job for Uncle Sam" [V–5], caricaturing

[V–3] Thomas Nast, "The Usual Summer Eruption," Harper's Weekly, *July 4, 1885.*

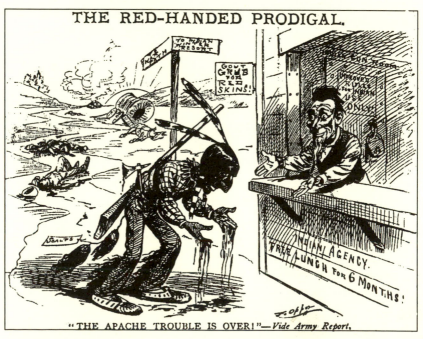

[V–4] Frederick Burr Opper, "The Red-Handed Prodigal," Puck, *October 19, 1881.*

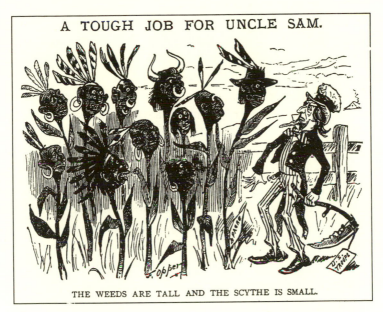

A TOUGH JOB FOR UNCLE SAM.

THE WEEDS ARE TALL AND THE SCYTHE IS SMALL.

[V–5] *Frederick Burr Opper, "A Tough Job for Uncle Sam,"*
Puck, April 11, 1883.

THE GREAT INDIAN ANTI-FAT REMEDY.
Satisfaction guaranteed, or flesh refunded.

[V–6] *E.S. Bisbee, "The Great Indian Anti-Fat Remedy,"*
Judge, December 6, 1884.

Apache warriors as grotesque noxious weeds. E.S. Bisbee's 1884 opus, "The Great Indian Anti-Fat Remedy" [V–6], depicting an Apache tomahawk severing a plump captive's arm, was representative of Indian filler art published in *Judge* during the period.[7]

When not engaged in rapine and pillage, the cartoon Indian of the era was portrayed as the most worthless of idlers waxing fat on the public dole. Opper's August 30, 1882, *Puck* back cover cartoon, "A Losing Business," featured a beleaguered reservation headwaiter Uncle Sam serving a motley Indian clientele from a menu of such entrees as "no-work pie," "idleness soup," "lie-off stew," "loafing chowder," "slouching hash," "nothing-to-do fritters," and "snooze shortcake." To reconcile this paradox between manic bloodlust and laziness, there evolved a theme in the dime humor weeklies and elsewhere that attributed to Indians a sort of seasonal schizophrenia, a lifestyle of spending "summers in slaughtering United States citizens and their winters in fattening on United States rations," as an 1883 *Judge* editorial proclaimed. A week earlier, *Judge* had run as its front cover Grant Hamilton's "Teller's Indian Grocery," depicting Secretary of the Interior Henry Teller as a shopkeeper for menacing braves above the subcaption "If we don't nourish these Indians well through the Winter, they won't be able to make war on us in the Spring." A companion essay complained of annual summer orgies of "rapine, murder, robbery, and crime of various kinds," after which "the cheerful Indians, warned by the approach of winter, return to their reservations, take a long and strong pull at the government rations, and then subside into tranquil, but by no means inexpensive quietude, till the lengthening days send them on the war path again."[8]

Although this hypothesis enabled bigots to characterize Indians as "dirty, thievish, murderous, and lazy," it was without much foundation in fact. As Robert Utley has detailed, many South Dakota Sioux did tend to move rather fluidly between agencies and nontreaty tribal bands, and reservation Ute, Bannock, and Cheyenne had rebelled under extraordinary provocation, but they were exceptions to the rule. Joseph's Nez Perce were nontreaty, although they were willing to live with an accord to which they had not acceded. Geronimo's Chiricahua Apache had sampled agency life, found it intolerable, and left the reservations for their mountain domain, to live apart in peace well before hostilities were forced upon them. Nevertheless, the prevailing image was compelling, somewhat akin to that of a deadly snake dozing in the sun until wakened to reptilian fury. Indeed, this motif was exploited by Hamilton in his June 20, 1885, *Judge* centerfold, "The Nation's Ward" [V–7]. His menacing Apache boa constrictor or python, crushing a helpless pioneer family while being spoon-fed government gruel by a doting Uncle Sam against the backdrop of a smoldering cabin, may be the most brilliant exploitation of anti-Indian prejudice in Gilded Age cartooning.[9]

This composite cartoon stereotype of the American Indian as dumb, drunken, dirty, and degraded was uncommonly demeaning, even in comparison to caricatures of other ill-fated minority groups during a period of retreat from early national and Civil War idealism. Cartoon Indians provided guffaws by proving too dense to distinguish a surveying glass from a liquor flask, a stick of dynamite from a bologna sausage, or a firecracker from a cigarette. Myriad cartoons, one-liners, and editorials depicted Indians as congenital sots committing drunken debaucheries on the war path or idling away winters in alcoholic stupors courtesy of Uncle Sam. Syd B. Griffin's February 18, 1891, *Puck* back cover, "The Artist's Mistake; or, a Spirited Drawing," portrayed in six panels an artist painting a fierce Indian warrior, stopping to take a pull from his whiskey bottle, and running off in terror as the Indian reached out from the painting to seize the bottle for a healthy swig! But in the cartoon lore of the period, an Indian's aversion to soap and a scrub-brush was even stronger than his aversion to sobriety. An 1885 *Puck* one-liner reported that a Minnesota Indian had been found in a bathtub and suggested that the information be sent to Washington, where the "government pensions original discoveries." Opper's 1891 *Puck* back cover cartoon, "The Servant-Girl Problem," portrayed a lineup of improbable domestics that included a "Sioux squaw—Willing to Do Anything but Wash." F.M. Howarth's 1893 *Puck* filler cartoon "A New Method" featured an Indian named "Man-Afraid-of-the-Soap."[10]

Only the bounds of artistic imagination limited portrayals of Indian degradation. An 1893 *Judge* filler piece portrayed the Pawnee "One-Shirt" as a dog-eater waxing fat on a prized setter entrusted to his care by a tenderfoot hunter. Even more demeaning was the two-panel 1888 *Judge* filler "In the Yellowstone Park" [V–8], with an eastern lass on a tourist train gushing to her mother, "See that magnificent specimen of the real American Indian. I know he's going to spear some fierce beast,"

[V–7] Grant Hamilton, "The Nation's Ward," Judge, June 20, 1885.
Photograph by Brian Campbell Fischer.

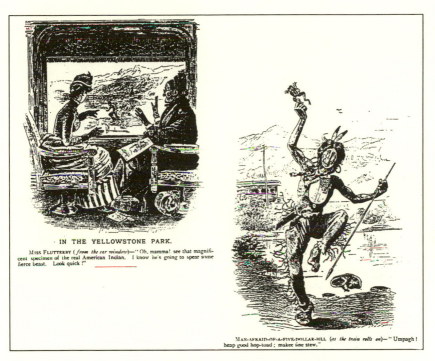

· IN THE YELLOWSTONE PARK.

MISS FLUTTERBY (*from the car window*)—"Oh, mamma! see that magnificent specimen of the real American Indian. I know he's going to spear some fierce beast. Look quick!"

MAN-AFRAID-OF-A-FIVE-DOLLAR-BILL (*as the train rolls on*)—"Umpagh! heap good hop-toad; makee fine stew."

[V–8] J.S. Sullivant, "In the Yellowstone Park," Judge, November 24, 1888.

and, in panel two, Man-Afraid-of-a-Five- Dollar-Bill holding up a toad, dancing in glee and exulting, "Umpagh! heap good hop-toad makee fine stew." Also exploiting the "noble savage" stereotype for comic purposes was the 1889 *Judge* filler cartoon "The Noble Indian" [V–9], featuring an Indian mournfully pondering a railroad track bereft of cigar butts while a tourist pontificated that he was a "once powerful chief, perhaps, brooding over the recent encroachments of civilization." In a similar vein, D.D. Smith's 1888 *Judge* filler "At Cheyenne" [V–10] portrayed a Boston matriarch and her daughter offering a scruffy Indian woman with a papoose on her back some luncheon leftovers, only to hear Howling Bad-Water's rejoinder, "No want grub; white squaw got any chew-to-bacco in her blanket?"[11]

This cartoon, of an Indian mother rejecting sustenance for her baby and herself in favor of a plug of tobacco, stands out as an especially brutal example of Indian degradation, at least as vicious as kindred car-

THE NOBLE INDIAN.

TOURIST (*on overland train*) —"A once powerful chief, perhaps, brooding over the rapid encroachments of civilization. How sad to see the proud head bowed in grief !"

ONCE POWERFUL CHIEF —" Ugh ! no find cigar stump. Injun no smoke."

[V–9] (Anon.), *"The Noble Indian,"* Judge, *July 18, 1889.*

toons of an Irishwoman sacrificing her children to save the family pig or Jewish couples rejoicing over a life insurance windfall from the death of an only son. In one sense this cartoon and others of its kind seem even more chilling than anything drawn during the period to lampoon the Irish, Jews, blacks, or any other ethnic group, for the underlying message is that of a people so degraded, so lacking in qualities of mind and character, that it is doomed to extinction. Other minority stereotypes convey quite the opposite impression. Blacks and the Irish were usually cartooned with platoons of children, and little doubt was left that black ingenuity in henhouse and melon patch, and Irish genius in monopolizing

AT CHEYENNE.

Mrs. Esmond (*of Boston*)—"Why, Violet, here's a real female Indian. Offer the poor thing some of the lunch."

Howling Bad-Water—"No want grub; white squaw got any chew-tobacco in her blanket?"

[V–10] D.D. Smith, "At Cheyenne," Judge, *June 9, 1888.*

urban political patronage, would provide for their progeny. If cartoon Jews had typically small families, often only little Ikey, congenital cunning and the floodgates of Eastern European immigration assured their survival. Indeed, Jewish domination was a persistent tenet of anti-Semitic cartooning. A bleak contrast is provided by filler cartoons of Indians spearing hop-toads or spurning food for tobacco.

This presumption of Darwinian doom was by no means limited to the cartoon art of the day. Indeed, long before Charles Darwin and his New World vogue, most Americans thought of the Indians as a race destined to disappear in the march of civilization westward. Berkhofer has noted that a pervasive theme in the ideal of the noble savage was a romantic nostalgia for a vanishing race. Thus, in 1841 artist George Catlin lamented that "the Indian and the buffalo . . . have taken up their last abode, where their race will expire and their bones will bleach together." Two years later Thomas Farnham described as "a melancholy fact" the axiom that "the Indians' bones must enrich the soil, before the plough of civilized man can open it." Even Andrew Jackson, no romantic idealist when it came to ancestral tribal domains east of the Mississippi, noted in 1830 during a rationale for his Indian removal agenda, "To follow to the tomb the last of his race and to tread on the graves of extinct nations excite melancholy reflections."[12] To avert or at least postpone such "melancholy reflections," the reservation was championed as a reform initiative that, as Wilcomb Washburn maintains, despite endemic abuses, at least "ran against a persistent current of thought that cared little whether aborigines disappeared from the face of the earth." In time disillusioned progressives would begin to regard the reservation itself as an agent of destruction and turned to a credo of assimilation.[13]

Only Nast, among his contemporaries, embraced even tentatively the assimilationist gospel, and no Gilded Age cartoonist portrayed the reservation in a kindly light. The idea that Indians were a doomed race was virtually unchallenged in the medium. This was true particularly of *Puck* and *Judge*, with the latter the more enthusiastic over the prospect and more likely to urge a hastening of its culmination. *Judge* editorials in 1883 declared that "not till the last one is dead will *The Judge* be willing to admit that there are any good Indians," and branded federal Indian policy a conundrum "that will probably continue so till the last

Indian solves it, and the great problem together, by dying," which it termed a "happy consummation."

More often than not the tenor was one of hurrying the natural process along through wholesale extermination of the Indians. In 1880 a *Puck* commentary on purported government coddling of renegade Sioux declared, "The Indian must be prevented from interfering with our alleged civilization, if we have to kill him to do it." A year later *Puck* urged a draconian reservation policy with the advice, "Shoot down every Indian that attempted to pass the line." In 1882, *Judge* urged President Chester Arthur to build "an army that can transform an Indian camp into a burying-ground at a moment's notice," and in an 1883 commentary accompanying the Hamilton centerfold "The Nation's Ward" suggested as an alternative to federal policy that "it would have been infinitely more kind and less expensive to have exterminated him by the short cut and wholesale."[14]

Although a majority of those Americans who purchased copies of the weekly *Puck* and *Judge* may well have agreed with such genocidal sentiments, it is nonetheless clear that the stock-in-trade of these publications was banal humor, and that such fulminations were not especially funny. The challenge, then, was to make fun of genocide—not an easy task. Combining the ingenuity of a Rube Goldberg with the ethical sensitivity of an oyster, cartoonists responded with a competition of sorts among various droll methods of extermination. The unsigned May 12, 1883, *Judge* centerfold "Solving the Indian Problem," suggested that six hundred prizefighters armed with revolvers might provide the answer, instead of an over-matched military. Two months later, Thomas Worth's *Judge* cartoon "The Solution of a Knotty Problem" proposed that the ultimate solution to the problems posed by the Indians and an antiquated Navy was to transport the wayward Apache to exile in Mexico on rotting naval hulks, with an implicit assumption that vessels and cargoes would be lost at sea. As a companion commentary argued, "Decidedly the two most useless, most expensive and most dangerous entities with which the country has to deal, are the Indians and its navy. If they could be made to destroy each other mutually, we would have taken a long step toward the millenium."[15]

In 1885, a New York City construction magnate named Buddensiek achieved notoriety for building substandard tenements that tended to collapse with a heavy loss of life. This perhaps suggested to *Judge* a parallel to Worth's epic on the Indians and the navy, for on August 15 appeared a Hamilton centerfold, "Uncle Sam's Extermination Policy: The Indian Problem Solved—Buddensiek the Boss Builder of the Plains," with Uncle Sam and Buddensiek examining plans for jerry-built tenements for the Ute, Apache, Sioux, and Cheyenne, in the hope that similar disasters would put an end to the Indian problem. As a companion essay declared, "In the absence of any original plan of extermination, why not adopt one of the means of destruction that have been tried and tested on white men?" On December 17, 1890, *Puck* featured on its back cover Opper's "Puck's Solution of the Indian Question," responding to a South Dakota Sioux threat by suggesting that if our bluecoats were not up to the mission, a Salvation Army detachment of the harridans and geezers of the "3rd Regiment Salvation Shooters" would bring the warriors to their knees. Its timing was even more unfortunate than its theme, for two days earlier Sitting Bull, the legendary Sioux leader, had been shot and killed accidentally by agency police. Worse yet was a *Judge* commentary on a Ghost Dance political parody centerfold that said of Sitting Bull, "We do not say that this ugliest and most ungrateful of savages can be hanged now for old offenses, but he should be watched closely for some new one that will enable him to meet his Messiah before the latter's arrival here."[16]

Just days later, the conflict ended in the tragedy of Wounded Knee, when soldiers of Custer's old 7th Cavalry surrounded Oglala and Brule hostiles. A rifle was fired, bedlam ensued, and twenty-five soldiers and nearly two hundred Sioux (almost half women and children) lay dead on the frozen plain. News from South Dakota shocked and sobered the nation and found echoes, however tinny, in humor weekly cartoons. On December 20, *Judge* had run a back cover cartoon deploring an Indian policy that starved them into hostile action and, on January 3, used as its front cover Bernhard Gillam's "Ever Our Indian Policy" [V–11], featuring Secretary of the Interior John W. Noble viewing dead Sioux on their funeral racks as vultures gathered. On January 18, *Puck* featured as its centerfold Joseph Keppler's "Consistency," contrasting Uncle Sam proffering bags of money and food to tropical natives, eastern Jews, and

[V–11] Bernhard Gillam, "Ever Our Indian Policy," Judge, January 3, 1891. Photograph by Brian Campbell Fischer.

starving Irish and Germans, but to dying Plains Indians only blazing revolvers and rotten provisions.[17]

But Wounded Knee produced only a temporary softening, if that, in humor weekly portrayals of Indian peoples. On January 17, *Judge* ran Eugene Zimmerman's back cover cartoon, "Several Ways of Solving the Indian Question," featuring eight purportedly comical genocidal vignettes—including annihilation by such ingenious means as free opium and liquor from Uncle Sam, college football, intertribal warfare, Irish home-rule reservations adjacent to Indian agencies, a lecture on Robert Browning poetry by a Boston debutante, a vaudeville rendition of "Annie Rooney," and three hundred pounds of "kill them with kindness" mixed candies. This cartoon ran two weeks or less after news of Wounded Knee reached New York and had to have been approved within three or four days of the first press reports. A week later, *Judge* featured a political centerfold portraying Senate Democrats as the "Democratic Free-Silver Sioux." Four days later *Puck* ran Opper's "Servant-Girl Problem," featuring a "Sioux squaw—Willing to Do Anything but Wash." On January 31, a *Judge* editorial blaming Wounded Knee on misguided federal philanthropy asked rhetorically, "Is the Indian capable of gratitude? Can he be trusted in any emergency? And is it right through a too merciful management to sacrifice white men and women year after year to his unconquerable savagery?"[18]

Yet, indirectly, Wounded Knee did effect real change in anti-Indian cartooning, not because of tender consciences but because it rang down the curtain on newsworthy western warfare and ushered in a long period in which Indians were almost wholly out of sight and out of mind for artists and their audiences alike. *Puck* and *Judge* cartoons and commentaries remained in vogue through the summer of 1891, then disappeared altogether for nearly two years. A May, 1893, *Judge* filler mocking the Pawnee as dog-eaters and a *Puck* filler two months later lampooning Indian aversion to soap, were the last of the genre. After Wounded Knee the Indian cartoon became a vanishing breed, like the stereotype it embraced.

VI

Cartoon
Culture

By its very nature, political cartoon art in a democratic society has been one of the purest artifacts of popular culture, seeking to influence public opinion through its use of widely and instantly understood symbols, slogans, referents, and allusions. The artist must exploit conventions in fundamental harmony with the "cultural literacy" of the public or risk almost certain failure, for obscurity and snob humor are fatal to the medium. Thus the context of the effective editorial cartoon, disregarding altogether its ideology or the issue at hand, can tell us much about the popular culture of its day.

Although popular culture is as old as civilization itself, its clear divergence from elite, folk, and other traditional categories of culture is a relatively recent phenomenon. Mozart composed and Shakespeare wrote for the pit as well as the boxes, exploiting familiar music and the great stories of folk tradition, the Bible, and classics as familiar to the unlettered as to the literati. Two icons of antebellum American popular culture were Charles Dickens, whose works blended fine writing with splendid storytelling, and Jenny Lind, the "Swedish Nightingale," who became a pop superstar by performing music that would be considered hopelessly "longhair" today. Indeed, the Germania Orchestra musicians who brought Beethoven to the New World in 1848 would have neither understood nor appreciated the Jekyll–Hyde relationship between the Boston Symphony and the Boston Pops, with the same musicians doing Igor Stravinsky one night under Erich Leinsdorf, and "I Saw Mommy Kissing Santa Claus" the next under Arthur Fiedler.

No clear dichotomy between elite and popular culture existed in the United States before the Civil War and was slow to develop after Appomattox. A distinctive popular culture began to evolve apace with

[VI–1] Steve Sack, "The Thinker," Minneapolis Star-Tribune, *1984.*
Reprinted with permission from the Star-Tribune, Minneapolis.

the Industrial Revolution, concomitant population growth in towns and
cities, a proliferation of leisure time and disposable income among ur-
banites, and an influx of European immigrants alien to the adage "Idle
hands are the Devil's workshop." For the most part, however, American
highbrows, middlebrows, and literate lowbrows continued to share a
rather traditional cultural heritage: Scripture, the fables of Aesop and
Arabian Nights, the mythology of Homer, the artistic and historical heritage of the ancients and the Renaissance, the writings of Shakespeare and
John Bunyan, and the adventures of Gulliver, Don Quixote, and Oliver
Twist. This was the milieu reflected in the art of Nast, Keppler, Gillam,
and their compeers.

That this common cultural matrix has waned to the point of extinction during the past century is made manifest by recent American political cartooning. Apart from such infrequent gems as a 1984 Steve Sack
effort drawing "new ideas" candidate Gary Hart as Rodin's "The
Thinker" with an empty thought bubble [VI–1] or a 1986 Jeff MacNelly
portrayal of the Gramm-Rudman deficit bill as "The Trojan Chicken,"[1]

the legacy of the classics has been virtually abandoned by cartoonists. The fables of Aesop and *Arabian Nights* have given way to those of Walt Disney and Hans Christian Andersen, and other fairy tales reincarnated as animated TV cartoons or feature films. The splendid creations of Hesiod, Homer, and Virgil no longer evoke visions of horror or heroics, for Hercules, Odysseus, and Aeneas have been replaced by Rambo and Superman, while the Cyclops, Hydras, and the Minotaur have been doomed to extinction by the likes of Darth Vader, Godzilla, and King Kong.

Also vanquished as cartoon allusions have been John Bunyan's ogre from *Pilgrim's Progress* and, despite some extraordinary inspiration in recent political high crimes and misdemeanors, Dante's *Inferno*. Shakespeare has not fared much better, with such compelling cartoon possibilities as Hamlet and the witches of *Macbeth* used rarely and Falstaff and Shylock not at all. Almost alone among the giants of contemporary cartooning with an affinity for the Bard is the *Los Angeles Times*'s Paul Conrad, whose magnificent 1973 portrayals of a beleaguered Richard Nixon as Hamlet casting aside the skulls of fallen lieutenants [VI–2] and as Richard II pondering his fallen state [VI–3] rank among the finest political cartoons ever produced in the United States. The sole survivor in recent cartoon art among so many memorable Dickens characters is Ebenezer Scrooge, much in vogue during the 1985 holiday season in the wake of a callous denial by Attorney General Ed Meese that hunger posed a problem in America. Don Quixote also puts in occasional appearances, undoubtedly due less to the literary legacy of Cervantes than to the modern musical extravaganza *Man of La Mancha*. Culturally literate political cartoon art is probably faring as badly in Canada as the United States, although Ed Uluschak's fine 1974 *Edmonton Journal* "Portrait of Dorian Nixon" provided one notable exception.[2]

Also exploited minimally in modern political cartooning has been the legacy of the Bible, with hundreds of characters and themes rich in potential now ignored altogether. For the most part, scriptural allusions are limited to personages and situations immediately recognizable to theological illiterates—Adam and Eve naked in Eden, Eve and the serpent, Moses with the commandments or parted sea, Jesus walking on water. During Nixon's Watergate difficulties cartoonists exploited his self-serving sanctimony by depicting him walking on mud or the heads of his abandoned subordinates. Mike Peters portrayed him brilliantly as

"ALAS, POOR AGNEW, MITCHELL, STANS, EHRLICHMAN, HALDEMAN, DEAN, KALMBACH, LA RUE, MARDIAN, STRACHAN, M'CORD, LIDDY, CHAPIN, HUNT, COLSON, KROGH, MAGRUDER YOUNG—I KNEW THEM..."

[VI–2] Paul Conrad, "Alas, Poor Agnew, Mitchell . . ." © *1973, Los Angeles Times. Reprinted with permission.*

[VI–3] Paul Conrad, "O that I were as great as my grief . . ." © *1973, Los Angeles Times. Reprinted with permission.*

O THAT I WERE AS GREAT AS MY GRIEF, OR LESSER THAN MY NAME! OR THAT I COULD FORGET WHAT I HAVE BEEN! OR NOT REMEMBER WHAT I MUST BE NOW.
KING RICHARD II. ACT III, SCENE III

a latter-day Moses, with edited tablets deleting three of the Ten Commandments. Another fine Peters Watergate effort, prompted by the Supreme Court ruling that Nixon must relinquish the tapes, featured the first couple as a naked Adam and Eve, with Nixon ditching the tapes under the accusing finger of God. Nixon's welfare cuts during the 1971 Christmas season inspired a deadly Nativity cartoon by Peters, and his 1979 attempt to buy into a Manhattan cooperative provided the same allusion for Doug Marlette, who has often used religious imagery to attack the Moral Majority and other televangelical insults to his Baptist heritage and flinty liberalism. On a few occasions Pat Oliphant cast born-again James Watt as a bald, maniacal Jesus walking on water or orchestrating the Second Coming during Watt's stormy stint at the Department of Interior.[3]

For the most part, though, the venerable characters of Scripture, classical mythology, Shakespeare, and the like have given way to the more familiar, instantly recognized icons of contemporary television, Tinseltown, the top forty, the comic strips, and other manifestations of popular culture. In 1972 Peters satirized the Nixon peace initiatives as "Cracker Jack Negotiations" (with a "Four More Years" button as a prize) and symbolized the disparity between the campaign organizations of Nixon and George McGovern by drawing the latter as a small gumball machine and the former as a huge slot machine dispensing Cabinet posts and ambassadorships in exchange for contributions. A decade later, in "Watt Man," Conrad portrayed Watt as an enormous Pac-Man gobbling up the United States, and in a pair of *Minneapolis Tribune* cartoons Steve Sack lampooned Watt's environmental agenda and Ronald Reagan's arms buildup by reducing them to bumperstickers ("I Brake for Developers," "Have You Hugged Your Warhead Today?").[4]

Many recent political cartoons have exploited the lyrics of popular songs. To lampoon Nixon's Watergate woes, Conrad portrayed him at the piano late at night belting out "Don't Blame Me," and in a *San Francisco Examiner* cartoon, Ken Alexander drew him with a banjo crooning mournfully, "Those Jury Calls are Breaking Up that O-o-o-ld Gang of Mine." Don Wright satirized Reagan's insensitivity to blacks with a cartoon depicting him treating the NAACP to a rendition of "Ol' Man River." A pair of fine 1980 Marlette *Wizard of Oz* cartoons featured Tin Man Reagan singing "If I Only Had a Heart," and Cowardly Lion Jimmy

Carter belting out "If I Only Had the Nerve." In 1982, parodies of the musical comedy *Annie* satirized Reagan's rosy economic forecasts: Marlette and Jack Ohman both drew a frizzle-haired "Ronnie" singing the upbeat "Tomorrow, Tomorrow" in a downpour. Country singer Willie Nelson's "Farm Aid" concert crusade inspired MacNelly in 1985 to draw Reagan as Nelson doing "In the Red Again" at a "Deficit Aid" gala, and Peters in 1986 to feature Reagan with guitar performing at a concert for "Contra Aid."[5]

Given the pervasive influence of television in contemporary American popular culture, it is inevitable that cartoonists draw heavily on it to convey their messages. Among the artists utilizing TV ads has been Dennis Renault, whose outstanding 1973 "I'm Ronnie—Fly Me" series in the *Sacramento Bee* parodied blatantly sexist and very popular National Airlines TV commercials to make mock of Reagan's neglect of gubernatorial duties while he positioned himself for a presidential bid. In their efforts to satirize Reaganomics, Herb Block parodied a popular E.F. Hutton commercial in 1981, and two years later Marlette did likewise with a DeBeer's diamond ad in "Deficits Are Forever." A 1973 Peters cartoon featured a hunkered-down Nixon being carried from the set of the popular TV game show "To Tell the Truth." In 1983 Sack critiqued superbly the Reagan invasion of tiny Grenada by portraying it as an episode in the TV series "Fantasy Island" and enjoyed success in 1987 presenting Reagan, Oliver North, John Poindexter, and other "Iranscam" miscreants as the cast of a bogus TV soap opera, "The Young and the Witless."[6]

Comic books and animated cartoons have also evolved into a useful source for inspiration. To lampoon the Machiavellian strategies and massive ego of Henry Kissinger, Marlette drew a series in comic-strip format entitled "The Professor and His Pals." Among the many parodies of Superman and kindred caped superheros have been Marlette's 1973 depiction of Nixon as "Law-and-Order-Man," clad in the cloak of executive privilege, and a 1981 Hugh Haynie effort portraying "Superreagan" reaping his comeuppance from the cane of a "Geriatric Juggernaut" after proposing cuts in Social Security entitlements.

As might be expected, the legacy of Walt Disney is too pervasive to have been neglected by political cartoonists. In 1973, Peters drew Nixon as Mickey Mouse with tape-reel ears, and as a pure and virginal Snow White [VI–4] unsullied by the Watergate mischief being committed

SNOW WHITE

[VI–4] Mike Peters, "Snow White," Dayton Daily News, 1973.
Reprinted with permission.

around him by John Mitchell and other subordinates, cast as the Seven
Dwarfs. Nixon's penchant for avoiding the unvarnished truth whenever
possible made the analogy with Disney's Pinocchio too tempting to pass
up for Haynie and New York Post cartoonist Joe Pierotti, both of whom
featured Nixon as a Pinocchio with a growing "Watergate" nose. Among
the more memorable Watt cartoons was a superb Peters effort featuring
him terrorizing two little children with a bedtime story of the execution
of Bambi and Thumper![7]

Of all varieties of contemporary popular culture, the movies have
provided cartoonists with the most numerous and, on the whole, the
most creative allusions for political commentary. Nixon was cast in many
Hollywood roles, most memorably as Casablanca's Bogie in MacNelly's
1972 "Play It Again, Sam," and as King Kong astride the Capitol in a
droll 1974 Jules Feiffer critique of the idea that impeachment could ruin
the republic. In 1972, Bob Beckett portrayed Nixon's "Phase IV" economic controls as Frankenstein's monster, a referent used adroitly by
Marlette to caricature Gerald Ford in his outstanding "Return of Frankenstein." Equally creative was Marlette's presentation of Henry Kissinger's self-serving memoirs as a poster for the film "Apackolies Now." Also

skillfully drawn was Haynie's 1982 portrayal of persistent unemployment defying "The Exorci$t." The characters of *Star Wars* and its two sequels, and the sinister Darth Vader in particular, have been appropriated extensively by cartoonists. In his 1983 "Return of the Jimmy," MacNelly drew the 1984 Democratic contenders as *Star Wars* characters. This parallel was enhanced by the dubbing of the Reagan anti-missile defense as "Star Wars" and Reagan's characterization of the Soviet Union as the "evil empire." Thus Reagan's "crack team of advisors" appear as Darth, robots R2 D2 and C–3PO, and E.T., and in two 1985 efforts, Andrei Gromyko was cast as Darth Vader by Peters and the Soviet military as the loathsome Jabba the Hutt by Bill Mauldin.[8]

The accession to the presidency of the Ronald Reagan of Warner Bros. and "Death Valley Days" rather predictably inspired a copious array of political cartoons based on Hollywood themes. Most of these were at first predicated mainly on the incongruity of having an actor (or cowboy) in the Oval Office and, as a result, were predictably mediocre as political satire. But as his presidency unfolded, the more creative cartoonists discovered ample opportunities to draw on Hollywood in lampooning Reagan and his agenda. A splendid 1981 Peters cartoon presented him with an Academy Award as "best actor in a supporting role" to the El Salvador junta. Robert Redford's role as middle-aged baseball rookie Roy Hobbs in *The Natural* prompted *Minnesota Daily* cartoonist Kevin Siers to caricature Reagan in baseball pin-stripes with a large "Commie Basher" bat. Reagan's hawkish foreign policy and the Sylvester Stallone epic *Rambo* provided cartoonists with a parallel too tempting to resist. Parodies portrayed "Ronbo" Reagan venting his ire on Nicaraguan Sandinistas and zapping Soviet missiles in outer space.[9]

As a lode of inspiration, Hollywood has been mined especially often, and effectively, by Steve Sack. Reagan's deficit woes prompted Sack in 1982 to draw him as "E.P. the Extra-Prezestrial" alone, lost, and "146,000,000,000 dollars from a balanced budget." His "gender gap" problems inspired Sack in 1983 to cast him as Rhett Butler romancing a "Women's Vote" Scarlett, but rebuffed with "Frankly, my dear, this time *I* don't give a damn." Much more caustic were a quartet of 1987 "Iranscam" parodies, with Reagan shooting himself in the foot in the *Platoon* spoof "Buffoon" [VI–5], debuting as "The Amnesiac" in the Oliver North *Untouchables* parody "The Uncontrollables" [VI–6], and starring

[VI–5] *Steve Sack, "Buffoon,"* Minneapolis Star-Tribune, *January 25, 1987. Reprinted with permission from the* Star-Tribune, *Minneapolis.*

[VI–6] *Steve Sack, "The Uncontrollables,"* Minneapolis Star-Tribune, *June 5, 1987. Reprinted with permission from the* Star-Tribune, *Minneapolis.*

in "Ronbo" and the William Casey-inspired *Tales from the Crypt*. Sack's
affinity for Hollywood allusions was again exhibited in 1988 parodies of
Who Framed Roger Rabbit, with George Bush cast as "Bushy Bunny,"
and *Gorillas in the Mist*, with Reagan trying to deal with Sandinista pri-
mates in "Guerillas in the Mist." Sack's 1991 "Home Alone II" featured
a deposed Mikhail Gorbachev, and in January 1992 he portrayed Sad-
dam Hussein as Frankenstein's monster [VI–7] and Fidel Castro as a for-
lorn "Prince of Tides" [VI–8].[10]

Without such sources for inspiration, the leading cartoonists of a
century ago relied on a more traditional and decidedly more elite pool of
cultural allusions. Nast ignored almost altogether the artifacts of contemporary popular culture. He was so partial to the trappings of antiquity,
in fact, that it is difficult to deduce from the corpus of his art whether the
toga or a business suit served as the typical dress of his day, or whether
the men who wore them dwelt in columned temples or brownstones! A
wicked 1879 James A. Wales *Puck* burlesque of Nast's style [II–1] featured his most overworked cartoon cliché, a stern female figure of Liberty
in classical attire "with a Roman sword in her hand, a Grecian cornice
on her head, and an expression of mingled agony, enthusiasm, and nau-
sea on her face."[11]

Some of Nast's first true cartoons cast the hated Andrew Johnson
as a cruel Roman emperor, although his most sinister portrayal of the
beleaguered Tennessean was as a menacing Medusa in his 1867 "Southern Justice." Another successful play on Greek mythology was his "Panic
in Session," an 1881 indictment of congressional budgetary chaos that
featured half-man, half-goat Pan astride the Capitol. Nast made use of
Diogenes and his lamp to impugn the integrity of the anti-Ulysses Grant
press corps, Horace Greeley, and Boss Tweed. After New York voters
ousted Tammany in 1871, Nast drew Tweed as a porcine, sulking Nero
sitting amidst the ruins of the Tammany temple [VI–9]. Cartoons of the
travails of Tweed, Johnson, and the apostate 1872 Liberal Republicans
as Ides of March scenes from *Julius Caesar* blended his fondness for antiquity with an equal affinity for Shakespeare. Nast parodies of *Othello*
portrayed Johnson, Jefferson Davis, and *New York Tribune* editor
Whitelaw Reid as Iago. He drew 1868 Democratic presidential nominee
Horatio Seymour as Lady Macbeth trying to wash away the bloodstains
of the 1863 New York draft riots, Britain's John Bull as a bloated

[VI–7] *Steve Sack, untitled,* Minneapolis Star-Tribune, *January 1, 1992. Reprinted with permission from the* Star-Tribune, *Minneapolis.*

[VI–8] *Steve Sack, "The Prince of Tides,"* Minneapolis Star-Tribune, *January 13, 1992. Reprinted with permission from the* Star-Tribune, *Minneapolis.*

[VI–9] Thomas Nast, *"What Are You Laughing At? To the Victor Belong the Spoils,"* Harper's Weekly, *November 25, 1871.*

Falstaff, Democratic party treasurer August Belmont as Shylock, and 1880 Greenback nominee James B. Weaver as Bottom, the *Midsummer Night's Dream* weaver transformed by Oberon into a jackass to punish fairy queen Titania.[12]

Nast borrowed from Austrian folklore in 1872 to cartoon the U.S.-British dispute over the Civil War "Alabama claims" by drawing William Tell as John Bull shooting an apple off the head of son Uncle Sam. In 1874 he borrowed from *Arabian Nights* to depict political gadfly Ben Butler as a menacing genie loosed from his bottle. Less fond of more recent cultural allusions, Nast did endow a cartoon mocking the 1872 Liberal Republicans with the Dickensian title "Great Expectations"; exploited Daniel Defoe's *Robinson Crusoe* and Jonathan Swift's *Gulliver's Travels* in cartooning Grant and Charles Sumner; and twice cast 1880 Democratic nominee Winfield Scott Hancock as Gulliver. His 1871 election-eve cartoon "The Tammany Tiger Loose" [I–4], which was praised to the skies by Albert Bigelow Paine and others for the shock value of its originality, was in fact a parody of a widely recognized canvas by French artist Jean-Léon Gérôme. Nast rarely drew on scriptural allusions, but did use the temptation of Christ to cartoon both feminist Victoria Claflin Woodhull [VI–10] and Horace Greeley, and on one occasion he dramatized racial discrimination by portraying a black Samson being shorn of hair and power by a Southern Democracy Delilah. One of his more memorable anti-Catholic cartoons, his 1869 "Pilgrim's Progress in the 19th Century," featured Pius IX as John Bunyan's decrepit ogre, grinning helplessly at passing Christian pilgrims from a cave strewn with the bones of the victims of his prime.[13]

The beginnings of a clear divergence between traditional and popular culture in political cartooning during the era were much more evident in *Puck* and *Judge*. Faced with a need to print three color cartoons a week with a minimum of trite banality, *Puck* and *Judge* artists found inspiration in a much more varied reservoir of sources than did Nast, including an array of cultural allusions and referents, both elite and popular, traditional and contemporary. Unlike Nast, the artists of *Puck* and *Judge* exploited the potential of an incipient popular culture to lampoon the foibles of their political foils. If Nast saw in the epic figures and contexts of antiquity an ideal vehicle for his strident moralism and stark black-and-white style, Keppler, his lieutenants, and his imitators found

[VI–10] *Thomas Nast, "Get Thee Behind Me, (Mrs.) Satan!,"* Harper's
Weekly, *February 17, 1872.*

in the exuberant banality of contemporary popular culture inspirations galore for the lighter satire and gaudy color of their fare.

Sports has provided a natural metaphor for political competition since crude, cluttered cartoons cast Jacksonians and Whigs as political runners and prizefighters.[14] In an era obsessed with spectator and participatory sports, *Puck* and *Judge* covers and centerfolds frequently portrayed political contests as boxing and tennis matches, baseball and football games, or races with bicycles, sailboats, sleds, and toboggans.[15] Other forms of competition exploited were horse and dog shows and produce exhibits at county fairs—cartoons likely to star Benjamin Butler, Roscoe Conkling, and other favorite targets as prize Clydesdales, whippets, or pumpkins. High fashion competition provided another tempting vehicle for lampooning leading public figures by drawing them as sissified fops—as Frederick Opper portrayed Conkling and Chester Arthur in his 1883 *Puck* front cover cartoon "The Original Political Dude Out-Duded"—or, even better, as outlandish society matrons in drag, as Victor Gillam savaged Grover Cleveland and David Hill in his 1888 *Judge* front cover cartoon "Easter Bonnets." Keppler seized on the same theme and the essential absurdity of beauty pageants to draw two dozen possible presidential contenders as hideous female impersonators in his 1884 *Puck* centerfold "The Contest of Beauty."[16]

Other popular-culture innovations of the era exploited by *Puck* and *Judge* artists for political satire included amusement park rides and beach activity, 4th of July fireworks displays, games and puzzles, and shows and theatrical productions of every stripe. Frank Beard debunked Cleveland's 1884 hopes by drawing him on a merry-go-round with six losing Democratic predecessors, and C.J. Taylor in 1888 lampooned French political instability by presenting rival leaders as riders on a Ferris wheel. A favorite approach was portraying leaders looking absurd in swimwear, splashing in the surf at Coney Island or beach resorts with a zany array of flotation devices. Predictable Independence Day cartoons featured public men as figural skyrockets fizzled, dead, or blazing skyward; April Fool's issues often depicted political wiles as schoolboy pranks; and nary a post-election December passed without cartoons of hopefuls hanging stockings in hopes of choice posts in the new regime.

Inspired by popular puzzles of the era were Wales's 1880 *Puck* back cover "15—14—13—The Great Presidential Puzzle," featuring Conkling stymied by the figural tiles of contenders in a "15-puzzle" variant, and Grant Hamilton's 1889 *Judge* cartoon "The Democratic 'Pigs in the Clover' Puzzle," with Louisville editor Henry Watterson trying to roll balls representing 1892 Democratic hopefuls into a miniature White House. The urban black cakewalk tradition provided artists with opportunities to draw their foils competing for the cake of political primacy in blackface, often with exaggerated African features.[17]

The popularity of minstrelry provided the *Puck* and *Judge* artists with additional opportunities to mix political commentary with white-supremacist chic, although virtually no variety of popular exhibition, show, or theatrical presentation was neglected. Comic opera in the Gilbert and Sullivan tradition was a natural for the opportunities it provided to dress characters in outlandish costumes and lampoon them in satiric librettos. The stage production of *Uncle Tom's Cabin*, the most ubiquitous melodrama of the era, was exploited by Bernhard Gillam, who drew Ben Butler as Topsy and the Democratic party as Miss Ophelia in his 1883 *Puck* cartoon "Incorrigible." He also portrayed the demise of the Cleveland administration as the play's tear-jerking finale in his 1889 *Judge* centerfold "The Last Scene in Uncle Grover's Cabin." Appropriating other vogues in popular entertainment, Gillam savaged the morally flexible Blaine as a carnival quick-change virtuoso in his 1884 *Puck* effort "A Lightning-Change Artist," and Cleveland as an improbable tightrope daredevil trying to cross Niagara Falls on a frayed rope while balancing cumbersome allies and issues in his 1888 *Judge* centerfold "Cleveland Will Have a Walk-Over." Punch and Judy puppetry provided an ideal vehicle for depicting political manipulation, with such figures as plutocrat Jay Gould and party bosses Tom Platt and Tammany's "Honest John" Kelly manipulating their marionette minions at will.[18]

Given the extraordinary influence in American popular culture of P.T. Barnum's attractions and their potential for caricature and satire, it was natural that cartoonists frequently exploited the circus, carnival, and freak show as a context for political commentary. A recurring theme in Bernhard Gillam's *Judge* cartoons during the 1888 campaign was the portrayal of Cleveland's re-election effort as a traveling circus and menagerie, with the corpulent president predestined for the role of Jumbo, "Sacred Civil Service Reform White Elephant." *Puck* artists countered with circus cartoons satirizing Republican inconsistency on the liquor issue and patronage squabbles between Blaine and Benjamin Harrison. Both humor weeklies used the carnival sideshow metaphor to poke fun at the splinter-party candidacies of Ben Butler and feminist Belva Lockwood—Bernhard Gillam in 1884 with his *Puck* piece "The Busted Side Show" and brother Victor in 1888 with his *Judge* centerfold "The Neglected Side Show." The advertising show was used as a referent; more commonly, ideologies and candidacies were cartooned as presentations of itinerant vendors of patent medicine. The freak show provided inspiration for what developed into the premier cartoon creation of the generation, the portrayal of Blaine as the tattooed man. In his April 16, 1884, *Puck* centerfold, "The National Dime Museum," Bernhard Gillam drew Blaine, tattooed head to toe with scandals and other compromises of probity, in league with Conkling as a bearded lady and other notables as sundry oddities of nature. This initiated a series so devastating that the Blaniacs spoke of lawsuits and censorship legislation, then finally exacted revenge by enticing Gillam from Keppler to draw Republican cartoons for *Judge*![19]

While these artists were creatively exploiting the conventions of contemporary popular culture, they made good use of more traditional resources as well. Keppler and Bernhard Gillam were fond of historical referents, with Keppler portraying Rutherford B. Hayes as Sir Walter Raleigh, lampooning arch-protectionist Samuel Randall as Canute trying to hold back the waves of tariff reform, and savaging commodity manipulators by depicting the crude but effective medieval remedy of nailing them by the ear to the door of a public building. The better Gillam cartoons of this genre include "The True Meaning of Republican Harmony" in 1883, comparing GOP tariff consensus to Rome's House of Tarquin trying to parlay a human sacrifice into a return to power, and "The Last Days of the Democratic Pompeii," an 1887 warning to the Democrats of the consequences of ignoring the labor vote. In other cartoons Gillam drew Cleveland as a reformist Cardinal Richelieu defying the Democratic royal court over civil service, as Brutus slaying a civil service Julius Caesar, and as Henry VIII courting a spoils-system Anne Boleyn. Other historical immortals used to lampoon the politicos of the day were Christopher Columbus, Napoleon Bonaparte, Louis XIV, and Lady Godiva.[20]

Folklore was also put to work. Gambrinus, a mythical Flemish ruler alleged to have invented beer, served Keppler, Grant Hamilton, and Taylor as a model for cartoons savaging Charles A. Dana, labor boycotts, John Bull, and Republican pension fraud. Aesop's fables and *The Arabian Nights* found new life in several cartoons, with rum-shop genies set loose from license law reform bottles; Democratic and Henry George donkeys starving between equally tempting piles of hay symbolizing political options; camels representing British free traders and cattle barons driving American labor and Plains Indians from their respective tents; and a puffed-up Ben Butler greenback bullfrog squashed by a "Solid Money" ox. In an especially clever Wales reprise of an Aesop fable, stork Roscoe Conkling invited Tammany bulldog John Kelly to share the spoils of collaboration, contained in an urn with a long, slender neck accessible only to the crafty stork.[21]

In sharp contrast to Nast, as well as to his own strong bent toward secular humanism, Keppler was inordinately fond of scriptural referents. His third English-edition centerfold immodestly featured young Puck as the political fulfillment of the prophecy of *Isaiah* 6:11, "And a little child shall lead them," in "The Millenium at Last." In 1880 he spoofed Ulysses Grant's third-term bid as "The Worship of the Golden Calf"; John Kelly of Tammany as Goliath routed by Samuel Tilden's reform Democrats at the Cincinnati convention and as Jonah tossed overboard by New York Democrats; and Democratic nominee Winfield Scott Hancock as baby Moses, and then Samson, first performing mighty feats and then in defeat being shorn of hair and power by a Republican Delilah. When Sarah Bernhardt was denounced during an American tour by censorious evangelists for having a bastard son, Keppler portrayed her as a "Modern Rizpah, Protecting Her Son from the Clerical Vultures" [VI–11], alluding to the story in *Samuel II* (21:8–11) of the heroic mother who saved her sons from the Gibeonites. As the fatally wounded James A. Garfield lay dying in August 1881, Keppler acidly drew such Republican rivals as Grant, Conkling, and Arthur as Roman soldiers casting lots for his robes in "A Humiliating Spectacle." This effort was less noteworthy for its unbridled venom than for its reliance on a New Testament allusion, although during the decade Bernhard Gillam depicted Cleveland as the Good Samaritan and apostate Republican George W. Curtis as the Prodi-

[VI–11] *Joseph Keppler, "Sarah Bernhardt, the Modern Rizpah, Protecting Her Son from the Clerical Vultures,"* Puck, *December 29, 1880. Photograph by Brian Campbell Fischer.*

gal Son, Hamilton portrayed Curtis and other reform renegades as "The Republican Pharisees," and Beard drew the Democratic party as Lazarus barred from a Republican patronage feast.[22]

Much more prevalent were allusions to the figures and tales of the Old Testament. Noah's Ark and the Flood, the struggles between Cain and Abel and David and Goliath, the saga of Samson and Delilah, and the temptation of Eve in the Garden of Eden all provided uncommon opportunity for political metaphor, as did the destruction of Sodom and Gomorrah for political corruption, and of the Tower of Babel for confusion or conflicting ideologies within a party or movement. To brand Cleveland a base hypocrite, Hamilton featured him in his 1888 "Cleveland's Coat of Many Colors" as Joseph parading in a patchwork cloak of contradictory positions. Mosaic analogies were especially ubiquitous. Appearing as baby Moses in the bulrushes were Cleveland, Hancock, and Hill. As Moses leading the exodus to the Promised Land, Ben Butler appeared, leading the Democratic Israelites to Washington. Uncle Sam was likewise cast, leading European pauper workers from bondage under pharoah John Bull to high wages in protectionist America in a Victor Gillam cartoon and, with exaggerated Semitic features, in a Keppler centerfold leading Eastern European Jews through the parted seas of bigotry to safe haven in the United States. One of the more creative biblical cartoons using rather obscure scriptural referents was the 1882 *Puck* centerfold "The Moloch of Arctic Discovery," in which Keppler drew *New York Herald* publisher James Gordon Bennett as the early Hebrew god infamous for decreeing the sacrifice of children (for Bennett's endowment of a polar expedition that sent several explorers to icy deaths). Another was the 1884 *Judge* centerfold "The Worship of Ananias," an acid postmortem that featured "mugwump" defectors from Blaine kneeling in homage to the champion liar struck dead for dishonesty in *Acts* 5.[23]

Exploited nearly as often and even more creatively was the secular tradition of antiquity, especially the heroes and wonderfully gruesome monsters of Homeric legend. In 1882, Bernhard Gillam cast anti-Chinese bigotry as the dog Cerberus, guardian of the infernal regions, with the three heads of a hooligan, a demagogue, and an Irishman. In 1885 he portrayed the tariff as the Minotaur "Protection Monster of Pennsylvania" being fed maidens symbolizing other states by congressmen William "Pig Iron" Kelley and Samuel Randall. In 1888 Keppler depicted trusts and the tariff as "A Hydra That Must Be Crushed," with each head a protected monopoly, and in 1895 Louis Dalrymple drew a "Free Silver Craze" Hydra with the heads of eight silverite senators. Wall Street was portrayed by Keppler as a poisonous Upas tree, and by *Puck* artist Friedrich Graetz as the temptress Circe. In "Between Scylla and Charybdis," Graetz cast Cleveland's patronage pests and his future mother-in-law as the Strait of Messina rock and whirlpool personified in mythology as deadly female monsters. Cleveland himself starred as a muscular Hercules in a pair of 1885 *Puck* cartoons, and as a corpulent Apollo playing a free trade lyre for the creatures of the forest in an 1888 *Judge* centerfold.[24]

In other cartoons Harrison appeared as Ajax, Bennett and Gould as rival Neptunes lobbing maritime muck at each other, and Conkling as Diogenes. Blaine starred as a tattooed Narcissus "mashed" on his own reflection [VI–12], an Apollo of corruption, and a Phoenix rising from the ashes of 1890 GOP misfortune. In Keppler's "Tantalus," he was chained to a rock and taunted by visions of an inaugural gala forever beyond his reach. Although in Greek mythology Tantalus had been condemned by his father Zeus to stand starving in water beneath a ripe fruit tree for revealing the secrets of Olympus, Keppler substituted the rock to symbolize the Little Rock & Fort Smith Railroad bonds Blaine had purportedly promoted as Speaker of the House. Keppler drew Susan B. Anthony, Lucy Stone, Elizabeth Cady Stanton, and other noted feminists as geese waddling to save Rome, a referent adapted by Wales to American Catholic bishops rescuing the Cincinnati archdiocese from financial ruin. In portraying (without explanatory text) Chester Arthur in drag with a leaking "Arthur Boom" barrel as a Danaïd, a daughter of Danaüs doomed to filling a perforated vessel for eternity, Graetz posed an honest challenge to the cultural literacy of *Puck* devotees. With Olympian irony, scrawny Peter Cooper was parodied as Atlas, a bloated Queen Victoria as Venus, and Irish machine kingpins Kelly of Tammany, Hughie McLaughlin of Brooklyn, and McManes of Philadelphia as "The Three Dis-graces," a ribald burlesque of the famed "Three Graces" statue of Aglaia, Euphrosyne, and Thalia, goddesses of beauty, charm, and feminine grace.[25]

Rarely was the compelling imagery of Dante exploited by *Puck* and *Judge* artists. Equally puzzling in light of the genre's potential and the

NARCISSUS; or, THE MAN WHO WAS MASHED ON HIMSELF.
J. G. B.—" The remarkable resemblance to George Washington is what strikes *me!*"

[VI–12] Bernhard Gillam, "Narcissus; or, The Man Who Was Mashed on Himself," Puck, *September 17, 1884. Photograph by Brian Campbell Fischer.*

affinity for opera shared by Keppler and several peers is the dearth of cartoons based on operatic themes. Along with some Carmen takeoffs, Keppler's 1887 parody on Wagner's *Ring of the Nibelungs* portraying Cleveland as "Siegfried the Fearless in the Political Dismal Swamp" provided an exception. Key literary figures exploited often were Cervantes' Don Quixote, Bunyan's aged ogre, Swift's Gulliver and Goethe's Faust and Mephistopheles. A splendid Goethe effort was Keppler's 1877 "The Erl King (New Version)," featuring Erl King Hayes riding through a swamp filled with macabre figural rotting trees to represent his intraparty rivals of the "Stalwart" faction. Equally superb was Bernhard Gillam's 1889 *Judge* Tennyson parody "The Mugwump Elaine—The Dead Steered by the Dumb," portraying Cleveland poling a dead mugwump Curtis up Salt River on a civil service funeral barge above suitably bastardized Tennyson stanzas. Dickensian referents included Pecksniff, Fagin, Oliver Twist, and the Micawbers. Shakespeare also yielded a rich harvest of referents. Keppler drew John Bull and Hancock as Hamlet,

[VI–13] Bernhard Gillam, "Phryne Before the Chicago Tribunal," Puck, June 4, 1884. Photograph by Brian Campbell Fischer.

Butler as Shylock demanding of Uncle Sam his pound-of-flesh veterans' pensions, and, in his excellent 1881 "A Grand Shakespearean Revival," Arthur as King Henry IV rebuking former cronies Conkling and Platt for unseemly familiarity. In 1889 Opper invoked the same theme in his "Going Back on the 'Blocks of Five'," featuring Harrison as Richard III spurning Buckingham as Indiana Republican kingpin W.W. Dudley, infamous for allegedly voting in "blocks of five" illicit nonresident "floaters." Bernhard Gillam's Shakespearean cartoons included *Puck* portrayals of Gould as Shylock and Kelly as Henry V eating the leek of repudiation, and *Judge* centerfolds starring Cleveland as Falstaff, Julius Caesar, and a lackey of Shylock John Bull.[26]

On other occasions, color cartoons drew inspiration from serious art. Bernhard Gillam's renowned June 4, 1884, *Puck* centerfold, "Phryne Before the Chicago Tribunal" [VI–13], portraying Whitelaw Reid exhibiting the tattooed Blaine to Republican leaders, parodied the 1859 Jean-Léon Gérôme oil *Phryne Before the Tribunal*, with Athenian orator Hypereides defending the lovely courtesan Phryne on the sole basis of her pulchritude. Keppler's 1885 inaugural salute, "Cleveland's Entry into

[VI–14] *Bernhard Gillam, "The Political 'Angelus,' " Judge, January 18, 1890. Photograph by Brian Campbell Fischer.*

Washington," reprised the 1878 Hans Makart work *Entrance of Charles V into Antwerp*, and his 1885 "Harmony and Envy" featured Reid, Blaine, and John A. Logan as the envious monks in Charles Garnier's *Jour de Fête*. Several 1885–89 Gillam centerfolds parodied the works of obscure European artists known mainly to Americans through cheap lithographed prints of their paintings. His 1885 "The Tribute to the Minotaur" parodied a work of the same title by Gendron, and his 1887 "The Democratic Henry VIII Makes Love to Anne Boleyn (Spoils System) to the Disgust of His Mugwump Cardinal" exploited a popular painting by Piloty to savage Cleveland and Maryland senator Arthur P. Gorman. In 1889 he portrayed Cleveland and Randall as Zamaçois' *The Rival Confessors*, drew Cleveland as a scandalized friar watching Hill court Miss Democratic Party on a park bench in "Shocking!," and satirized free-trade attacks on McKinley tariff initiatives in a parody of Gilbert Gaul's *Bringing Up the Guns*. Gillam's 1890 "The Political 'Angelus' " [VI–14], featuring Cleveland and Hill as a peasant couple sowing the seeds of sham reform in a barren winter field to the tolling of a village church bell, parodied Jean-François Millet's 1859 *The Angelus*, a work *Judge* was making even more familiar to its devotees by awarding lithographed reproductions of it as premiums for subscription renewals.[27]

Judge's choice of premium does much to shed light on the dilemma posed by color cartoons that demanded what would be regarded today as an extraordinary level of cultural literacy. Clearly, cartoons predicated on an immediate, widespread recognition of the works of Millet and Zamaçois, the legends of Canute and Gambrinus, the evil of Moloch and the Minotaur, and the travails of Tantalus, the Danaïdes, and Rizpah either mirrored faithfully the prevailing cultural heritage of the day or failed as political cartoon art through elitist obscurity. Weighing against the latter hypothesis were press runs in six figures per issue, the resulting fortunes accumulated by Keppler and *Judge* publisher William J. Arkell, and the absence of a compelling motive to spend a dime for the ads and feeble humor in the twelve pages that surrounded the cartoons! To be sure, cartoonists frequently "fudged" by providing reams of explanatory text. Nast especially did so, although he avoided such hedges as often as not, and in instances where his art came encumbered with encyclopedic copy, he was probably only indulging a characteristic affinity for the type of caption derided by *Puck* as "a chapter from the Patent-Office reports."[28] Culturally challenging allusions were less frequently given explanatory notation in *Puck* and *Judge*, and there seems to have been little correlation between the use of didactic text and the obscurity of a referent. As cases in point, no guidance was given for Gillam's "A Sop to Cerberus," Graetz's study of Arthur as a hapless Danaïd or his "Between Scylla and Charybdis," or Keppler's "Tantalus"—and the only verbiage explaining his tribute to Sarah Bernhardt as "The Modern Rizpah" came in editorial notes fourteen pages distant.

Such cartoons can tell us much about American culture during a remarkable generation when, to judge from the graphic art of political criticism, the traditional, essentially elite, cultural heritage of our ancestors still competed on an equal footing with the aborning phenomenon of contemporary popular culture, and that it did so with the same creative, imaginative exuberance we commonly associate with pop culture. For Keppler, Gillam, and their compeers, the heritage of classical mythology, of Shakespeare and Scripture, and of Dante and Dickens was not some dry-as-dust medicine to ward off the atrophy of western civilization, but rather a living legacy rich in dynamic parallels to the political world they satirized. For those who lament the eclipse of this heritage or construct cultural equivalents of Gresham's Law, there are lessons to be learned.

VII

Liberty

For more than a century, Auguste Bartholdi's massive *Liberty Enlightening the World* has graced Bedloe's (Liberty) Island in New York harbor, arguably our most hallowed national icon and, as a result, a useful device for editorial cartoonists. Unlike other cartoon conventions explored in this volume, Liberty was born to serve as a symbol on both sides of the Atlantic, as a tribute to Franco-American friendship and to a global political ideal. By its 1886 installation and dedication, however, Emma Lazarus's poem "The New Colossus" and the personal crusade of Hungarian-born presslord Joseph Pulitzer to fund and erect the pedestal were tranforming Liberty more into a welcoming symbol for millions of Old World refugees "yearning to breathe free." The nation's rise to the status of a superpower prompted American cartoonists in the new century to use Liberty mainly as an icon of national glory and patriotic purpose against the likes of Kaiser Bill, Hitler, Mussolini, and Stalin—a rather brittle goddess of holy war and "my country right or wrong." In recent years, a trend among cartoonists has been to exploit Liberty less reverently and more creatively, often as a device to promote humanitarian ideals. In the beginning, though, Liberty was cartooned primarily as a gigantic, improbable curiosity.[1]

A gargantuan 151 feet from torch to toe, Bartholdi's creation prompted the *New York Times* to suggest using "a fat woman for the right thumb nail" and *Puck* to observe, "It is lucky for us that the Colossus of Rhodes committed suicide when he did. He might have come over here and eloped with our Statue of Liberty." One caustic art critic likened Liberty to "a bag of potatoes with a stick projecting from it"; a Catholic essayist denounced her as a manifestation of pagan idolatry like "Nabuchodonoser's great statue of old"; and reactionary southern Protestants saw in the project dire portents of heathenism and political subversion. Suspicious of the French and their machinations in Mexico during our Civil War, many Americans questioned subsequent French altruism, some noting that Liberty was as hollow as the Trojan horse. One Jeremiah branded her a French conspiracy to bankrupt the United States! Bartholdi's selection of a site in New York harbor inspired controversy, his admission that he had modeled Liberty's face on his mother's evoked derision, and his premature execution of the torch and right hand for display at Philadelphia's 1876 Centennial Exhibition prompted the *Times* to suggest that a "really able and earnest sculptor" would have begun with the boots and worked up! The long, frustrating drive to pay for the pedestal gave rise to slurs against the patriotism and generosity of leading citizens and whole communities and classes.[2]

A similar spirit of raucous irreverence characterized most early Liberty cartoons. After the torch and hand were displayed in Philadelphia and then in New York's Madison Square, Americans assumed that their wait for the finished monument would be brief. In 1879, James A. Wales made fun of the delay in a *Puck* cartoon of Bedloe's Island featuring torch and hand lashed crudely to a long stick. In 1881 a Frederick Opper *Puck* cartoon urged actress Sarah Bernhardt to pinchhit for the still-missing Bartholdi statue instead of sailing away to Europe. In 1882 another *Puck* cartoon suggested mounting hand and torch atop the partially constructed Washington Monument to provide "an easy way of completing Geo. Washington's monument, and ridding Madison Square of an ugly ornament at the same time." Work on the statue was finally completed in Paris in 1884, but in the United States, a faltering campaign to fund the pedestal threatened further delays, a theme exploited superbly by one cartoonist who portrayed Liberty as a shriveled, decrepit, thousand-year-old hag still awaiting her pedestal![3]

Among the cartoons tendering tongue-in-cheek advice for improved fundraising were two Opper *Puck* efforts. One in 1883 substituted for Bartholdi's statue one of popular prizefighter John L. Sullivan, and an 1885 back cover cartoon depicted Liberty festooned with such advertising gimmicks as sunglasses, silk top hat instead of crown, umbrella in lieu of torch, magnum of champagne in place of a tablet, and handbills hawking sundry wares. In 1885 cartoons by C.G. Bush in *Harper's Weekly* and Eugene Zimmerman in *Puck* made fun of the pedestal drive by portraying panhandlers, bootblacks, and *Puck* soliciting coins from passersby, customers, and *New York Herald* publisher James Gordon Bennett (who declined because Bartholdi had not dubbed his work "Liberty Enlightening the *Herald*," favoring instead Pulitzer's *World*).[4]

Bartholdi's inspiration for designing Liberty as a woman brandishing a torch also engendered some creative cartoons. In his 1885 "Not Presented by France," Opper attributed the genesis of Liberty's design to a besotted husband sneaking home late to find an angry wife on the landing with her kerosene lamp aloft, "the old familiar family Bartholdi statue, seen only on lodge-night." An 1884 *Puck* cartoon by Walt McDougall drew on press accounts that Liberty had indeed been inspired by Bartholdi's mother, portraying her holding high a shoe ready to descend on the backside of a squirming boy.[5] It is likely that Mme. Bartholdi would have been cartooned more often if it had been known that she was a domineering religious zealot who drove one son to suicide for trying to marry a Jewish woman and kept Bartholdi from marrying until he was forty-two and on the brink of scandal.

In his 1881 *Harper's* cartoon "A Warning Light" [VII–1], Thomas Nast drew Liberty as a skeletal death figure, "an Admonition of Pestilence and Death in our Harbor." Motivated by a mass rally to protest Tammany indifference to decaying piles of garbage thought by New Yorkers to be responsible for recent epidemics, Nast parodied Bartholdi's design by depicting Liberty as Death with warning lights instead of a crown, a horn in place of a torch, and a "roll of death" in lieu of a tablet.[6] Here he pioneered a simple formula that has been followed for more than a century to create the most successful of all Liberty cartoons: retaining the familiar pose but making wholesale substitutions of figures and devices to fit the theme of the cartoon.

Several of Nast's contemporaries followed his formula to protest political corruption, also with excellent results. In his 1884 Currier & Ives lithograph "Barsqualdi's Statue Liberty Frightening the World" [VII–2], Thomas Worth used a grotesque black woman with a smoldering firebrand and a "New York Port Charges" ledger to decry notorious corruption in the New York Custom House.[7] "Bartenders' Statue of License Lightening New York" [VII–3], an 1885 *Judge* back cover cartoon by Daniel McCarthy, featured Liberty as a dishonest policeman with a book of broken rules and a horn of shakedown coins atop a pedestal of

[VII–1] *Thomas Nast, "The Warning Light,"* Harper's Weekly, *April 2, 1881.*

BARSQUALDI'S STATUE
LIBERTY FRIGHTENING THE WORLD.
BEDBUGS ISLAND. N.Y. HARBOR.

[VII–2] Thomas Worth, "Barsqualdi's Statue Liberty Frightening the World," Currier & Ives, 1884. Photograph by Brian Campbell Fischer.

[VII–3] Daniel McCarthy, "Bartenders' Statue of License Lightening New York," Judge, May 23, 1885. Photograph by Brian Campbell Fischer.

opium joints, dime dancehalls, gin mills, and and other sleazy enterprises bribing a police force under attack for tawdry scandals involving murder and the sexual molestation of young girls. Victor Gillam's 1886 "Erecting the New York Political Statue" [VII–4], also a *Judge* back cover, cast as Liberty the late Tammany sachem Boss Tweed with a moneybags torch. He is being pieced together by five current Tammany spoilsmen in a public-works boondoggle similar to the city aqueduct construction contract that had just been awarded to two of the figures, metropolitan Public Works Commissioner Maurice B. Flynn and state Democratic party chairman John O'Brien.[8]

In addition to these cartoons burlesquing Liberty to protest corruption—and the Opper works casting Liberty as John L. Sullivan, Sarah Bernhardt, an advertising agent's fantasy, and a toper's angry spouse—other artists took indecent liberties with Bartholdi's design. In an 1882 *Puck* centerfold, Joseph Keppler portrayed Liberty as Miss New York in shackles, chains, and prison stripes to protest restrictive laws imposed on the city by straitlaced sabbatarians and rural "hayseed" legislators in Albany. The 1884 Friedrich Graetz *Puck* cartoon "Timely Art" featured Liberty as "Livery Enticing the Girls," an opportunistic Yonkers equestrian in riding togs with a marriage license and moneybags in lieu of the tablet and torch. The 1886 Bernhard Gillam *Judge* centerfold "Judge's Wax Works—the Political Eden Musée," inspired by a Statue of Liberty tableau at New York's famous Eden Musée wax museum, cast as Liberty Joseph Pulitzer, the driving force behind the campaign to finance the pedestal.[9]

Not all early Liberty cartoons were so blithely irreverent or so contrary to the statue's symbolic thrust. The cartoonists of the day ignored almost completely such symbolic themes as abstract liberty, Franco-American friendship, and the New World as a haven for Europe's "huddled masses." But even before Liberty was put in place, cartoonists began to exploit her as a representation of American nationalism and republican civic virtue. Several 1884 and 1885 Nast cartoons portrayed Liberty in a reverent manner and the July 4, 1885, McCarthy *Judge* front cover work featured Liberty chiding three wealthy New York dandies for their slavish imitation of aristocratic English fashions and manners, and their lack of respect for their nation's birthday. Portrayals of Liberty as a patriotic icon were especially prevalent during her dedication week in October

[VII–4] F. Victor Gillam, "Erecting the New York Political Statue," *Judge, September 4, 1886. Photograph by Brian Campbell Fischer.*

1886. *Judge* printed as its centerfold a Bernhard Gillam creation featuring a majestic Liberty, a corona of heavenly light radiating from her crown, and Bartholdi and his coterie of American supporters in the foreground. *Puck*'s centerfold tribute was C. Jay Taylor's "Our Statue of Liberty—She Can Stand It" [VII–5], portraying Liberty as a curious amalgam of Bartholdi's figure and the traditional Miss Columbia with Phrygian liberty cap, standing firm against the forces of political evil and radicalism trying to pull her down.[10]

Although these centerfold accolades clearly foreshadowed the metamorphosis of Liberty into a sacred symbol, her transformation in cartoon art from oddity to icon was not a sudden one. After her torch had been temporarily extinguished to make its light more visible, the *Judge* filler cartoon "A Smoker's Question Illustrated" featured a darkened Liberty shrouded in heavy fog, pleading, "Can I trouble you for a light?" But when a brighter torch killed waterfowl flying into it, *Puck* responded more reverently, with a Louis Dalrymple front cover portraying the birds as anarchists and nihilists "Rushing to Their Own Destruction" in Liberty's flame. During the next few years Nast featured her as a monument to giant corporate trusts and as a grotesque Hibernian Miss Tammany; Zimmerman drew her as an Irish leprechaun with jug and candle atop a whiskey barrel; and Victor Gillam portrayed Liberty as a bright blue prude, torch snuffed out by a lamp damper and her pedestal a stack of "blue law" books in a protest against Sunday "blue laws." Increasingly more common, however, were cartoons treating her with the dignity due a revered symbol of national glory.[11]

By the turn of the century, irreverent Liberty cartoons had become uncommon. By World War I, when such cartoons as William A. Rogers' "To France!" featured her leading American doughboys into battle against the Huns and posters portrayed a stern, warlike Liberty demanding, "YOU Buy a Liberty Bond Lest I Perish!," truly disrespectful Liberty cartoons had become almost unthinkable. Indeed, her evolution into a generic symbol of American patriotism was so nearly complete by then that she was rarely if ever invoked against wartime and postwar suppressions of civil liberties and the push to curtail the flow of "huddled masses" into the United States—both blatant mockeries of ideals she had been created to symbolize! Perhaps the only truly iconoclastic Liberty cartoon from this period appeared, oddly enough, in the January 24,

[VII–5] C. Jay Taylor, "Our Statue of Liberty—She Can Stand It," Puck,
October 27, 1886. Photograph by Brian Campbell Fischer.

1919, edition of *Stars and Stripes*. In "My, How She Has Changed!,"
A.A. Wallgren drew Liberty as a dried-up Prohibition spinster with a
"U.S. Bone Dry" tablet and upside-down wine-glass torch, greeting a
thirsty doughboy returning from France.[12]

Since then, Liberty has been featured in hundreds of editorial cartoons, very few of them rivaling Wallgren's or the better 1880s examples
of imagination and intellectual integrity. Until recently, in fact, most
modern Liberty cartoons have exhibited little more creative genius than
the typical recruiting poster or postage stamp. In many instances Liberty
has been rendered less a caricature than an almost mechanical replica-
tion, much more in the tradition of Liberty Bond poster art than that of
Nast, Keppler, and the Gillams. Typically, she has been exploited as a
simplistic patriotic convention to cheer on a succession of martial endeavors, promote defense expenditures and "big stick" diplomacy, celebrate our political and economic systems, disparage a rogue's gallery of
terrorists and totalitarian despots, greet distinguished visitors and refugees, and welcome home returning soldiers, statesmen, prisoners-of-war,
and hostages. Thus Liberty was used in 1973 by Charles Brooks (*Bir-
mingham News*) to honor Alabama POW Jeremiah Denton; in 1976 by
Karl Hubenthal (*Los Angeles Herald-Examiner*) to pay homage to the
Bill of Rights [VII–6]; in 1979 by *Lawton* (Oklahoma) *Constitution &
Press* artist Vern Thompson to protest unruly Iranian student demonstrators [VII–7]; and in 1984 by Art Wood of the *American Farm Bureau
News* to celebrate a bountiful supply of foodstuffs.[13]

Where cartoonists of such traditional mindset have been moved to
modify Liberty's likeness at all, most frequently it has been to accent her
virginal femininity by portraying her as a sweet, wholesome lass symbolizing pristine national virtue. During the 1950s, Roy Justus exploited
Liberty in this manner in his *Minneapolis Star* cartoon "Perverted Use
of the Torch" to decry the menace of international communism. In his
Cincinnati Enquirer cartoon "A Woman Always Feels Better in a New
Hat," L.D. Warren explored the outer limits of both Cold War ideology
and male chauvinism by drawing a lovely Miss Liberty with hand mirror
beaming her approval of a new spiked crown festooned with Safeguard
missiles![14]

Other overworked Liberty cartoon clichés have also emphasized
her essential femininity. She has been drawn hiding her head in her hands

[VII–6] *Karl Hubenthal, "Liberty's Crown,"* Los Angeles Herald-Examiner, *December 8, 1976. Reprinted with permission.*

THE FOREIGN GUEST ABUSING THE SANCTITY OF HIS HOST

AMERICAN FREEDOMS

VIOLENT IRANIAN STUDENT DEMONSTRATIONS

THE LAWTON CONSTITUTION

[VII–7] *Vern Thompson, "The Foreign Guest Abusing the Sanctity of His Host,"* Lawton *(Okla.)* Constitution & Press, *January 1979. Reprinted with permission.*

in sorrow or shame to render commentary on such events as the 1961 Bay of Pigs fiasco, the 1981 attempt on the life of President Reagan, and the drowning of refugees from Haiti braving stormy seas in flimsy boats. In his 1941 *Detroit Free Press* cartoon "Americans All!," Art Poinier drew her as a comforting mother welcoming to her bosom a horde of youngsters ("My Children!") representing various white ethnic constituencies. In 1973 Charles Werner and Draper Hill followed suit in *Indianapolis Star* and *Memphis Commercial Appeal* cartoons depicting Liberty bestowing maternal hugs on returning Vietnam War POWs. Probably the ultimate feminine cliche has been that of Liberty shedding tears. *Minneapolis Tribune* artist Scott Long drew Liberty weeping in grief over the assassination of Martin Luther King, Jr., in 1968, as did *Arizona Republic* cartoonist Reg Manning in 1973 over the experiences endured by American prisoners-of-war in Vietnam. After the release of

"..CAME THOSE RIBBONS, YELLOW RIBBONS, LOVELY RIBBONS FOR HER HAIR."

[VII–8] Ray Osrin, ". . Came Those Ribbons, Yellow Ribbons, Lovely Ribbons for Her Hair," Cleveland Plain Dealer, *January 1981. Reprinted with permission.*

embassy hostages by the Ayatollah Khoumeini in 1981, *Cleveland Plain Dealer* cartoonist Ray Osrin paid tribute with a cartoon [VII–8] featuring Liberty shedding tears of relief over a caption reprising the Harry Belafonte ballad "Scarlet Ribbons"—a reference to the display of yellow ribbons during their ordeal.[15]

Another common cartoon theme was the extinction of Liberty's flame, the most renowned example of which remains Herblock's terse 1949 *Washington Post* classic "Fire!," with a representation of anti-communist hysteria climbing up a ladder with water to douse the flame of freedom. A 1965 Tom Little *Nashville Tennessean* piece portrayed the flame as a casualty of a Tennessee state senate bill to sanction covert committee meetings. The attempted assassinations of George Wallace and Ronald Reagan prompted Charles Werner in 1972 and Drew Litton *(El Paso Times)* in 1981 to create cartoons of bullets streaking toward Liberty's torch or blasting away her right arm. In 1973 WGN-TV (Chicago) cartoonist Don Moore reprised the Herblock classic with a cartoon of Vice President Spiro Agnew threatening the flame with a garden hose. That year Roy Justus drew Liberty rotting away atop a festering mound of Watergate garbage, and two years later, in "Inside Job," *St. Louis Post-Dispatch* cartoonist Tom Engelhardt represented CIA and FBI invasions of privacy as "snooping" termites eating away Liberty's arm and torch. Another common ploy, suggested by her proximity to the waters of New York's harbor, has been to depict Liberty sinking slowly into seas representing such various ills as industrial pollution, municipal debt, and isolationist diplomacy. A wry variant on this cliché was Steve Sack's July 2, 1986, *Minneapolis Star-Tribune* cartoon "Give Me Your Tired. Give Me Your Poor. Give Me a Break." Run two days before David Wolper's tasteless centennial extravaganza, it featured Liberty torch-deep in the rubble of commemorative glitz, schlock, hype, schmaltz, and TV tripe![16]

Such refreshing irreverence has been all too rare in Liberty cartoons since her passage from oddity to icon, but why this has been the case is anyone's guess. One reason for so many trite, unimaginative Liberty cartoons, of course, is that many of them have been created by trite, unimaginative men, artists of the sort once disparaged by Bill Mauldin as "the pants-pressers in this business." This may have been especially true of cartoonists who drew patriotic platitudes for conservative or reactionary publications. One need not be a political liberal or radical to be a creative cartoonist, for from Nast through Jeff MacNelly and Steve Benson, tough-minded conservatives have more than held their own. By its very nature, however, the editorial cartoon works best as a vehicle for irreverent iconoclasm and wry satire, not as a sanctifier of the status quo or patriotic icons. MacNelly's dictum that "many cartoonists would be hired assassins if they couldn't draw" was not made entirely in jest. It must also be conceded that the statue itself has posed challenges. Charles Press has noted that static symbols present special problems of immobility, stolidity, and solemnity for cartoonists, and 151 feet and 225 tons atop a massive pedestal surely qualify Liberty as a static symbol.[17] Moreover, Bartholdi's choice of a metal that would take on an ice-green patina, and his knowledge of the firestorm of controversy surrounding Eugene Delacroix' superbly sensual painting of a bare-breasted *Liberty Leading the People* did not prompt him to endow his Liberty with a surplus of sexuality or vibrant feminine warmth.

Still, Liberty is an anthropomorphic figure, and not exactly a gargoyle at that. Her distinctive pose, uplifted torch, and spiked crown provide the element of instant identification prized in a cartoon convention, and her icy visage would seem to invite the sort of visual and thematic incongruity on which the better cartoonists thrive. A more compelling reason for the difficulty in cartooning Liberty creatively is her venerable status as a patriotic icon—a secular equivalent to the Blessed Virgin in Roman Catholic cultures. Just as it is almost impossible to envision Mary taking cartoon pratfalls or engaging in bawdy or bathroom activities, or even giving vent to human emotions other than maternal love and grief and Christian piety and compassion, American cartoonists drawing for mass audiences have found it consistently difficult to defy personal and societal restraints and take truly indecent liberties with this First Lady of American national symbolism. A century ago our cartoonists labored under no such handicaps. Another parallel is provided by the large body of Liberty cartoon art drawn by foreign artists. Dani Aguila's useful 1986 anthology, *Taking Liberty with the Lady*, features 167 cartoons from more than forty foreign nations, collectively notable only for routinely portraying Liberty in ways most Americans would find outrageously offensive—grossly pregnant, grotesquely flabby with sagging breasts, as a Soho strumpet, and worse![18]

During the past twenty years or so, the quality of Liberty cartoons appearing in American newspapers has improved dramatically as creative art and as political commentary. This has been due in large part to fundamental changes in the profession of American editorial cartooning. The boom in higher education has created unprecedented opportunities for student satirists to hone their skills on college dailies, but simultaneously the number of newspapers that keep an editorial cartoonist on staff has diminished appreciably due to consolidation and attrition. One result has been a sharp reversal in the laws of supply and demand, with a growing pool of talented cartoonists competing for a shrinking number of choice positions. Thus many of Mauldin's "pants-pressers" have given way to younger, more imaginative cartoonists, many of them products of campus culture during an era when Vietnam, Watergate, and subsequent catalysts of disillusionment made iconoclasm fashionable and blind fealty to sacred cows unthinkable. At the same time, publishers, attracted to the potential for prestige and revenue that comes from having in house a nationally syndicated cartoon artist, have given maverick cartoonists an unprecedented degree of ideological latitude. Thus the stodgily conservative *Los Angeles Times* has made a congenial home for Paul Conrad, whose talented trashing of Republican reactionaries from Barry Goldwater through Ronald Reagan has won him three well-deserved Pulitzers while countering every *Times* editorial endorsement and earning him an equally prominent place on a Richard Nixon enemies' list!

Simultaneously, their audiences have adjusted apace. Since the assassination of John F. Kennedy, and in particular since Vietnam and Watergate, newspaper readers have evinced a growing tendency toward partisan independence, political alienation, and skepticism toward institutions and attitudes formerly embraced as holy writ. The upshot has been a renaissance in creative editorial cartoon art unlike anything witnessed since the heyday of Nast and Keppler, including a number of mildly risqué Liberty cartoons nearly unthinkable a generation before. Jimmy Carter's bizarre 1976 confession to a *Playboy* interviewer that he had "lusted in my heart for many women" inspired Conrad to draw one of the finest of all modern Liberty efforts [VII–9], featuring Carter pruriently fantacizing Liberty as a voluptuous nude. A 1977 blackout in New York City prompted Dennis Renault to depict Liberty stripped down to her lace panties and bra by looters. Renault, Ken Alexander, and Don Wright have portrayed Liberty as pregnant, by no means the cliché among American cartoonists it is for foreigners. In 1984 John Backderf drew her as a nude (with only her legs visible, however) in spoofing the possible consequences of having *Penthouse* publisher Bob Guccione on the statue's restoration committee.[19]

Many contemporary cartoonists have turned out fresh and imaginative Liberty cartoons by utilizing the formula pioneered by Nast a century ago: presenting incongruous substitutes for Bartholdi's lady, often with supporting devices and Emma Lazarus parodies to match. In 1974 Renault cast Watergate gossip Martha Mitchell as Liberty, holding aloft a telephone in lieu of a torch. In 1975 Andy Donato, prompted by Gerald Ford's poor-mouthing, portrayed him in his *Toronto Sun* piece "State of the Union" as Liberty in tattered rags, with pencils instead of tablet and tin cup in place of torch. Two years later Doug Marlette drew Jimmy Carter as a grinning Liberty, holding in one hand the torch of "Human Rights" and in the other a neutron bomb. Similarly, Scott Willis por-

[VII–9] *Paul Conrad, untitled,* Los Angeles Times, *1976.* © *1976* Los Angeles Times. *Reprinted with permission.*

GIVE ME YOUR TRULY TIRED, YOUR TRULY POOR, YOUR TRULY HUDDLED MASSES,...

[VII–10] Mike Peters, "Give Me Your Truly Tired, Your Truly Poor, Your Truly Huddled Masses," Dayton Daily News, 1981. Reprinted with permission.

trayed Ronald Reagan in 1982 as Liberty with a spiked crown of nuclear missiles and a torch exploding in a mushroom cloud. In 1983 Conrad rendered Reagan as Liberty with a snuffed torch of "Public Information." The most lethal Reagan Liberty cartoon, however, was probably Mike Peters's "Give Me Your Truly Tired, Your Truly Poor, Your Truly Huddled Masses" [VII–10], a *Dayton Daily News* critique of Reagan's claims that his draconian domestic spending cuts would not really harm those whom he had characterized as the "truly needy."[20]

Detroit News cartoonist Draper Hill, also the most knowledgeable living authority on Nast, has made a virtual cottage industry of Liberty cartooning according to the formula established by the master. In 1978 he drew the Internal Revenue Service as a Liberty medieval torture device with sharpened pencil and stack of revised 1040 tax forms, on a pedestal inscribed with the Lazarus burlesque "Give me your tired. Your con-

National Health Program

[VII–11] Draper Hill, "National Health Program," Detroit News, *May 16, 1980.* © *1980* Detroit News. *Reprinted with permission.*

fused. Your inflation-tossed. The wretched refuse of your sluggish economy." Prompted by the 1979 Joseph Califano offensive against cigarette smoking, he portrayed the habit as a skeletal Liberty death figure puffing merrily away, with an "Enjoy!" tablet and a pack of smokes in place of the torch. In May, 1980, inspired by Fidel Castro's diabolical response to a Carter human-rights propaganda blitz—sending to Florida boatloads of felons, the terminally ill, and the criminally insane—Hill drew "National Health Program" [VII–11], portraying Castro as Miss Liberty with castanets, gleefully belting out a calypso Lazarus parody offering as a bonus his "nasties," "loonies," and "sickies." Later that year, as

Democratic party delegates came together in New York, Hill drew as Liberty the Democratic donkey with a Lazarus parody summoning "your bruised, your uncertain, your folded, stapled, spindled masses." In his 1982 cartoon "Let There Be Light . . . ," Hill cast a maniacal Menachem Begin as Liberty, holding a "Mind Your Own Business!" tablet and standing outside the barbed wire of a Palestinian refugee camp. Following a petulant Lee Iaccoca speech on Japanese trade policies in 1985, he drew "The Statue of Reciprocity," with the Chrysler chairman as Liberty puffing on a cigar and holding a tablet that read "Buy American, Dammit!"[21]

Other examples of creative Liberty cartooning include a pair of 1984 efforts portraying her as Reagan's sweetheart, the Marlette "Deficits Are Forever" parody on a DeBeer's diamond commercial, and Pat Oliphant's "America's Back and Reagan's Got Her!," a takeoff on the "Gable's Back and Garson's Got Him" promotion of the 1954 MGM film *Adventure*. In 1979 John Trever drew a nonplussed Liberty sporting a huge baseball glove instead of her torch, a droll comment on NASA assurances that a dying Skylab satellite posed no hazard to public safety, and Clyde Wells lampooned that summer's fuel shortage by portraying Liberty hitchhiking with an empty gas can. The sanctuary provided in this country for deposed Philippine autocrats Ferdinand and Imelda Marcos inspired a splendid 1986 Oliphant cartoon picturing the pair passing an under-repair Liberty with several lackeys toting their plunder. As Ferdinand grandly flips a coin into a "restoration fund" coin box, little Punk the Penguin yells that they have stolen the golden door! More recently Sack portrayed Liberty as a smiling World War I flyboy in "Ace!," flashing a thumbs-up above painted symbols of fallen communist regimes in Poland, East Germany, Hungary, Czechoslovakia, Yugoslavia, Bulgaria, Romania, and Nicaragua.[22]

As Liberty cartoons have become more blithely irreverent, they have also tended to exploit Liberty not as a patriotic platitude, but rather as a symbolic challenge to Americans to nurture ideals central to her genesis—"melting-pot" ethnic diversity and respect for human rights. When during the 1920s Congress slammed shut the golden door for all but a miniscule privileged elite, our corps of cartoonists (nearly all native-born, unlike Nast, Keppler, the Gillams, and many of their contemporaries) signaled a silent acquiescence by ignoring the symbolic dimension given Liberty by Emma Lazarus. With the exception of a few cartoons welcoming European refugees after World War II and commemorating the ill-fated Hungarian uprising in 1956, this tradition continued until recently. Then an influx of Vietnamese refugees and a virtual tidal wave of Mexican illegals, Mariel boat people from Castro's Cuba, Haitians, and other Latins fleeing civil wars, repression, and poverty put to the acid test a faith in ethnic diversity of a nation already wracked by social tensions and economic ills. One result had been a few Liberty cartoons incongruously urging restriction, and a much larger number true to the Lazarus tradition. Among the latter have been a Paul Szep *Boston Globe* cartoon of Liberty holding aloft a "No Gooks" sign, a similar effort by *Orlando Sentinel* artist Dana Summers featuring a "No More Wetbacks" sign, and a Sack cartoon featuring Liberty with a "New Haitian Policy" tablet and, in lieu of a torch, a fan for blowing refugee rafts back to Haiti.[23]

Liberty's meaning as a symbol of unalienable individual rights has never been ignored altogether by cartoonists, although until recently they were less likely to use her to protest internal threats to civil liberties than those posed by foreign adversaries from the Kaiser through the Ayatollah. Nonetheless, during the post-World War II hysteria over the "red menace," such libertarians as Daniel Fitzpatrick, Herblock, and Ross Lewis of the *Milwaukee Journal* exploited Liberty to good advantage against Joseph McCarthy and his cohorts. Herblock, Bill Mauldin, Conrad, John Fischetti, and many others followed suit to protest threats of repression inspired by Vietnam, 1960s domestic dissent, the divisive opportunism of Richard Nixon, and the alliterative smears of Spiro Agnew. Renault, Jimmy Margulies, Conrad, Tom Englehardt, and others used Liberty to decry invasions of privacy by the FBI and CIA; Bill Sanders and Hy Rosen to condemn attacks on the press in the guise of national security; Englehardt and Bill Graham to protest federal harassment of Salvadorean sanctuary activists; and Renault, Ben Sargent, and Clifford Baldowski to promote the Equal Rights Amendment or lament its demise. *Philadelphia Inquirer* artist Tony Auth drew Liberty with a clothespin on her nose, dutifully upholding the right of Nazis to parade in 1978 in the heavily Jewish Chicago suburb of Skokie.[24]

During the last decade, Liberty cartoons drawn to defend individual rights and civil liberties, at home and abroad, have become almost

[VII–12] *Bill Day, untitled,* Detroit Free Press, *1985. Reprinted with permission of the* Detroit Free Press.

[VII–13] *Steve Sack, untitled,* Minneapolis Star-Tribune, *December 13, 1989. Reprinted with permission from the* Star-Tribune, *Minneapolis.*

commonplace. The cartoon Liberty has passed not from a conservative to a liberal icon, but rather from an establishment symbol to a libertarian one. Thus heavy-handed Reagan administration attempts to please Christian conservatives by championing public-school prayer initiatives inspired a Herblock cartoon of the statue upside-down on a pedestal inscribed "Freedom of Religion is Government-Sponsored Prayer in the Public Schools," and a fine Bill Day *Detroit Free Press* cartoon [VII–12] featured the newly restored Liberty brandishing a cross instead of her torch. After George Bush opted to abjure sanctions against the Chinese regime of Deng Xiaoping following the crushing of student protests with tanks in Beijing, Oliphant drew Bush as Liberty moving to club Chinese dissidents with the torch, and Sack portrayed Bush racing to toast Deng over a prone Liberty gushing blood from Deng's dagger through the heart [VII–13].[25] Such cartoons make clear that after a century of service to American cartoonists, first as an intriguing curiosity and then as an icon of national glory, Liberty has at long last attained the status of a symbolic challenge to further those human ideals championed by her promoters a century ago.

VIII

The "Monumental" Lincoln

It remains one of the few political cartoons so powerful that a generation of Americans will carry the image to their graves [VIII-1]: Bill Mauldin's Lincoln Memorial likeness, head in hands, mourning the assassination of John Fitzgerald Kennedy. Mauldin had finished his daily cartoon that gray November day when he was told of the shooting in Dallas. Returning to his drawing board at the *Chicago Sun–Times*, he pondered how to render comment on such a "monumental" tragedy and from the word "monumental" he derived his inspiration. Racing a deadline, he finished it in two hours. In stark simplicity, Mauldin's masterpiece captured precisely the national mood of wrenching grief seasoned with a pinch of shame. According to a *Sun–Times* promotional blurb, more than 150,000 copies were requested in the eight months following the assassination. Another key to the greatness of this cartoon was the appropriateness of its analogy. Both Lincoln and Kennedy had served as uncommonly strong presidents much maligned in turbulent times, in part for their commitments to human rights for black Americans. Both had been gunned down in their political primes by mentally unstable ideologues, JFK just three days after the centennial of the Gettysburg Address.[1]

To judge from an anthology of 1963 assassination cartoon art—in which Mauldin's effort was not included—several other American editorial cartoonists used the parallel, including Don Wright and Jim Berryman. Especially successful were Lincoln–Kennedy tributes by Wright and *Dayton* (Ohio) *Journal-Herald* artist (and noted Lincoln enthusiast) Lloyd Ostendorf exploiting the theme of JFK's Pulitzer prize-winning *Profiles in Courage*. In these cartoons, Lincoln was drawn as a profile, a bust, a full-bodied figure, and an agent of apotheosis in the clouds—but

[VIII–1] *Bill Mauldin, untitled,* Chicago Sun-Times,
November 23, 1963. Reprinted with permission.

only once in "monumental" form, in the clouds above the Kennedy cas-
ket.[2] If this Associated Press effort and Mauldin's were uncommon in
this respect, they did reflect faithfully a tradition of more than a century
of cartooning Lincoln as a monument, an inanimate representation of
the American nation, an icon of American political ideals. This inspiration flowed not from Lincoln the prairie rail-splitter or the savior of the
Union, martyred on the altar of sectional discord and racial strife, but
instead from the august white marble figure by Daniel Chester French
that graces Henry Bacon's shrine at the foot of the mall in Washington,
the Lincoln Memorial exploited so poignantly by Frank Capra in his

1939 masterpiece *Mr. Smith Goes to Washington.*[3] For two generations before the dedication of the memorial in 1922 and three since, American editorial cartoonists have tended to draw Lincoln not as flesh-and-blood caricature but as a bronze or marble representational sculpture.

It wasn't always so. The living Lincoln had, during the course of his 1860 candidacy and troubled presidency, served as a very human foil in many cartoons, ranging from whimsical Currier & Ives lithographs to the caustic satire of John Tenniel and his *Punch* compatriots and the venomous characterizations of arch-Confederate artist Adalbert Volck of Baltimore. As mean-spirited and scabrous as many of these creations seem in retrospect, they did suggest in the lean, craggy beanpole with a wicked wit a ripe figure for creative caricature. One student of American national symbolism has suggested that Lincoln served cartoon artists here and in London as a prototype for Uncle Sam.[4] But then, on the morning of April 15, 1865, he passed on to the ages and, as David Donald has noted, grieving countrymen "suddenly discovered that the President had been the greatest man in the world."[5] To portray a Lincoln of foibles and flaws became for American cartoonists not just what would be called today. "politically incorrect," but out-and-out sacrilege. There appear to be no posthumous Lincoln cartoons that mock or disparage him and, until recently, few that even subject him to the gentlest of humor. Since political cartooning is an inherently negative medium thriving on barbed satire, this universal reverence accorded the martyred Lincoln has made him of rather limited use to cartoonists.

An inventory of the cartoons in *Puck* and *Judge* yields no more than two dozen Lincoln cartoons from 1877 through 1900, barely one a year. Nast, despite Lincoln's immense potential as the ultimate Union icon and Nast's own penchant for scourging Democrats and the South with the graphic art of the "bloody shirt," rarely drew him at all during his career at *Harper's Weekly.* An exception, and a somewhat "nasty" one at that, was his November 1868 "Wilkes Booth the Second," featuring Democratic vice-presidential nominee Frank Blair and New York Democrat editor "Brick" Pomeroy sneaking up with swords to assassinate Ulysses Grant, as under a portrait of Lincoln he scans a scroll reading "With malice toward none and charity for all. . . . Let us have peace."[6] Only in his sunset years, during the 1892 and 1896 campaigns, did Nast use Lincoln, along with Grant, as a stereotypical cartoon con-

vention to measure (and find wanting) the stature of Democratic nomin-
ees Grover Cleveland and William Jennings Bryan.

In his 1947 essay "The Folklore Lincoln," David Donald described
Lincoln's posthumous evolution as an American folk icon as a lengthy
struggle over essential definition. Grateful freedmen sought to define him
as a New World Moses, New England clergymen as a blend of Washington and Jesus ("somewhat like a Gilbert Stuart painting with a halo
dubbed in by later, less skillful hands"), and westerners as a Bunyanesque
but lazy practical joker, "teller of tall and lusty tales." Gilded Age cartoons attest instead to an apotheosis more sudden and less complicated,
an almost instantaneous transformation into a national civic deity as suggested by Mark Neely, Gabor Boritt, and Harold Holzer in *The Lincoln
Image*, and in greater detail recently by Merrill Peterson in *Lincoln in
American Memory*. It should be remembered that in its infancy political
cartooning was primarily a New York phenomenon, owing more to the
urban centers of the Atlantic seaboard and Europe than to American
regional folklore. Thus the martyr slain on Good Friday for the sins of
sectionalism was never a theme in Lincoln cartooning, and not until the
later emergence of such native midwestern editorial artists as John T.
McCutcheon and Jay N. "Ding" Darling would Lincoln be drawn, and
seldom at that, as a frontier folk figure. More indicative of the thematic
exploitation of Lincoln as a cartoon convention has been Peterson's the-
sis that his place in the national memory has hinged on five salient facets:

> Lincoln as Savior of the Union, Great Emancipator, Man of the Peo-
> ple, the First American, and the Self-Made Man. Nationality, Hu-
> manity, Democracy, Americanism, and the individual opportunity
> which is its essence; these are the building blocks of the Lincoln
> image.[7]

A revealing parallel to this genesis of Lincoln as a folk icon was the apotheosis of George Washington. In his cogent essay "The Flawless American," Lawrence J. Friedman perceptively analyzed the invention of
Washington by eulogists as the ultimate American deity, lauded by historian John Kingston in 1813 as "the statesman's polar star; the hero's
destiny; the boast of age; the companion of maturity; and the goal of
youth." The pillar of probity, compassionate conqueror, and exemplar
of republican virtue and common sense, and even in death an immortal

mortal, the mythic Washington became to Americans a measure of human perfectibility by which future generations of would-be statesmen were to be judged. In 1822 the *Richmond Enquirer* exulted, "His character is the scale by which the people will graduate the measures and conduct of his successors."[8] Inspiration does not always make for excitement or intimacy. In explaining away or simply ignoring Washington's human failings, his eulogists rendered him, as Donald has noted, "so dignified and remote that it was hard to think of him as a man, much less as a boy; he was a portrait by Peale or a Houdon bust."[9] Yet cartoon portrayals of Lincoln during the generation after his death followed suit almost identically, by casting him as less man than monument, the ultimate yardstick or scale by which a later generation of public figures was to be measured.

The first victim of such cartoon measurement was Lincoln's Confederate counterpart, Jefferson Davis, whose 1881 autobiography inspired the acid James A. Wales *Puck* front cover cartoon "A Dead Hero and a Live Jackass" [VIII–2], contrasting a monumental "Malice Toward None" Lincoln with Davis (clad in a bonnet, shawl, and hoopskirt to recall his humiliating escape from Fortress Monroe), hawking his *History of Treason* outside a "Secession Cemetery." When Davis died eight years later, a *Judge* front cover cartoon drawn by Bernhard Gillam [VIII–3] featured Miss South mourning the rebel chieftain as a "patriot and statesman" while the shade of Lincoln mused, "If he was a PATRIOT, what was I?" Although such cartoons demonstrate the potential utility of Lincoln for disparaging the South and the Democracy, such was not the case in the ferocious 1884 Cleveland–Blaine contest, although the Blaine forces resorted to strident "bloody-shirt" appeals to wartime passions in speeches and print. The lone Lincoln "bloody-shirt" cartoon that year in *Puck* or *Judge*, in fact, was an anti-Republican *Puck* centerfold by Gillam savaging Blaine's running mate John Logan for his antebellum zeal for hunting down fugitive slaves! *Judge* exploited Lincoln only once that year as well, among a quartet of tattooed figures (with Washington, Blaine, and James A. Garfield) in a rather lame Grant Hamilton attempt to rebut the celebrated *Puck* series lampooning Blaine as the "tattooed man" of political sleaze and scandal.[10]

Why *Judge* artists neglected to exploit Lincoln as a "bloody shirt" icon until after the election defies logic, but Cleveland's selection of ex-Confederates for key administration positions and other purported out-

[VIII–2] James A. Wales, "A Dead Hero and a Live Jackass," *Puck*, June 22, 1881, 267. Photograph by Brian Campbell Fischer.

[VIII–3] *Bernhard Gillam, "The Truth of 1861 Is the Truth of To-day,"* Judge, *December 21, 1889, 169. Photograph by Brian Campbell Fischer.*

rages against the Lincoln legacy guaranteed him steady work as a cartoon convention beginning in 1885. Cleveland's pilgrimage to Gettysburg that May, reported by the *New York Sun* as an orgy of gluttony and beer guzzling, prompted the Daniel McCarthy Memorial Day cartoon, "Two Presidents at Gettysburg," portraying Cleveland ordering up more beer as he feasted with secretary Daniel Lamont on "Solid South" beef against a backdrop of Lincoln delivering his immortal address. Even more outrageous as sectional demagoguery was Gillam's 1887 Independence Day cartoon, "Halt!," fueled by the return of some rebel battle flags as a conciliatory gesture. Protesting the surrender of flags from Antietam, Gettysburg, Vicksburg, and Appomattox to Lucius Lamar and a scruffy Solid South representation, Lincoln's specter ("Spirit of the War for the Union") declares, "Had you fought for those flags, you would not be so quick to give them away!" This reminder of Cleveland's purchase of a substitute to avoid donning Union blue is met with a protest, "They're rubbish anyhow." Other "rubbish" in the room includes Redcoat flags and muskets; a Mexican cannon; a whip for slaves; the bonnet, shawl, and hoopskirt of Jefferson Davis; and—pièce de résistance—the pistol of John Wilkes Booth![11]

Both vicious and patently dishonest, the cartoon illustrates an irony in Lincoln cartooning, then and since: the exploitation of "Honest Abe" as a device for wholesale deception. This was Lincoln, after all, author of "malice toward none, charity for all," a man who on the evening of Lee's surrender had graciously requested the Marine Band to play "Dixie." Other *Judge* cartoons deploying Lincoln as a weapon against the Democrats include an 1890 Hamilton Memorial Day centerfold and the October 11, 1890, F. Victor Gillam centerfold "The Same Old Sneaking Deserter." When in 1890 a measure to provide federal protection to black voters in the South fell victim to Democratic Senate opposition, Victor Gillam adorned a centerfold of Miss Columbia facing down a motley array of Democratic ward-heelers and Dixie bigots with a Lincoln portrait inscribed "My work was not in vain." Just months earlier, a *Judge* editorial by publisher William J. Arkell had mocked black political participation as "the gift of a jewel to a barbarian unaware of the difference between a bead and a diamond" and had urged instead strict literacy tests to weed out most black and immigrant voters! As late as 1896, Lincoln was used as a "bloody-shirt" device against William Jennings

Bryan by *Puck* and *Judge* alike. Victor Gillam's September *Judge* centerfold "Forbear!" portrayed Lincoln's ghost demanding of Bryan, "Halt!
How dare you try to revive a war of sections?," while Louis Dalrymple's
October *Puck* centerfold "History Repeats Itself" featured a vignette of
Jefferson Davis defying Lincoln and the Union at Fort Sumter as a parallel to Bryan and his scruffy Dixie and radical minions denouncing federal
interference in local affairs.[12]

Lincoln's image as the Great Emancipator was occasionally used
more benignly by period cartoonists. A bookmark bearing his bust
adorned Grant Hamilton's *Judge* centerfold "Two Pages in History," a
tribute to the 1885 New Orleans Exposition that contrasted slaves toiling
in a cotton field under the whip with freedmen casting votes in Ohio. A
Joseph Keppler, Jr., *Puck* centerfold, "The New South—The Triumph of
Free Labor," a salute to the 1895 Atlanta Exposition, featured whites
and blacks paying respects to a statue of Lincoln. Hamilton's "1863–
1898, History Repeats Itself" [VIII-4], a *Judge* tribute to Cuban liberation, paired a marble monument of William McKinley freeing Miss Cuba
with similar background statuary of Lincoln with Proclamation freeing a
Negro slave. Hamilton's January 1899 accolade to McKinley for extend-
ing federal care to Confederate parts of Civil War cemeteries, "Great
Men Make Great Nations," linked McKinley ("Fraternity—Care for
Confederate Dead") and Grant ("Let Us Have Peace") with Lincoln
("Liberty—Emancipation").[13] As did the Mauldin assassination cartoon,
these efforts portrayed Lincoln as a symbolic expression of the fundamental ideals of the American experiment, above party or faction. The
vast majority of Lincoln cartoons then and since, however, have been
both partisan and pejorative. Yet even at a time when memories of the
war and concomitant party battles were yet undimmed, the cartoon Lincoln was never exclusively a device used by Republicans to denigrate
Democrats.

In his 1951 essay "Getting Right with Lincoln," David Donald
noted that the tug-of-war over the martyr's shroud began almost at once
and, despite the manifest advantages enjoyed by the GOP in laying claim
to the Lincoln legacy, rarely did they do so by default.[14] Four 1885–91
Puck centerfolds co-opted the image of Lincoln to bash his party heirs.
Bernhard Gillam's 1885 "A Great Past and a Pitiful Present" used a background monument to David Farragut, Grant accepting Lee's sword, and

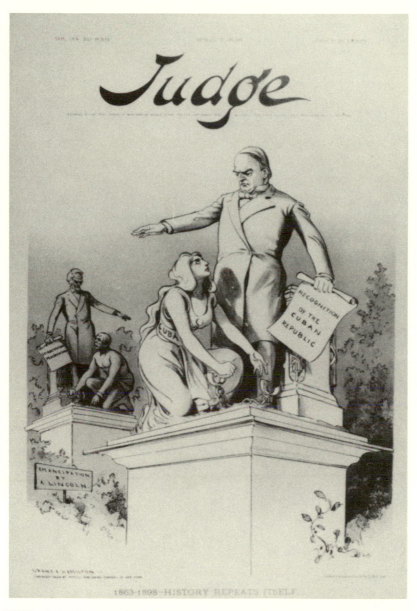

[VIII–4] *Grant Hamilton, "1863–1898, History Repeats Itself,"* Judge,
April 2, 1898, 211. Photograph by Brian Campbell Fischer.

Lincoln freeing the slaves to counterpoint the then-current GOP slough of scandal and fraud, while Uncle Sam protested in subtext below, "It's no use lifting me up to look at your Monumental Record, gentlemen; what can you give me to stand on Now?" Joseph Keppler's 1887 "The Lesson of the Past" summoned the ghost of Lincoln to comfort a beleaguered Cleveland: "They call me martyr, chief among the dead, and speak my name with reverence. In my life no curse too vile, no word of spite too wild they found to cast upon me." Keppler's 1887 "The Ideals of 1863 and the Idol of 1887—The Decadence of a Great Party" employed marble background statues of Lincoln and Charles Sumner as reminders of a noble tradition debased by a current GOP party idol representing the politics of the bloody shirt, pension fraud, and patronage spoils. In "The Old Leaders and the New" four years later, Keppler exploited this formula to debase Republican chieftains George Frisbee Hoar, "Czar" Reed, Matt Quay, and Benjamin Harrison as unworthy of party patriarchs Sumner, William Seward, Salmon Chase, and Lincoln.[15]

Like their pro-Republican *Judge* counterparts, these *Puck* centerfolds suggest the evolution of a pat formula for Lincoln cartooning: the gross unworthiness of one or more contemporary politicos is compared to the legacy of Lincoln, often accentuated by casting him as a larger-than-life marble or bronze monument. In some instances, the specific issues or character traits informing the invidious comparisons might make sense—Union, civil rights, integrity, for example—while in others they were strained or downright silly. It mattered little. If no analogy came to mind, the cartoonist could simply portray his target as woefully deficient in stature, a midget in the shadow of the giant. Thus, after poet-reformer James Russell Lowell saluted Cleveland as "the best representation of the highest type of Americanism that we have seen since Lincoln," *Judge* ran the Bernhard Gillam cartoon "An Aggravated Case of Big-Head" [VIII–5] on January 28, 1888, portraying the president as a puffed-up, froglike gnome dwarfed by bronze statues of Lincoln and Grant. Later that year, a Hamilton election-eve cartoon on the front cover of *Judge* presented an even tinier Cleveland casting by candlelight a huge shadow over a bust of Grant, a statue of Jefferson, and portraits of Franklin, John Quincy Adams, Washington, and Lincoln. Victor Gillam's October 1896 *Judge* centerfold "The Sliding Scale" portrayed a linear regression in size from Washington and Lincoln through Cleveland and Bryan. Hamilton's

[VIII–5] Bernhard Gillam, "An Aggravated Case of Big-Head," Judge, *January 28, 1888, 1. Photograph by Brian Campbell Fischer.*

September 1900 *Judge* cartoon "Bryan Is Entitled to Another 'Think' " [VIII–6], prompted by Bryan's affinity for quoting Lincoln, provides a textbook example of the formula, with wee Bryan preening on tiptoes alongside a massive marble bust of Lincoln.[16]

Despite Lincoln's many demonstrated uses, his popularity as a cartoon convention did not soar appreciably after the decline of the humor weeklies and the advent of daily newspaper editorial cartooning. This transition in technology, art, individual autonomy, and daily deadline pressures did help bring about greater flexibility in Lincoln's graphic exploitation by twentieth-century cartoonists. In his acid 1924 cartoon

[VIII–6] Grant Hamilton, "Bryan Is Entitled to Another 'Think,'"
Judge, *September 22, 1900, 1. Photograph by Brian Campbell Fischer.*

"The Republican Party Down to Date," Art Young used the same formula as Grant Hamilton did on Bryan and Lincoln to draw a minuscule
Calvin Coolidge dwarfed by a massive marble bust of his party's progeni-
tor.[17] On the whole, however, the pioneer newspaper cartoonists did effect a partial liberation of Lincoln from his "monumental" bronze and
marble confines, even as Americans were tending to associate him with
the magnificent French figure, dedicated in 1922 and destined to become, as Merrill Peterson has described it, "the nation's foremost sculp-
tured icon." Throughout the twentieth century, daily editorial cartoon
artists would divide their efforts rather evenly between the monumental
motif (increasingly French's seated figure) and anthropomorphic forms
when they used Lincoln as a convention.

The concurrent genesis of a national holiday on February 12 to
honor Lincoln's birthday gave rise to the phenomenon of the birthday
cartoon. Predictably, most of these efforts were cartoons the world
would (and should) little note nor long remember, disappointing as art
and commentary alike, short on incisive irony and long on noble sentiment. Since these cartoons were inspired not by timely events but by the
calendar, appropriate counterpoints rarely obliged. When Lincoln was
trotted out as a yardstick, then, it was to deplore the likes of pettifogging
politicos, immigrant extremism, and laziness. This annual rite was the
forte of such native midwesterners as *Chicago Tribune* artist John T. Mc-
Cutcheon and *Des Moines Register* mainstay Jay N. "Ding" Darling,
exemplars of a folksy, somewhat benign style of cartooning. Representative of such birthday offerings was Darling's 1921 *Collier's* opus [VIII–7]
improbably portraying Lincoln, an agnostic with three months of formal
schooling, prescribing "the little red schoolhouse and the white church"
as antidotes to radical agitation. A contemporary McCutcheon *Tribune*
cartoon [VIII–8] had a young rail-splitter deliberating between upward
mobility and sloth.[18]

Another midwesterner, Daniel Fitzpatrick of the *St. Louis Post-Dispatch*, executed in 1943 a rare Lincoln birthday cartoon transcending
such banality, "That These Dead Shall Not Have Died in Vain" [VIII–9].
A distinctive crayon-on-grained-paper rendering of the Lincoln visage in
the smoke of a smoldering planet, it evokes not a simplistic yearning for
peace in the midst of war but a gritty resolve that this peace be worth
preserving and worth its horrible cost, much like Lincoln's challenge to

From One Who's Familiar with the Roads

"Turn back two miles to the little red schoolhouse and the white church, then straight ahead"

[VIII–8] John T. McCutcheon, "When Lincoln Made His Choice
Between Mediocrity and Immortality," John McCutcheon's Book, 267.
Reprinted with permission of the Chicago Tribune.

Opposite: [VIII–7] Jay N. "Ding" Darling, "From One Who's Familiar
with the Roads," Collier's Weekly, February 12, 1921, 17.

"THAT THESE DEAD SHALL NOT HAVE DIED IN VAIN"
FEBRUARY 12, 1943

[VIII–9] *Daniel R. Fitzpatrick, "That These Dead Shall Not Have Died in Vain,"* St. Louis Post-Dispatch, *February 12, 1943; from* As I Saw It, *90. Reprinted with permission of the* St. Louis Post-Dispatch.

AT THE GRASS-ROOTS CONVENTION
JUNE 11, 1935

[VIII–10] *Daniel R. Fitzpatrick, "At the Grass-Roots Convention,"* St. Louis Post-Dispatch, *June 11, 1935; from* As I Saw It, *5. Reprinted with permission of the* St. Louis Post-Dispatch.

the nation at Gettysburg. Unrivaled during his generation as a master of the medium, Fitzpatrick, a fiery progressive, was also capable of wry drollery. In 1935 the Republican party, hitting rock bottom in public approval at the nadir of the Great Depression, staged a "grass-roots" conclave in Lincoln's Springfield to affirm party origins. Fitzpatrick's burlesque of bloated GOP plutocrats masquerading in Lincoln masks, "At the Grass-Roots Convention" [VIII–10], surgically conveyed Fitzpatrick's impression that "nothing important came out of this show and they fooled no one but themselves." In a similar vein, *Baltimore Sun* cartoonist Richard Q. Yardley exploited Lincoln in 1949 and 1951 birthday drawings to lampoon a Republican party mired in defeat and caught in the crossroads between its conservative and moderate camps.[19]

The use of Lincoln in American political cartooning has remained somewhat selective, despite cogent parallels that have seemed to beg for his presence. Although many cartoonists appropriated him to render commentary on John Kennedy's assassination, there seem to be none who did so in the wake of the 1968 slayings of Robert Kennedy or Martin Luther King, Jr., or the attempted assassinations of Gerald Ford and Ronald Reagan, occasions ripe for analogies to Lincoln's death. Cartoon comparisons of the Great Emancipator to black struggles against Jim Crow were few, an exception being Richard Q. Yardley's 1964 *Baltimore Sun* drawing "His Soul Goes Marching On," portraying a smiling Lincoln seated with the new rights legislation in hand. Two weeks later Yardley lampooned Senate Republican kingpin Everett Dirksen as "Abe Lincoln Dirksen in Illinois" for his capitulation to the Barry Goldwater insurgency. This abrupt departure from the GOP's Lincoln pedigree prompted *Louisville Courier-Journal* artist Hugh Haynie to reprise Tenniel's immortal 1890 Bismarck–Kaiser Wilhelm masterpiece, with a malevolent Goldwater supplanting Lincoln on the deck of "S.S. Grand Olde Party," and Herblock to portray a Goldwater partisan with muddy boots trampling a Lincoln portrait under the wry caption "We Stand upon Our Historic Principles —." Watergate inspired very few Lincoln cartoons, despite the compelling contrast provided by "Tricky Dick" Nixon and "Honest Abe." Ray Osrin did just that in a 1974 *Cleveland Plain Dealer* cartoon portraying the two men seated next to one another in the pantheon of history, with Lincoln inquiring, "They called me 'Honest Abe.' What do they call you?" Vic Roschkov exploited Gerald Ford's self-deprecating "I am a Ford, not a Lincoln" in a *Windsor* (Ontario) *Star* cartoon of the two worthies, plus Nixon as "Edsel"![20]

Perhaps Lincoln has been used so sparingly through the years because, with few exceptions, cartoons that did exploit him did so in such a reverent way. Cartoonists must draw to earn paychecks, but they take pride in creative subtlety and find enjoyment in using symbols with which they can have fun. Unlike the actual Lincoln, a man of deadly one-liners and risqué humor, the somber, monumental Lincoln can scarcely be considered a "fun" fellow. For more than a century, cartoonists used him to have fun with foils, but they did not have very much fun with him. Most of these cartoonists had, as schoolboys, memorized the Gettysburg Address and the second inaugural. Thus Lincoln's symbolic stature tended to limit his use to those causes and events of proper magnitude. Mauldin's 1963 classic, for example, made perfect sense for mourning a martyred president, but would have been a ridiculous vehicle for lamenting a Chicago alderman slain during a shakedown, just as Fitzpatrick's Lincoln in the smoke of a burning planet required World War II, not a Grenada or a Panama.

Moreover, those qualities of character for which the mythic Lincoln has become a symbol—rigid integrity, compassion for the disadvantaged, lofty national idealism—provide contrasts lacking subtlety. His use as an icon of integrity requires a Nixon as a foil, just as his use as an exemplar of Union needed a Jefferson Davis. Foils so inviting come along less frequently than cartoonists might wish. Finally, cartoonists seem to have been intimidated, and understandably so, by a pervasive sense of sadness evoked by the Lincoln mystique, casting what Charles Press has aptly described as a "certain blackish pall over the proceedings." The wonder may not be that he has been cartooned so seldom, but that he has been cartooned at all.

Press has written of the troubles cartoonists have encountered in exploiting inanimate national monuments as dynamic symbols, for they "suggest solemn dignity and gravity, but they are always at rest and this limits somewhat the range of emotions they can express."[21] A useful parallel to the "monumental" Lincoln might be the Statue of Liberty. The statue first served cartoonists superbly during an era when it was popularly regarded as a French engineering oddity or a New York tourism boondoggle, then evolved into a sacred symbol drawn primarily for purposes of eagle-screaming patriotism. Only recently has a new generation of cartoonists forsaken high moral dudgeon for zany iconoclasm and recaptured an element of irreverent wit, epitomized by Paul Conrad's superb 1976 portrayal of Liberty as a voluptuous nude [VII–9] in a prurient Jimmy Carter fantasy.

If a cartoon portraying the Great Emancipator sitting jaybird-naked in his memorial seems a trifle far-fetched, a witty 1990 Steve Benson cartoon [VIII–11] suggests that it need not be an impossibility. His

[VIII–11] *Steve Benson, untitled, April, 1990,* Tacoma Morning News-Tribune. *Reprinted with permission of Tribune Media Services.*

portrayal of an anguished monumental Lincoln stripped down to polka-dot briefs over the legend "Four Score and Several Hundred Billion Dollars Ago" underscored at once a decade of American fiscal irresponsibility as well as a crisis in banking. It epitomizes two recent trends in political cartooning: an even greater shift from moral indignation to irreverent satire, and an increasing flexibility in the use of national symbols for wry commentary. As a result, Lincoln has emerged as a cartoon symbol either emancipated from his monumental straitjacket or, as in Benson's piece, given a wide latitude of burlesque within it.[22]

In 1980, for example, Jimmy Carter's labored apologia for refusing to debate third-party candidate John Anderson prompted Mike Peters to evoke the Lincoln–Douglas debates in a *Dayton Daily News* cartoon featuring a TV producer dictating to a bemused Lincoln the Carter conditions on behalf of Douglas. When in 1982 Reagan indicated his support for tax breaks for racially segregated private academies, Pat Oliphant drew him as an actor playing Lincoln, but balking over emancipation ("I free the *WHAT???*"). Similarly, Reagan's opposition to sanctions against the Union of South Africa for racial apartheid inspired Ed Stein's 1986

[VIII–12] *Steve Benson, "What If Geraldine Ferraro Had Been Abraham Lincoln's Speech Writer?" (1984) from* Fencin' with Benson, *68. Reprinted with permission of* Tribune Media Services.

cartoon in Denver's *Rocky Mountain News*, "The Great Emancipator Meets the Great Communicator," with Reagan perched on the arm of a disgusted monumental Lincoln as he prattles on about quiet diplomacy. Geraldine Ferraro's 1984 waffling on the abortion issue prompted the wry Benson riposte "What If Geraldine Ferraro Had Been Abraham Lincoln's Speech Writer?" [VIII–12], with Lincoln fudging on emancipation. The tenor of modern politics and a soured American electorate was captured well in Jack Ohman's 1985 *Portland Oregonian* effort "If Abe Lincoln were President Today. . ." [VIII–13]. Scott Stantis lampooned the George Bush–Michael Dukakis debates in a 1988 *Memphis Commercial Appeal* effort depicting Lincoln and Douglas viewing them on television with looks of disgust. After Bush vetoed a 1990 civil rights bill with a bent for racial preference quotas, Ohman responded with side-by-side statues of Lincoln ("Freed the Slaves 1863") and Bush ("Freed the Owners 1990") [VIII–14]. Evoking shades of Nast, Benson rendered him as "John Wilkes Bush" lurking outside Lincoln's theater box.[23]

As contemporary cartoonists have begun to "lighten up" on Lin-

[VIII–13] Jack Ohman, "If Abe Lincoln Were President Today . . .,"
Portland Oregonian, *February, 1985. Reprinted with permission.*

[VIII–14] Jack Ohman, *untitled,* Portland Oregonian, *1990. Reprinted
with permission.*

coln, they have helped transform him from a monumental icon of limited utility into a much more flexible "man for all seasons" as a cartoon convention. When genetic research prompted speculation in 1991 that human life (including Lincoln expressly) could be cloned through DNA reconstruction, M.G. Lord (*Newsday*) and Ohman both responded with cartoons, Lord to mock Democratic desperation for a savior and Ohman to lampoon Republican anxieties over another run with Dan Quayle! Ohman that year also chided Mario Cuomo and other Democrats wavering between candidacies and bleacher seats in his "If These People Had Been Democratic Presidential Hopefuls." In the cartoon, Paul Revere cancels his midnight ride as too dangerous; Martin Luther King, Jr., abandons his dream because of high negatives; and Lincoln forsakes his 1860 quest for the presidency because polls show the Union cause less popular than he had believed. During the 1992 campaign, while Bush vacillated over committing American forces to beleaguered Bosnia, an *Akron Beacon-Journal* cartoon by Bok portrayed Lincoln learning that a party focus group opposed committing ground troops to a civil war. Following his inauguration, Bill Clinton sought to run the White House as he had his campaign—relying heavily on media talk shows and town meetings to ensure that the winds of popular acclaim blew steadily at his back. Don Wright drew a caustic critique featuring Lincoln scanning print-outs and opting not to free the slaves after all![24]

Although the editorial cartoonists of today have largely liberated the mythic Lincoln from the rigid confines of bronze and marble, they continue in the long tradition of their medium. They rely on him as a measure, perhaps the ultimate yardstick, of public figures and of qualities that transcend the banalities of TV "talking heads," sound bites, daily headlines, and the ubiquitous "spin doctors." A splendid example of this came in June 1993, when Clinton, reeling from popular disapproval, sought to ameliorate his poisonous relations with the White House press corps. He admired a reporter's Mickey Mouse necktie, then put it on and mugged for the cameras. Unimpressed by such patently phony Disneyland populism, *Detroit News* cartoonist Draper Hill executed "With Malice Toward None, With Charity for All" [VIII–15], which featured a nonplussed monumental Lincoln sporting a garish Mickey Mouse tie, to suggest a gentle but deadly contrast between Lincoln and this latest

[VIII–15] Draper Hill, untitled and unpublished, June 20, 1993.
Reprinted with the permission of the artist.

successor. This cartoon, like Benson's savings-and-loan effort exploiting
the Memorial image of Lincoln while wryly lampooning its limits, con-
veys both the enduring power of Lincoln as a cartoon convention and
myriad possibilities for future exploitation.[25]

IX

The Lucifer
Legacy

The graphic portrayal of evil has long posed something of a paradox for political cartoonists. On the one hand, evil has always been the mother's milk of their vocation, like beauty to Emerson's rhodora "its own excuse for being." On the other, it is a complex phenomenon, encompassing the spectrum of human defects from picayune peculations and deceptions to the sickening atrocities of Hitler, Stalin, Idi Amin, Pol Pot, and their ilk. Like goodness, malfeasance cannot be cartooned with a universal generic symbol. To caricature the architects of the Holocaust and kindred acts with the same graphic imagery used to portray petty grafters, cheats, timeservers, and demogogues would be to trivialize the former, overkill the latter, and serve up art of such banality as to scarcely justify the newsprint and ink to purvey it.

Eighteenth-century cartoonists were infatuated with the image of Lucifer, a figure of compelling importance to the intensely religious culture of early America, a symbol of depravity instantly recognized and morally consonant with the fanatical acrimony inspiring most early cartoons. During the 1760s Benjamin Franklin and James Dove cast each other as lackeys of Lucifer, and Paul Revere drew Satan to pillory pro-Parliament Massachusetts assemblymen. A generation later, Jeffersonian and Federalist artists followed suit to disparage opposition figures.[1] Satan's utility as a convention waned with his role in Christian imagination, although Nast used him to savage Horace Greeley and Victoria Woodhull [VI–10] during the 1870s. In 1896 Grant Hamilton drew William Jennings Bryan as a scarlet Satan tempting a farmer with a world awash in silver coins in his *Judge* centerfold, "The Temptation," and on rare occasions Lucifer still graces modern political cartoons. His main rival as a symbol of evil through the ages has been the macabre skeletal image of

death, the Grim Reaper. A problem for cartoonists is that these are difficult conventions to exploit without overkill. Lucifer works well for ep-
ochal human evil, as does Mr. Death for truly apocalyptic horrors, but
neither serves successfully in cartooning routine political spats or run-
of-the-mill moral shortcomings, topics that require subtlety, not sledge-
hammer condemnation.

It requires little creative genius, for example, to render an effective
cartoon of a grinning Satan or Reaper overlooking a Nazi concentration
camp, or Stalin's Gulag, or the killing fields of Cambodia or Rwanda.
Fortunately, such occasions are rare. For lesser sins against the body poli-
tic, these symbols do not suffice. Cases in point are Nast's Greeley and
Woodhull cartoons and Hamilton's "Temptation"—despite fine imagery
and artwork, invoking Satan to pillory opposition to the Grant scandals,
gender discrimination, and the gold dollar rings fundamentally false.
Similarly, Nast's portrayal of the Russo–Turkish War as a two-faced
"Temple of Janus" skull devouring both of the armies is splendid, but his
use of Mr. Death to portray American trade unionism, European communism and anarchism, and Dennis Kearney's California underclass radicalism seems patently silly.[2] Appropriate images for the handiwork of Hitler
or Vlad the Impaler, Lucifer and Mr. Death work poorly as symbols for
lesser venality in a political democracy—where rascals must exhibit some
endearing human qualities to earn the chance to betray the public trust!

Joseph Keppler, Bernhard Gillam, and their colleagues at *Puck* and
Judge exhibited a much more subtle creativity in portraying political
wrongdoing. They often cast corporate trusts, urban machines, and the
Roman Catholic hierarchy as octopuses or serpents. Drawing on their
affinity for antiquity, Keppler and his contemporaries used the Hydra,
the Minotaur, and Cerberus to symbolize silver coinage, a protective tariff, and the "yellow peril." In lampooning individual shortcomings, Narcissus did nicely for vanity [VI–12] and parodies of Diogenes served for
cartooning duplicity. But neither the classics nor Scripture provided these
artists with a generic symbol of that congenital rottenness of soul we
refer to as "sleaze." Hermes, Greek god of slick dealing and petty pecula-
tion, was much too obscure, and Judas Iscariot was depressingly heavy
and lacked the requisite visual image.[3] Even the modern popular culture
of Hollywood, television, and comic books has failed to provide cartoonists with such a generic sleaze symbol. Perhaps the very nature of petty

sleaze is lacking in Homeric or Biblical dimensions: the only adequate referent for sleaze is sleaze itself. From Nast through the moderns, most cartoonists have avoided symbolism and resorted instead to the simple expedient of directly portraying malefactors committing their purported misdeeds.

For a sinner to evolve into a generic symbol of political venality, therefore, would require uncommon ethical breaches worthy of widespread and unforgettable notoriety. Although creative cartoonists could play a role in this process, their efforts would have to dovetail with consensus cultural prejudice and the larger verdict of historical memory. The failure of James G. Blaine to achieve such stature after his 1884 celebrity as the tattooed man provides a good example. He was targeted by *Puck* cartoonists in the most effective running gag in the history of the medium, marked head to toe with tattoos representing the "Mulligan Letters" and other alleged ethical lapses. The sequence attracted extraordinary attention, prompted angry Blainiacs to threaten lawsuits and legislation, and may have decided an election hinging on the loss of New York by a bare thousand votes. But it did not create a generic cartoon convention. Why the device of the tattoo failed to become a stock vehicle for cartooning sleaze remains a mystery, for it offered artists simplicity, flexibility through the text of tattoos, and ready association. Contemporary cartoonists still use the device on lazy days to connote embarrassing beliefs, actions, or endorsements. Why Blaine himself failed to evolve into such a symbol is hardly a mystery. Less corrupt than simply careless and obtuse to rumors of scandal, he may have been vulnerable to allegations of sleaze in 1884, but he was not stigmatized sufficiently to gain immortality as a generic symbol for the ages.[4]

Indeed, in the long annals of American political cartooning only two men have done this: Boss Tweed of Tammany and Richard Nixon of Watergate. Each achieved this dubious distinction through enduring notoriety for memorable misdeeds real or invented, with appreciable assists from Mother Nature and crusading cartoonists. With Tweed, Nast did more than merely assist, of course. Through powerful cartoon satire and brilliant caricature, he transformed the propaganda of George Jones and other New York Tammany critics into the improbable but compelling mythic ogre that history texts have accepted as gospel for more than a century. Whatever transgressions the real Tweed did or did not commit, it was Nast's Tweed the American public came to love, and to loathe. This was the machine mastermind who turned Tammany into a veritable merchandise mart for offices, contracts, and police favors that cost New Yorkers some $200 million, made Gotham his personal fiefdom with a nefarious 1870 city charter, and then arrogantly taunted his critics, "What are you going to do about it?" This powerful symbol of "urban rot, malodorous, the embodiment of all that is evil and cancerous in American municipal and political life," as Leo Hershkowitz has characterized Nast's creation, was far too compelling to fade away after the mortal Tweed had passed from the scene.[5]

Soon after his death in New York's Ludlow Street jail in 1878, Tweed evolved into a generic prototype of political corruption in the color cartoons of *Puck* and *Judge*, invariably drawn as a spectral version of the Nast caricature, even by Keppler and other rivals who disliked Nast and resented his celebrity. To the rampant Republican partisans of *Judge*, Tweed's affiliation with the Democratic party was sufficient cause to extend the stigma of his venality to anyone casting a Democratic ballot at any level. On one occasion they did so by similtaneously pirating and pillorying Nast as well. When in 1884 Nast joined in a "mugwump" defection from Republican ranks to support Democratic reform nominee Grover Cleveland, the *Judge* centerfold "Anything to Beat Blaine" [IX–1] parodied an 1872 Nast anti-Greeley cartoon. Frank Beard drew Nast as the organ-grinder's monkey of *Harper's* editor George W. Curtis, embracing "across the bloody chasm" of sectional and partisan strife the ghost of Tweed, who assures the artist, "Go right along, gentlemen; you are now arrayed against my old enemy, the Republican party. Our spirits bless you and we all forgive you." Another 1884 *Judge* cartoon presenting Tweed as a ghost of Democracy past was the unsigned "In the Democratic Graveyard," featuring sexton Charles A. Dana and a resurrected Thomas Hendricks against a backdrop of monuments to past party sins, including Tweed's in the upper left.[6]

Most cartoon materializations of Tweed's ghost, however, were inspired by municipal corruption and machine rule. Probably the first of these, James A. Wales's 1881 *Judge* front cover "Philadelphia Imitating New York," which was prompted by disclosures of tax fraud in Philadelphia, featured Tweed's specter challenging a trio of reformers, "What are you going to do about it?" This dictum possessed sufficient notoriety to

[IX–1] Frank Beard, "Anything to Beat Blaine," Puck, July 12, 1884, 8–9. Photograph by Brian Campbell Fischer.

stand alone as a Tweed cartoon referent, as it did in subtitles for Keppler's 1884 Puck "Solid for Another Year" portrait of "Honest John" Kelly, Tweed's successor as Tammany czar, and Beard's 1884 anti-Tammany effort "The Board of Aldermen."[7]

In 1882 Wales used it for the title of a Judge centerfold featuring Hubert O. Thompson, Tweed's successor as New York's public works commissioner, seated on an empty city safe with his cronies under an 1870 oil painting of Tweed and his lieutenants in a similar pose. Although Thompson had risen through the ranks of the county organization and not Tammany, had never been a Tweed intimate, and was probably no more corrupt than most other municipal politicians of his day, his office and his physiognomy conspired to make him the butt of cartoons portraying him as Tweed's legatee. A week later, Wales followed with "Of Public Interest," featuring Thompson by a looted treasury safe, surrounded by vignettes of him wining and dining the influential to illustrate the subtitle, "He's a good fellow; he's just like Tweed." Thompson's death in 1886 inspired Keppler's Puck centerfold "Pandora Grace Opens His Little Box," featuring Thompson's welcome to the "Department of

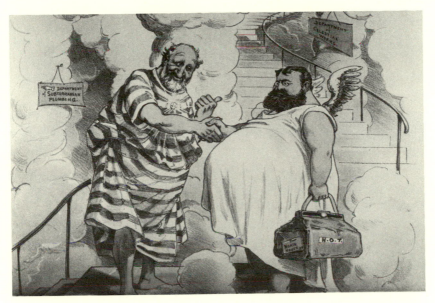

[IX–2] *Upper detail from Joseph Keppler, "Pandora Grace Opens His Little Box,"* Puck, *392–93. Photograph by Brian Campbell Fischer.*

Celestial Works" by the spirit of Tweed in prison stripes [IX–2]. A week later, Frederick Burr Opper's *Puck* cartoon "Rough on America's Great Cartoonists" featured Keppler and Nast pleading for mercy from the Grim Reaper, who holds a scroll with the names of Tweed, Thompson, Kelly, and other departed miscreants who had inspired their art. In 1889, hints that "Boston Strongboy" John L. Sullivan might seek political office prompted Hamilton in "The Slugger's Political Ambition" to draw Sullivan comparing himself favorably to some notorious spoilsmen in a room accented with a portrait of Thompson and a bust of Tweed.[8]

Just weeks after Thompson's death and weeks before the dedication of the Statue of Liberty, *Judge* carried an outstanding posthumous Tweed cartoon, F. Victor Gillam's "Erecting the New York Political Statue" [VII–4]. Inspired by the awarding of a lucrative aqueduct contract by such spoilsmen as state Democratic chairman John O'Brien and Thompson successor Maurice B. Flynn to a construction firm in which the two were partners, Gillam portrayed the project as a boondoggle to put together a shrine to Tweed. Less subtle by far was Hamilton's 1891 savaging of New York governor David Hill in "Tweed's Protégé and

Successor" [IX–3], featuring Hill lounging alongside Tweed's tombstone with trophies of spoils as Tweed's materialized spirit confers the blessing, "Dave, old pard, you beat me hollow. Like you, *I* did my own counting in, and appointed judges to do my bidding; but, after being steeped in corruption, *I* did not have the cheek to aspire to the Presidency."[9]

In 1897 a threat by New York Republican kingpin Tom Platt to enact a repressive anti-cartoon bill prompted Hearst cartoonist Homer Davenport to feature Platt twice with a Nast-like caricature of Tweed— first, in "They Never Liked Cartoons," a reference to Tweed's reputed plea to "Stop them damned pictures!," and again in a subsequent cartoon gloating over the failure of Platt's legislation. But then cartoons using Tweed as a generic symbol of arrogance and sleaze alike appeared less often as his contemporaries, politicians and cartoonists alike, began to pass from the scene. These cartoons ceased almost entirely after the system of municipal machine politics fell casualty to civil service, bureaucratic centralization, and ethnic acculturation. Two rare exceptions are the parodies on Nast's legendary Tweed portrait "The Brains" done by Paul Conrad in 1978 [IX–4] to savage the General Services Administration, and a 1987 portrayal of Detroit Mayor Coleman Young [IX–5] by Draper Hill. Disclosure in 1993 of a secret slush fund and other improprieties involving Dominic Jacobetti, longtime chair of Michigan's House Appropriation Committee, prompted Hill to expand on the analogy of Nast's "Brains." In "We Are Not a Crook" [IX–6], Hill drew the shadow of the "Godfather" as a creative combination of the Tweed body, money-bags head, and garish diamond stickpin, and the Nixon trademark "waggle-V" gesture and classic denial.[10]

For a century after Tweed's downfall, despite no discernible lack of political venality, no public figure attained a similar status in cartoon art. Then came Nixon—for cartoonists a gift from the gods. Dirty tricks, distortion, innuendo, rampant red-baiting, and a genius for the politics of fear and division exemplified his public service and his campaigns. Voracious for material gain, Nixon was surrounded by the taint of scandal, from the early slush fund that gave rise to the 1952 "Checkers" speech through a scheme to milk millions from his presidential papers. His Watergate "high crimes and misdemeanors" were without parallel in the life of the nation. For more than a quarter century—from the vicious red-baiting campaign that brought him to the Congress in 1946 to his

[IX–3] Grant Hamilton, "Tweed's Protégé and Successor," Judge, December 19, 1891, 635. Photograph by Brian Campbell Fischer.

[IX-4] *Paul Conrad, untitled,* Los Angeles Times, *1978.* © *1978,* Los Angeles Times. *Reprinted with permission.*

[IX-5] *Draper Hill, "Words to Live By,"* Detroit News, *February 17, 1987.* (C) *1987,* Detroit News. *Reprinted with permission.*

[IX–6] Draper Hill, "We Are Not a Crook," Detroit News, January 21, 1993. © 1993, Detroit News. Reprinted with permission.

mawkish "My mother was a a saint" valedictory, in which he equated his loss of political office with Theodore Roosevelt's loss of a young wife—his legacy was, as George Will noted in a candid obituary, "terrifying testimony to the toll that ambition can take on character."[11]

Even in political exile, new grotesqueries continued to bubble to the surface, including a suggestion made to aides in 1972 that the apartment of George Wallace's failed assassin be salted with phony evidence implicating the Democrats! Nixon was seen by Americans as so singularly devoid of such redeeming qualities as a sense of humor or spark of spontaneity that three decades in the national spotlight won him no nickname save "Tricky Dick." He rendered himself even more vulnerable to satirists with his penchant for patent incongruity, sleaze wrapped in sanctimony, the lying tremolo of "Let me make this perfectly clear"— even a coverup dubbed "Operation Candor."

So obsessed by hostile cartoonists that in 1960 he spoke of his unsavory reputation as his "Herblock image," and later put *Los Angeles Times* artist Paul Conrad on an official "enemies list," Nixon surely provided the most tempting of targets. Unlike Nast with Tweed, modern cartoonists rarely had to resort to wholesale invention. As Mike Peters reminisced fondly of Watergate, "There wasn't a day I didn't come down from the bedroom, open the door, pick up the newspaper, and the headline would become the cartoon." Moreover, even better than Tweed, Nixon provided the natural ingredients of caricature: ski-jump nose, beady eyes, jowls, thin shoulders—above all, his affinity for slouching with arms uplifted and fingers in a trademark double-V waggle. As *Newsweek* noted in 1980, "Never has nature so perfectly molded physiognomy to personality." Doug Marlette once said of him, "Nixon was to cartooning what Marilyn Monroe was to sex. Nixon looked like his policies. His nose told you he was going to bomb Cambodia." In short, he inspired good cartoonists to greatness and mediocre ones to adequacy. As Peters noted wistfully, "He was our Camelot."[12]

Not all cartoonists shared this feeling. As *Rocky Mountain News* artist Ed Stein confided, "I was so sick of him and so relieved when he left, I vowed never to draw him again." The majority opinion, however, was exemplified by a 1984 *Minneapolis Star-Tribune* resignation anniversary cartoon by Steve Sack featuring demonstrators chanting "We Want Nixon" and urging a comeback, as Nixon mused "Damned cartoonists!" During the decade following Nixon's exile, cartoonists did not let him go gently into the dark night but instead exploited him at every turn. Any mention of Nixon in the headlines, or a salient anniversary of the Watergate break-in or his resignation, invariably elicited Nixon cartoons by Sack, Peters, and others. In 1978 Nixon's junkets to Europe and Kentucky inspired derisive cartoons by Peters, and publication of a Nixon memoir prompted another Peters effort, this one of a group of fairy-tale favorites laughing uproariously as Mother Goose reads to them from the volume. In 1980, release of new Nixon tapes inspired Jerry Fearing to portray him as Darth Vader in a *St. Paul Dispatch* cartoon. On the tenth anniversary of the Watergate burglary, Pat Oliphant drew a solitary Nixon with a birthday cake with ten candles, and Peters portrayed him bedridden with a tape recorder as his wife Pat tendered regrets to a Watergate reunion, "Sorry, he can't come to the reunion . . . He's in bed with a bug."[13]

A decade in oblivion did little to diminish Nixon's attractiveness to opportunistic cartoonists. In 1984 a Supreme Court ruling on wiretaps inspired a Peters cartoon of Nixon bugging a telephone call from the Supreme Court to Pat, and another of him bugging the proceedings and grousing, "I should've used a Betamax." A series of TV interviews that year at $500,000 apiece prompted Sack to portray him as a figural Watergate vending machine, and Peters to feature him in the television series "Bloopers, Blunders, and Practical Jokes." His 1985 stint as arbitrator of a baseball umpires' strike led to a Sack panel of Nixon daydreaming of world peacemaking glory, as the parties argued about scented soap in washrooms, and a fine Peters cartoon of Nixon behind home plate fudging a call on a baserunner with Watergate rhetoric. Publication of his 1990 volume, *In the Arena*, prompted Sack to portray Nixon coating himself with whitewash. The dedication that summer of his presidential library in Yorba Linda, California, inspired a Sack cartoon of visitors experiencing eighteen-and-a-half minute gaps in their walking-tour tapes during the Watergate exhibit, and a Hill cartoon of Nixon consoling Gerald Ford, Ronald Reagan, and George Bush with, "They just don't make enemies the way they used to." Some unsought, self-serving 1992 Nixon advice to Bush on negotiating with the Soviets prompted acid cartoons by Sack and Steve Benson. Later that year, the twentieth anniversary of the burglary led to another Sack "damn cartoonists" effort, and Nixon's ongoing attempts to sequester Watergate records for personal profit inspired Sack to cast him as "RumpelNixon" reaping gold coins from a tape-reel spinning wheel.[14]

All the while, his writings and occasional public appearances fueled speculation of a return from Elba. This prompted cartoonists to use Nixon as a generic symbol for the manic political ambition he had displayed, despite setbacks that would have sent any other mortal scurrying to the practice of law, a university sinecure, or the nearest golf course. The dust had barely settled from his exit when in 1975 Fearing portrayed a terrified GOP elephant out on a window ledge evading Nixon announcing a comeback. In 1980, speculation that Reagan wanted Ford as a running mate prompted Peters to draw Nixon telephoning Reagan with

word of his availability. Following Reagan's victory, John Fischetti drew
him with Henry Kissinger loitering outside the White House gate. Ap-
pointment of former Nixon major domo Alexander Haig as secretary of
state, prompting talk of a Nixon role in the new regime, inspired Oliphant to caricature Nixon superbly as a piece of baggage and as a vul-
ture. After Coca-Cola caused a furor in 1985 by altering its hallowed
formula, Peters wickedly lampooned both the soft drink giant and the
ritual of proclaiming a reformed "New Nixon" during each comeback
from an ethical lapse or political defeat by drawing him in an Edsel at a
fast-food window [IX–7] ordering a "new Coke." Gary Hart's quixotic
return to the 1988 presidential campaign after a bizarre sequence of esca-
pades with a "bimbo" prompted Sack to draw a GOP elephant laughing
at the news as Nixon comes knocking. Peters struck again with his droll
"Forget It, Dick," showing Pat dissuading a Nixon with arms raised in
the classic pose. Word that Bush would "sleep on" a choice for a 1988
running mate inspired Peters to portray Nixon on a stepladder outside his bedroom [IX–8] cooing, "Niiixxxon . . . You Waaannt
Niiixxxon. . . ."[15]

Nixon's utility as a generic cartoon convention was not limited to
the theme of ambition, for his career suggested other compelling parallels. When Jimmy Carter granted asylum to the ailing Shah of Iran in
1979, Doug Marlette acidly portrayed the Shah with his friend Nixon as
"Two Peas in a Pod." That same year, the Chinese invasion of Vietnam
prompted Peters to draw Nixon telephoning the Chinese premier with a
secret plan to end the war, à la his 1968 pledge of a fictitious arrangement
for U.S. withdrawal from Vietnam. When an embattled Jimmy Carter
sought to win re-election in 1980 by resorting to patent demagoguery,
Oliphant portrayed him with a chemistry set, adding vile character attri-
butes until, like Hyde from Jekyll, he is transformed into a Nixon proclaiming, "When the going gets nasty, the nasty get going." Disclosures
that Franklin Roosevelt had used a primitive recording device in the
White House inspired Steve Benson to draw him in a 1982 *Arizona Republic* cartoon [IX–9] as "Richard Milhous Roosevelt." When the Israeli
regime of Menachem Begin was implicated in a 1982 massacre of Leba-
nese refugees, Conrad drew Nixon telephoning Begin, "Menachem, you
should have burned the bodies." Disclosures in 1983 that Reagan's campaign staffers had stolen a Carter briefing notebook before their 1980

[IX–7] Mike Peters, "Strange . . He's the Only Guy Who Orders the New Coke," Dayton Daily News, 1985. Reprinted with permission.

[IX–8] Mike Peters, "Niiixxxon . . . You Waannt Niiixxxon . . .," Dayton Daily News, December, 1987. Reprinted with permission.

[IX–9] Steve Benson, "Richard Milhous Roosevelt," Arizona Republic, January, 1982. © 1982, The Washington Post Writers Group. Reprinted with permission.

debate prompted *Duluth News-Tribune* cartoonist Steve Lindstrom to draw Nixon as Lucifer with horns and tail, urging Reagan, "Deny everything, erase the evidence, tell them you're not a crook!" The celebrated 1985 Pepsi commercial made by Geraldine Ferraro for a $500,000 fee inspired Sack to suggest such parallels as Nixon promoting Memorex tape.[16]

The "sleaze factor" that plagued Reagan's presidency provided a number of occasions to trot out Nixon as a generic referent. In 1984, while "Easy Ed" Meese was under attack for ethics less lofty than one might wish for an attorney general, and Secretary of Labor Raymond Donovan was under indictment on racketeering charges, Peters drew Nixon in the classic pose to mislead his readers while asking them to name "the only administration in U.S. history sleazy enough to have a cabinet officer indicted." The Nixon parallel became compelling in 1987 with "Contragate," a Byzantine blend of covert and patently illicit derring-do, destruction of evidence, perjury, and stonewalling that made it truly Son of Watergate. Conrad depicted Nixon effusing to Reagan, "Thanks, Ron . . . I never thought they'd forget Watergate!" Tom Toles drew a fine *Buffalo News* cartoon [IX–10] featuring Reagan roller-skating down a Nixon figural nose ski jump of sleaze in the "Richard M.

[IX–10] Tom Toles, untitled, Buffalo News, *May, 1987.*
© *1987,* Buffalo News. *Reprinted with permission of*
Universal Press Syndicate.

Nixon Amusement Theme Park." After Reagan agreed to turn over some
of his personal papers, Sack drew Nixon in combat gear with a machine
gun guarding his National Archives papers and proclaiming his successor
a "piker." Dana Summers drew a slouching Nixon reading of the "Ollie
Mania" cult inspired by Colonel Oliver North and recalling in disgust
"those awful days when the American people thought that lying was
wrong." Speculation that Reagan would give pardons to North and other
indicted aides inspired Marlette to portray Nixon and North simultaneously exclaiming "Pardon!" as they meet at a junction of two sewers,
North with the Constitution in his shredder and Nixon with such Watergate paraphernalia as a tape recorder and impeachment citations.[17]

After Reagan's retirement, events continued to conspire to elicit generic Nixon cartoons. Reports that key members of the George Bush
1988 campaign were apparently Nazi sympathizers and avid anti-Semites
prompted a Draper Hill cartoon depicting Bush receiving unwanted advice on the subject from Nixon, whose tapes had borne evidence of a

[IX–11] *Steve Benson, "Running Mate?,"* Arizona Republic, *May, 1992.*
Reprinted with permission of Tribune Media Services.

persistent, almost pathological prejudice against Jews. Bush administration willingness to overlook the Chinese massacre of dissident students
in Beijing inspired Sack to draw Nixon, in a tub of rotting dead fish,
toasting Deng Xiaoping, in a tub of blood: "To America's short memory,
the triumph of expediency over evil, and your eventual return to respectability." A 1991 Marlin Fitzwater press release on a check of White
House water by plumbers after an illness afflicted Bush and his wife Bar-
bara prompted a Sack cartoon featuring a trio of masked Nixon "plumbers" and Fitzwater's hope to "have the bugs out soon." In May 1992,
speculation over a possible running mate for independent Texas billion-
aire Ross Perot inspired Steve Benson to draw a tiny Perot backed by a
huge, menacing Nixon, arms uplifted in the classic pose [IX–11], suggesting a Perot penchant for megalomania and carelessness with the truth. In
1993, Bill Clinton's assurance that he would consult with former presidents led to Sack's drawing him as he discovers Nixon installing taping
equipment: "Your Expertise, Mr. Nixon. I told you we wanted you here
to tap your Expertise!" After the Clinton presidency became bogged
down in allegations over the Whitewater controversy and other rumored

Arkansas improprieties, Benson drew the Clintons as cavalrymen hunkering down against enemy arrows with Nixon urging, "Stick with Me."[18]

That more than twenty years after the Watergate break-in, American readers still recall the Watergate cast of characters, White House buggings with eighteen-and-a-half minute gaps, "plumbers' " harassment of Daniel Ellsberg, and other Watergate arcana attests to the enduring horror of these high crimes and misdemeanors, and to an enduring fascination with political hanky-panky and sleaze. Nonetheless, as the years have passed and collective memory has faded, a more simplistic composite Nixon stereotype has developed that serves better the needs of cartoonists. Stripped to its bare essentials, it symbolizes best the politics of denial exemplified by Nixon from Checkers through Watergate, and it exploits the bare essentials of the Nixon image—hunkered down with arms raised in the trademark double-V and the classic plea of denial, "I am not a crook." Thus a reader need not be versed in the details of Watergate to recognize this formulaic Nixon figure as a mirror opposite of Parson Weems's little George Washington with hatchet in hand alongside the doomed cherry sapling.

So in 1988, as Republican televangelist Pat Robertson sought the votes of the faithful while allaying the fears of the secular, in the midst of proliferating scandals involving other television ministries, Marlette drew him in the classic Nixonian pose proclaiming, "I am not a televangelist!" Hill drew beleaguered Speaker of the House James Wright with his purported memoir in the Nixon pose, [IX–12] insisting, "I am not a crook." Later that year, as Democratic nominee Michael Dukakis reeled under attacks linking him with his party's left wing, both Bob Gorrel and Michael Ramirez [IX–13] featured him striking the classic Nixon pose to declare, "I am not a liberal!" As Mikhail Gorbachev scrambled in 1990 to reform Soviet government, Benson drew him as Richard Milhous Gorbachev in the Nixon pose insisting, "I am not a dictator." A tawdry scandal arising from the attack on American Olympic figure-skating hopeful Nancy Kerrigan by agents of her rival Tonya Harding prompted Marlette to portray Tonya as Nixon. And as the gathering storm of Whitewater began to envelop the Clinton presidency, two cartoonists, Kevin Siers in the *Atlanta Constitution* and Carl Moore in *Heterodoxy* [IX–14], drew First Lady Hillary Clinton as Nixon, Siers

[IX–12] Draper Hill, "I Am Not a Crook," Detroit News, June 13, 1988. © 1988, Detroit News, 1988. Reprinted with permission.

[IX–13] Dennis Ramirez, "I Am Not a Liberal!," Copley News Service, August 3, 1988. Reprinted with permission.

LUNA BEACH By Carl Moore

[IX–14] Carl Moore, "Luna Beach," Heterodoxy, March, 1994. Reprinted with permission.

with the trademark pose and Moore with the classic disclaimer, "Hillary Rodham Clinton is not a crook!"[19]

Like Boss Tweed, Nixon has served as a generic symbol of political venality for more than two decades following his loss of office. His appeal to editorial cartoonists has withstood a decided decline in loathing for the man personally among the American populace and much of the media. Nixon aged with uncharacteristic grace, was called upon from time to time to play the role of elder statesman with concomitant respect, and enjoyed a generous measure of rehabilitation in reputation. Yet his "Herblock image" has survived unabated, sprouting anew on the op-ed pages whenever cartoonists are confronted with tempting parallels of political sleaze or duplicity. Indeed, the Whitewater, Tonya Harding, and Hillary Clinton efforts followed an outpouring of sympathy for Nixon after the 1993 death of his loyal, long-suffering wife, Pat.

A month after the Hillary cartoons saw print, Nixon died, and Republicans and Democrats vied to pay tribute to a longtime leading player on the world stage. As TV commentaries and the print media portrayed Nixon with respect bordering on reverence, cartoonists maintained a stubborn independence with their obituary tributes. Jules Feiffer executed a panel of Nixon plotting one last comeback. *Cincinnati Enquirer* artist Jim Borgman drew St. Peter ordering, "Cancel my appointments . . . This one may take awhile." Longtime Nixon nemesis Draper Hill exhibited both respect and an ongoing mystification by portraying the Nixon gravesite as that of Arlington's unknown soldier, "an American president known only but to God." Perhaps the collective cartooning verdict was rendered most faithfully by *Atlanta Constitution* artist Mike Luckovich, who drew Mount Rushmore with Nixon's visage sculpted between those of Teddy Roosevelt and Lincoln, and a tourist declaring, "I say the revisionists have gone too far."[20]

Like Tweed, Nixon may in time earn a respite as Peters, Conrad, Marlette, Sack, Hill, and other masters of the generation he served as "*our* Camelot" are replaced by youngsters whose knowledge of Nixon comes only from history books. It should be noted, however, that many of the cartoonists who have used Nixon most skillfully in recent years as a generic symbol are young men with long, brilliant careers yet ahead, those like Peters and Marlette who came to greatness as professionals during Watergate, or even younger artists who first encountered Nixon as collegians. Upon such talents may well depend whether Nixon some-day follows Tweed into cartoon oblivion or, instead, lives on as a graphic symbol of sleaze, as useful to cartoon artists of the future for portraying the venial sins of the political process as Lucifer and the Grim Reaper have been for the truly apocalyptic horrors.

Notes

CHAPTER 1: "THEM DAMNED PICTURES"

1. See Alexander B. Callow, Jr., *The Tweed Ring* (New York, 1966), 268, 290–91; Denis Tilden Lynch, *'Boss' Tweed: The Story of a Grim Generation* (New York, 1927), 364, 400–01; Albert Bigelow Paine, *Thomas Nast: His Period and His Pictures* (New York, 1904), 137–201, 335–37; J. Chal Vinson, *Thomas Nast: Political Cartoonist* (Athens, Ga., 1967), 15–22; and Stephen Hess and Milton Kaplan, *The Ungentlemanly Art: A History of American Political Cartoons* (New York, 1968), 12–14, 95–99.

2. Thomas C. Leonard, *The Power of the Press: The Birth of American Political Reporting* (New York, 1986), 97.

3. Perhaps no figure in American political history, not even fellow New Yorker Aaron Burr, remains so shrouded in mystery or mistruth as Tweed, but three exceptions should be noted. Leo Hershkowitz, *Tweed's New York: Another Look* (New York, 1977), however abrasively argumentative and at times uncritical in its devil's advocacy, remains the only serious scholarly effort to use municipal records and other primary documents to sort fact from fiction on Tweed and his allies and adversaries. One need not accept its arguments chapter and verse to concede its usefulness as a point of departure in discovering the essential Tweed. Seymour J. Mandelbaum, *Boss Tweed's New York* (New York, 1965), 66–86, persuasively places the controversy in a larger context of ethnic and cultural conflict and the evolution of municipal government. Leonard's splendid *Power of the Press*, 97–131 and 240–44, provides cogent insights into Tweed's improbable transformation from benign politico into monster for the ages.

4. Hershkowitz, *Tweed's New York*, passim; Charles Wingate, "An Episode in Municipal Government," *North American Review*, July 1875, 150; *Harper's Weekly*, August 26, 1871.

5. Hershkowitz, *Tweed's New York*, 5, 174–75; Paine, *Thomas Nast*, 169, 173; Hess and Kaplan, *The Ungentlemanly Art*, 13; Morton Keller, *The Art and Politics of Thomas Nast* (New York, 1968), 177; Mandelbaum, *Boss Tweed's New York*, 58, 66; Roger A. Fischer, "The Lucifer Legacy: Boss Tweed and Richard Nixon as Generic Sleaze Symbols in Cartoon Art," *Journal of American Culture*, XIII (Summer, 1990), 6.

6. Hershkowitz, *Tweed's New York*, xiii–xx. Essential to an understanding of the mythic power of Nast's Tweed is Henry Nash Smith, *Virgin Land: The American West as Symbol and Myth* (Cambridge, Mass., 1950).

7. Leonard, *Power of the Press*, 110–16.

8. Mark Wahlgren Summers, *The Era of Good Stealings* (New York, 1993), 62–85.

9. Quoted in Keller, *Art and Politics of Nast*, 4.

10. Gerald W. Johnson, *The Lines Are Drawn: American Life Since the First World War as Reflected in the Pulitzer Prize Cartoons* (Philadelphia, Pa., 1958), 13.

11. Quoted by Richard Samuel West in *The Puck Papers*, II (Fall 1979), 5.

12. Quoted in Paine, *Thomas Nast*, 150.

13. Hess and Kaplan, *The Ungentlemanly Art*, 47–49, 107, 127; Herbert Block, *Herblock Special Report* (New York, 1974), 39, 54; Alan Westin, ed., *Getting Angry Six Times a Week: A Portfolio of Political Cartoonists* (Boston, 1979), 106–07.

14. Hess and Kaplan, *The Ungentlemanly Art*, 22; Westin, *Getting Angry*, 38; Bill Watterson, "The Cartoonist's License," *Target: The Political Cartoon Quarterly*, 2 (Winter 1982), 18; Charles Press, *The Political Cartoon* (Rutherford, N. J., 1981), 251; Johnson, *The Lines Are Drawn*, 14.

15. *The Puck Papers*, I (Winter 1979), 10; Watterson, "Cartoonist's License," 18.

16. The literature on this phenomenon is too voluminous to detail and too familiar to warrant it, but two volumes are especially rich in insights: John William Ward, *Andrew Jackson: Symbol for an Age* (New York, 1955), and Joe McGinniss, *The Selling of the President, 1968* (New York, 1969). The classic psychological treatise on the subject remains Gordon W. Allport and Leo Postman, *The Psychology of Rumor* (New York, 1947).

17. Allan Nevins and Frank Weitenkampf, *A Century of Political Cartoons: Caricature in the United States from 1800 to 1900* (New York, 1944), 10; Charles Brooks, ed., *Best Editorial Cartoons of 1972* (Gretna, La., 1973), x; Bob Gorrell, "A Responsibility to Fairness," *Target*, 1 (Autumn 1981), 12; Johnson, *The Lines Are Drawn*, 15; Press, *The Political Cartoon*, 19.

18. Westin, ed., *Getting Angry*, 96, 129; Bill Mauldin, *What's Got Your Back Up?* (New York, 1961), ii; Jules Feiffer, "Interview," *Target*, 6 (Winter 1983), 5; Watterson, "The Cartoonist's License," 18; *Newsweek*, October 13, 1980, 83.

19. Press, *The Political Cartoon*, 19; *Target*, 11 (Spring 1984), 2.

20. A good selection of Nast's anti-Catholic cartoons preceded by a rather flawed essay may be found in Keller, *Art and Politics of Nast*, 159–75. For other discussions of Nast's religious biases and leanings, see Paine, *Thomas Nast*, 150, 190–91; Hess and Kaplan, *The Ungentlemanly Art*, 99; Press, *The Political Cartoon*, 246–47; and Kendall B. Mattern, Jr., "A Degree of Intolerance: The Anti-Catholic Cartoons of Thomas Nast and Joseph Keppler," *Target*, 11 (Spring 1984), 14–18. For dissenting interpretations of the nativist proclivities of the Harper brothers and their role in the publication of Maria Monk's *Awful Disclosures*, see Ray Allen Billington, *The Protestant Crusade, 1800–1860* (New York, 1938), 101–02, 214, 343, and Eugene Exman, *The Brothers Harper* (New York, 1965), 185–89.

21. Billington, *The Protestant Crusade*, 142–57, 292–95, 315–16; John Higham, *Strangers in the Land: Patterns of American Nativism, 1860–1925*, rev. ed. (New York, 1963), 28–29; Mandelbaum, *Boss Tweed's New York*, 34, 69–70.

22. Alice Felt Tyler, *Freedom's Ferment: Phases of American Social History from the Colonial Period to the Outbreak of the Civil War* (Minneapolis, Minn., 1944), 86–107.

23. Apparently existing only as an undated original drawing on scratchboard in the archives of the Library of Congress, the cartoon has been printed in Gary L. Bunker and Davis Bitton, *The Mormon Graphic Image, 1834–1914* (Salt Lake City, Utah, 1983),

85. Although the Mormon Tabernacle in Salt Lake City had been completed with much fanfare in 1867, and Nast devised the bishop-as-crocodile motif in 1871, political cartoonist and Nast scholar Draper Hill believes that the signature and other stylistic features suggest a much later date. For an earlier Nast portrayal of Mormonism as a Tabernacle turtle, see *Harper's Weekly*, January 9, 1886.

CHAPTER II: "MUGWUMP'S MONKEY"

An earlier version of this essay appeared in *The Journal of the Thomas Nast Society*, 4 (1990), 3–14, and is reprinted with permission of the Thomas Nast Society.

1. An excellent case in point is the reaction of Pat Oliphant to the 1987 Pulitzer Prize for Editorial Cartooning awarded to Berke Breathed for his cartoon strip "Bloom County" and Breathed's response to Oliphant. See Richard Samuel West, "The Pulitzer War," *Target*, 24 (Summer 1987), 13–16.

2. See Paine, *Th. Nast*, 262–86; and Vinson, *Thomas Nast*, 23–33.

3. *Puck*, March 14, 1877, 1; January 1, 1879, 16; June 4, 1879, 208; August 6, 1879, 344–45; September 29, 1880, 58. For an informative discussion of anti-Nast cartooning in *Puck*, see Draper Hill, "Trashing Nast (Puckishly)," *Association of American Editorial Cartoonists Notebook* (Winter 1988), 12–14.

4. Useful on the differences between Nast and Keppler, both as artists and as political critics, is Press, *The Political Cartoon*, 244–59. During 1882 and 1883 a Keppler obsession was creation of a "New Independent Party" made up of what he regarded as the best elements of the Republican and Democratic parties, with no ideological focus other than political purity, civil service and tariff reform, and a dismantling of corporate monopolies. See Richard Samuel West, *Satire on Stone: The Political Cartoons of Joseph Keppler* (Urbana, Ill., 1988), 235–38, and *Puck*, August 20, 1882, 396–97; October 25, 1882, 120–21; November 1, 1882, 129; November 15, 1882, 168–69; November 22, 1882, 184–85; November 7, 1883, 152–53.

5. *Puck*, March 10, 1880, 3.

6. For a succinct but cogent assessment of Blaine's character and personality, see H. Wayne Morgan, *From Hayes to McKinley: National Party Politics, 1877–1896* (Syracuse, N.Y., 1969), 63–71.

7. *Harper's Weekly*, March 15, 1879; May 8, 1880; Paine, *Th. Nast*, 473–508.

8. *Harper's Weekly*, June 14, 1884; June 21, 1884; Paine, *Th. Nast*, 494–96.

9. *New York Daily Graphic*, June 24, 1884, 1; *Judge*, June 28, 1884, 1; July 5, 1884, 1, 8–9.

10. *Harper's Weekly*, November 23, 1872; January 31, 1874.

11. *Judge*, July 12, 1884, 8–9; August 30, 1884, 5; *Wasp*, October 11, 1884, 8–9.

12. *Harper's Weekly*, June 8, 1872; *Harper's Weekly Supplement*, July 6, 1872. Draper Hill has drawn my attention to an 1852 cartoon by Frank Bellew lampooning Greeley, Winfield Scott, and the *New York Times* in a similar manner, although Nast (twelve at the time) may not have been aware of it. See *Lantern*, August 21, 1852.

13. *Wasp*, July 26, 1884, 8–9; *Judge*, July 26, 1884, 8–9; August 2, 1884, 16; August 30, 1884, 8–9; September 13, 1884, 8–9; October 4, 1884, 8–9, 16; October 25, 1884, 8–9, 16, November 1, 1884, 1; November 8, 1884, 1, 8–9, 16.

14. *Judge*, November 22, 1884, 8–9; December 6, 1884, 1; December 13, 1884, 8–9; January 17, 1885, 8–9; March 7, 1884, 8–9; November 28, 1885, 8–9; January 2, 1886, 8–9.

CHAPTER III: RUSTIC RASPUTIN

This essay appeared originally in *Kansas History*, 11:4 (Winter 1988–89), 222–39, and is
reprinted with the permission of the Kansas State Historical Society.

1. For two examples, see Roger A. Fischer, "William Windom: Cartoon Centerfold,
   1881–91," *Minnesota History*, 51:3 (Fall 1988), 99–109, and Fischer, " 'Holy John'
   Wanamaker: Color Cartoon Centerfold," *Pennsylvania Magazine of History and Biography*, 115:4 (October 1991), 451–74.

2. Peter Argersinger, *Populism and Politics: William Alfred Peffer and the People's Party*
   (Lexington, Ky., 1974), 105.

3. *Puck*'s visceral response to the May, 1886, Haymarket bombing in Chicago provides
   an excellent case in point; see *Puck*, May 12, 1886, 168–69; May 19, 1886, 184–85;
   192, May 26, 1886, 197, 200–01; June 23, 1886, 272; July 14, 1886, 312–13; July
   21, 1886, 328–29, 336; July 28, 1886, 337.

4. *Puck*, April 8, 1891, 104–05; July 8, 1891, 312–13; December 30, 1891, 324–25;
   January 30, 1895, 408–09; January 6, 1897, 8–9; *Judge*, October 28, 1893, 264–65.

5. *Judge*, September 19, 1891, 390–91.

6. *Puck*, August 19, 1891, 409; December 30, 1891, 324–25; November 22, 1893,
   216–17; February 7, 1894, 424–25; March 13, 1895, 56–57; June 19, 1895, 280–81;
   November 4, 1896, 8–9; January 6, 1897, 8–9; *Judge*, July 4, 1891, 206–07; August
   8, 1891, 292–93; December 31, 1892, 472–73; July 29, 1893, 56–57; March 30,
   1895, 200–01; April 20, 1895, 252–53; July 9, 1895, 152–53; December 26, 1896,
   436–37; March 11, 1899, 152–53.

7. *Judge*, April 11, 1891, 8–9; April 25, 1891, 33; June 6, 1891, 131; October 3, 1891,
   422–23; *Puck*, July 8, 1891, 312–13; August 19, 1891, 409.

8. *Judge*, August 8, 1891, 292–93; September 5, 1891, 356–57; September 19, 1891,
   390–91; *Puck*, December 30, 1891, 324–25.

9. *Judge*, January 2, 1892, 8–9; April 9, 1892, 242–43; December 31, 1892, 472–73;
   Puck, May 8, 1892, 208.

10. *Judge*, August 12, 1893, 88–89; August 26, 1893, 120–21; September 9, 1893,
    152–53; October 21, 1893, 241; October 28, 1893, 264–65; *Puck*, August 30, 1893,
    32; October 11, 1893, 120–21; November 1, 1893, 168–69; November 22, 1893,
    216–17; December 20, 1893, 312–13; January 31, 1894, 408–09.

11. *Puck*, February 7, 1894, 424–25; February 14, 1894, 440–41; August 22, 1894, 8–9;
    October 10, 1894, 113; *Judge*, November 10, 1894, 296–97.

12. *Judge*, February 23, 1895, 120–21; March 30, 1895, 200–01; April 20, 1895, 252–53;
    Puck, March 13, 1895, 56–57; June 12, 1895, 264–65; June 19, 1895, 280–81; July
    3, 1895, 312–13; November 30, 1895, 216–17.

13. *Puck*, August 12, 1896, 1, 8–9; September 23, 1896, 8–9; September 30, 1896, 8–9;
    November 4, 1896, 8–9.

14. *Puck*, January 6, 1897, 8–9; *Judge*, December 26, 1896, 436–37; March 11, 1899,
    152–53. For a cogent account of Peffer's partisan musical chairs after his departure
    from the Senate, see Argersinger, *Populism and Politics*, 285–301.

15. See Argersinger, *Populism and Politics*, 269.

16. For an outstanding synopsis of Peffer's consistent position on free silver as economic
    dogma and party strategy, his adamant opposition to fusion, and his alienation within
    the movement as a consequence, see Argersinger, *Populism and Politics*, 91–92, 120–
    29, 152–56, and 194–259.

17. Argersinger, *Populism and Politics*, 106, 193; O. Gene Clanton, *Kansas Populism: Ideas and Men* (Lawrence, Kans., 1969), 294n; Walter T.K. Nugent, *The Tolerant Populists: Kansas Populism and Nativism* (Chicago, 1963), 63.

18. *Puck*, July 8, 1891, 306, 312–13.

19. *Alliance Bulletin* (Harper), September 26, 1890; *Weekly Kansas Chief* (Troy), July 30, 1896; *Emporia Gazette*, October 1, 1896, quoted in Clanton, *Kansas Populism*, 85, 189–90, and 191 respectively.

20. For 1894 Coxey color cartoon art, see *Judge*, April 14, 1894, 234–35, and May 12, 1894, 291; and *Puck*, April 18, 1894, 136–37, and July 25, 1894, 360–61. For succinct, informative character sketches of Simpson and Lease, see Clanton, *Kansas Populism*, 73–78, 83–87; O. Gene Clanton, "Intolerant Populist? The Disaffection of Mary Elizabeth Lease," *Kansas Historical Quarterly*, 34 (Summer 1968), 189–200; and Nugent, *The Tolerant Populists*, 76–78, 80–84.

21. Argersinger, *Populism and Politics*, 104–05. After Peffer began to decline in importance in the estimation of the press, according to Argersinger, the term *Pefferism* gradually became a synonym of sorts for the apocalyptic "calamity howl" lamentation for which the movement was notorious, although Zimmerman's use of a "dead populistic Peffer tree" as late as 1899 to symbolize the party's demise would seem to indicate a lingering linkage between man and party in the public mind.

22. Clanton, *Kansas Populism*, 63; Argersinger, *Populism and Politics*, 105.

CHAPTER IV: ALIENS

1. *Puck*, April 28, 1880, 128; March 21, 1883, 39; *Judge*, March 11, 1882, 3; September 6, 1884, 12; January 31, 1885, 4; April 30, 1887, 10.

2. For perceptive analyses of the worst tenets of racism during the period, see Claude Nolen, *The Negro's Image in the South: The Anatomy of White Supremacy* (Lexington, Ky., 1967), 3–50, and Lawrence J. Friedman, *The White Savage: Racial Fantasies in the Post-bellum South* (Englewood Cliffs, N.J., 1970), 3–76.

3. Thomas Nelson Page, *The Negro: The Southerner's Problem* (New York, 1904), 64. Should the distinction between the South and New York appear to resolve the dictotomy, it should be noted that D.W. Griffith's luridly racist film *The Birth of a Nation*, based on the Thomas Dixon, Jr., novel *The Clansman*, drew—at a stiff two dollars a ticket—a New York audience of 800,000, a figure undoubtedly under-reported by theater owners.

4. The best extant guide to black cartoon stereotypes and their significance is Joseph Boskin, *Sambo: The Rise & Demise of an American Jester* (New York, 1986), 121–47. This volume is valuable especially for its creation of a context for such caricature within vaudeville, minstrelsy, and other contemporary forms of popular entertainment.

5. An outstanding study of the Anglo-American tradition in Irish cartooning, although tilted heavily toward British art, is L. Perry Curtis, Jr., *Apes and Angels: The Irishman in Victorian Caricature* (Washington, 1971). A cogent analysis of the intellectual context in Britain for this phenomenon is Curtis, *Anglo-Saxons and Celts: A Study of Anti-Irish Prejudice in Victorian England* (Bridgeport, Conn., 1968), 49–65. Useful as an introduction to the genre is John J. Appel, "From Shanties to Lace Curtains: The Irish Image in *Puck*, 1876–1910," *Comparative Studies in Sociology and History*, 13:4 (October 1971), 365–75, a study flawed by a condescending willingness to concede "a kernel of reality" in *Puck*'s stereotypes of a people "prone to fights" who "loved a

drink." It also tends to inflate a softening of *Puck* satire after 1894 into an evolutionary trend in Irish upward mobility, a phenomenon linked less to sociological trends than to the untimely death of the Celtophobic Joseph Keppler.

6. The most thorough study of the subject remains Rudolf Glanz, *The Jew in Early American Wit and Graphic Humor* (New York, 1973), in which Glanz downplays ideological differences between the ambivalent *Puck* and the more anti-Semitic *Judge* and *Life* to focus on a composite Jewish stereotype in American humor of the period. John J. Appel, "Jews in American Caricature, 1820–1914," *American Jewish History*, 71 (September, 1981), 103–33, provides a convenient historiographic overview and useful insights of its own, although the relatively benign color art and editorial commentary of *Puck* is somewhat overemphasized.

7. Oscar Handlin, "American Views of the Jew at the Opening of the 20th Century," *Publications of the American Jewish Historical Society*, 40 (June 1951), 324–45; Richard Hofstadter, *The Age of Reform* (New York, 1956), 78, 80; John Higham, *Strangers in the Land: Patterns of of American Nativism*, 1860–1925 (New Brunswick, N.J., 1955), 26–27, 66–67, 92–94; Higham, "Anti-Semitism in the Gilded Age: A Reinterpretation," *Mississippi Valley Historical Review*, 43 (March 1957), 559–78; Higham, "Social Discrimination Against Jews in America," 1830–1930, *Publications of the American Jewish Historical Society*, 43 (September 1957), 1–33; Higham, "The Cult of the 'American Consensus:' Homogenizing our History," *Commentary*, 27 (February 1959), 93–100.

8. Glanz, *The Jew in Early American Wit and Graphic Humor*, 237; Michael N. Dobkowski, *The Tarnished Dream: The Basis of American Anti-Semitism* (Westport, Conn., 1979), 235.

9. Curtis, *Apes and Angels*, 94.

10. Robert F. Berkhofer, Jr., *The White Man's Indian: Images of the American Indian from Columbus to the Present* (New York, 1978), 26–27.

11. A proliferating body of "politically correct" revisionist scholarship debunks the notion of a single American character as a sexist, racist, "Eurocentric" delusion. I reject this ancestral, victimological concept of American nationality for a synthesis of the experiential approach of Daniel Boorstin, *The Americans: The Colonial Experience* (Chicago, 1959), and the transforming creedal interpretation of Arthur M. Schlesinger, Jr., *The Disuniting of America* (New York, 1991).

12. Irvin G. Wyllie, *The Self-Made Man in America: The Myth of Rags to Riches* (New Brunswick, N.J., 1954); John G. Cawelti, *Apostles of the Self-Made Man* (Chicago, 1965), 1–164; Richard Weiss, *The American Myth of Success from Horatio Alger to Norman Vincent Peale* (New York, 1969), 3–96; John William Ward, *Andrew Jackson: Symbol for an Age* (New York, 1955); Robert Gray Gunderson, *The Log-Cabin Campaign* (Lexington, Ky., 1957); and Eric Foner, *Free Soil, Free Labor, Free Men: The Ideology of the Republican Party Before the Civil War* (New York, 1970), 11–39.

13. *Judge*, April 11, 1885, 13; May 14, 1892, 322; *Puck*, May 24, 1885, 271; July 18, 1888, 22; January 4, 1893, 322.

14. *Judge*, September 17, 1892, 190; August 11, 1894, 82, August 25, 1894, 115; September 1, 1894, 131; January 20, 1894, 48; *Puck*, June 26, 1889, 290.

15. *Puck*, March 5, 1884, 12; April 21, 1886, 117; August 22, 1888, 441; January 22, 1890, 377; April 15, 1891, 117; September 23, 1891, 70; January 11, 1893, 329; May

10, 1993, 186; March 20, 1895, 70; *Judge*, November 15, 1884, 10; June 30, 1888, 184; November 10, 1888, 76; July 12, 1890, 228; July 4, 1891, 208; October 6, 1894, 211.

16. *Puck*, May 22, 1889, 215; May 27, 1891, 213; January 10, 1894, 363; *Judge*, September 30, 1893, 208.

17. *Puck*, January 21, 1880, 758; November 30, 1881, 196; February 15, 1882, 378; May 9, 1883, 145; July 19, 1890, 55; July 12, 1893, 325.

18. Higham, *Strangers in the Land*, 26; *Puck*, October 19, 1881, 97; October 26, 1881, 115; May 24, 1882, 194; March 7, 1883, 3; February 6, 1884, 363, March 12, 1884, 19, April 28, 1886, 130; *Judge*, December 9, 1893, 29.

19. Outstanding on this theme is Dobkowski, *The Tarnished Dream*, 78–112.

20. *Puck*, November 7, 1889, 220; December 31, 1890, 327; April 22, 1891, 138; October 14, 1891, 138; February 24, 1892, 6; December 14, 1892, 269; March 1, 1893, 26; January 23, 1895, 394; January 29, 1896, 405; March 25, 1896, 4; April 22, 1896, 4; June 10, 1896, 6; July 29, 1896, 2; August 11, 1897, 7; September 15, 1897, 11; *Judge*, August 29, 1885, 6; September 30, 1893, 202; April 27, 1895, 266; February 8, 1896, 100.

21. Higham, *Strangers in the Land*, 26–27; *Judge*, August 19, 1882, 8–9; September 15, 1888, 367; May 12, 1894, 297; *Puck*, October 17, 1888, 117; May 28, 1890, 213; December 10, 1890, 42; June 21, 1893, 278; August 2, 1893, 374; September 9, 1896, 7; September 22, 1897, 4.

22. *Puck*, January 12, 1887, 337; May 2, 1888, 167; October 5, 1892, 102; December 10, 1992, 417; January 18, 1893, 348; February 8, 1893; 401; April 19, 1893, 138; June 14, 1993, 258; August 2, 1893, 370; February 21, 1994, 3; May 16, 1994, 197.

23. Jacob Riis, *How the Other Half Lives* (New York, 1890), 79; *Judge*, May 29, 1886, 10; August 21, 1886, 10; December 10, 1892, 418; *Puck*, November 15, 1882, 297; September 11, 1889, 37; April 9, 1890, 100; November 14, 1894, 202; March 6, 1895, 38.

24. *Puck*, April 26, 1882, 118.

25. Quoted in K.T. Erikson, *Wayward Puritans: A Study in the Sociology of Deviance* (New York, 1966), 13.

CHAPTER V: BETTER DEAD THAN RED

1. Outstanding in its analysis of white attitudes toward Indians is Robert F. Berkhofer, Jr., *The White Man's Indian: Images of the American Indian from Columbus to the Present* (New York, 1978). Also of value are Roy Harvey Pearce, *Savagism and Civilization: A Study of the Indian in the American Mind*, 2d ed. (Baltimore, 1965), and Bernard W. Sheehan, *Seeds of Extinction: Jeffersonian Philanthropy and the American Indian* (Chapel Hill, N.C., 1973). A judicious synopsis of white-Indian relations during the period is Wilcomb E. Washburn, *The Indian in America* (New York, 1975), 209–45. On the dynamics of western conflict between the tribes and the federal military, Ralph K. Andrist, *The Long Death: The Last Days of the Plains Indians* (New York, 1964), is both excessively melodramatic and prematurely "politically correct," but Robert M. Utley, *Frontier Regulars: The United States Army and the Indian, 1866–1891* (New York, 1973), is very informative and judiciously evenhanded. Utley, *The*

Lance and the Shield: The Life and Times of Sitting Bull (New York, 1993) is superb on conflict between the Sioux and the federals. For the parallel I suggest to the Mormons, Bunker and Bitton, *Mormon Graphic Image*, makes the case convincingly.

2. Berkhofer, *White Man's Indian*, 26–30, 88–105.

3. *Puck*, March 13, 1889, 40–41.

4. *Puck*, January 20, 1886, 321; August 29, 1888, 8–9; August 19, 1891, 409; *Judge*, January 24, 1891, 286–87; March 4, 1893, 142–43. See also *Puck*, April 27, 1881, 125; and *Judge*, August 23, 1884, 8–9; November 21, 1885, 8–9; July 31, 1886, 8–9.

5. See *Puck*, August 22, 1877, 16; August 7, 1878, 16; January 22, 1879; 1, September 14, 1881, 24–25; August 30, 1882, 420; August 19, 1885, 400; January 21, 1891, 372–73; and *Judge*, June 17, 1882, 16; December 8, 1883, 1; December 20, 1890, 214.

6. Keller, *Art and Politics of Nast*, 108, 124, 219–20, 230–33; *Harper's Weekly*, August 10, 1878, 625; February 28, 1880, 144; September 24, 1881, 655; February 18, 1882, 109; April 29, 1882, 272.

7. *Harper's Weekly*, July 4, 1885, 436; Utley, *Frontier Regulars*, 332–42, 369–96; *Puck*, October 15, 1879, 506; October 22, 1879, 534; October 19, 1881, 100; May 10, 1882, 156; April 11, 1883, 84; *Judge*, December 6, 1884, 4. See also *Judge*, April 8, 1882, 16; May 13, 1882, 2, 8–9; October 25, 1884, 4; and *Puck*, September 29, 1886, 69.

8. *Puck*, August 30, 1882, 420; *Judge*, December 8, 1883, 1, 2; December 15, 1883, 2.

9. *Judge*, December 15, 1883, 2; June 20, 1885, 8–9; Utley, *Frontier Regulars*, 236–54.

10. *Judge*, August 31, 1889, 333; January 10, 1891, 250; July 4, 1891, 362; *Puck*, January 21, 1885, 323; February 18, 1885, 396; January 28, 1891, 396; February 18, 1891, 444; July 26, 1893, 359; September 23, 1896, 5.

11. *Judge*, June 9, 1888, 142; November 24, 1888, 107; July 20, 1889, 242; May 27, 1893, 332.

12. Catlin quoted in Berkhofer, *White Man's Indian*, 88; Jackson and Farnham quoted in Pearce, *Savagism and Civilization*, 57, 65.

13. Washburn, *Indian in America*, 209, 236–43; Berkhofer, *White Man's Indian*, 29–30, 88–92; Pearce, *Savagism and Civilization*, 49–69, 165–222. Wilcomb E. Washburn, ed., *The Indian and the White Man* (New York, 1964), 377–85, excerpts a perceptive 1874 report by John Wesley Powell on the reservation and assimilation as weapons against Indian extinction.

14. *Puck*, September 1, 1880, 450; September 14, 1881, 18; April 11, 1883, 84; *Judge*, May 13, 1882, 2, May 12, 1883, 2, December 8, 1883, 2; June 20, 1883, 2.

15. *Judge*, May 12, 1883, 8–9; July 14, 1883, 2, 16.

16. *Judge*, August 15, 1885, 2, 8–9; December 20, 1890, 200; *Puck*, December 17, 1890, 300; Utley, *Lance and Shield*, 291–307.

17. *Judge*, December 20, 1890, 479; January 3, 1891, 481; *Puck*, January 21, 1891, 372–73. The definitive study of Wounded Knee remains Dee Brown, *Bury My Heart at Wounded Knee* (New York, 1971). See also Utley, *Frontier Regulars*, 397–413, and Andrist, *Long Death*, 338–54.

18. *Judge*, January 17, 1891, 278; January 24, 1891, 286–87; January 31, 1891, 296; *Puck*, January 28, 1891, 396.

19. *Judge*, February 21, 1891, 346; February 28, 1891, 362; July 4, 1891, 205; May 27, 1893, 332; *Puck*, February 18, 1891, 444; August 19, 1891, 409; July 26, 1893, 359.

CHAPTER VI: CARTOON CULTURE

This essay appeared originally in Ray B. Browne, Marshall W. Fishwick, and Kevin O. Browne, eds., *Dominant Symbols in Popular Culture* (Bowling Green, Ohio, 1990), 181–208, and is reprinted with permission of The Popular Press, Bowling Green State University.

1. *Minneapolis Star–Tribune*, April 13, 1984, and July 30, 1986.

2. Paul Conrad, *Pro and Conrad* (San Rafael, Calif., 1979), 23, 27; and Charles Brooks, ed., *Best Editorial Cartoons of the Year*, 1975 Edition (Gretna, La., 1975), 61.

3. Mike Peters, *The Nixon Chronicles* (Dayton, Ohio, 1976), 48, 137, 150; Doug Marlette, *Drawing Blood* (Washington, DC, 1981), 57, 157, 172; Pat Oliphant, *Ban This Book!* (Kansas City, Mo., 1982), 28, 122.

4. Peters, *Nixon Chronicles*, 54, 56; Charles Brooks, ed., *Best Editorial Cartoons of the Year*, 1983 Edition (Gretna, La., 1983), 112; Carew Papritz and Russ Tremayne, eds., *Reagancomics: A Cornucopia of Cartoons on Ronald Reagan* (Seattle, Wash., 1984), 65; *Minneapolis Star-Tribune*, March 5, 1982.

5. Ed Salzman and Ann Leigh Brown, eds., *The Cartoon History of California Politics* (Sacramento, Calif., 1978), 110; Charles Brooks, ed., *Best Editorial Cartoons of the Year, 1974 Edition* (Gretna, La., 1974), 43; Marlette, *Drawing Blood,* 12, 150; Doug Marlette, *It's a Dirty Job . . . . But Somebody Has to Do It!* (Charlotte, N.C., 1984), 30; *Duluth* (Minn). *News–Tribune & Herald*, September 10, 1985, 12B; *Newsweek*, March 17, 1986, 15.

6. Salzman and Brown, *Cartoon History of California Politics*, 134–35; Papritz and Tremayne, *Reagancomics*, 93, 104; Peters, Nixon Chronicles, 96; *Minneapolis Star–Tribune*, May 7, 1987, 17A.

7. Marlette, *Drawing Blood*, 71; Brooks, *Best Editorial Cartoons, 1974*, 7, 2l; *Newsweek*, June 1, 1981, 22; Peters, *Nixon Chronicles*, 92, 105; Carew Papritz, ed., *100 Watts: The James Watt Memorial Collection* (Seattle, Wash., 1983), 45.

8. Charles Brooks, ed., *Best Editorial Cartoons for the Year 1972* (Gretna, La., 1973), 52; Marlette, *Drawing Blood*, 55, 128; *Newsweek*, April 4, 1983, 21, June 13, 1983, 19, and January 21, 1985, 25; *Target: The Political Cartoon Quarterly*, 10 (Winter 1984), 13.

9. *Newsweek*, February 27, 1984, 22; *Minneapolis Star–Tribune*, January 25, 1987, June 5, 1987, and July 3, 1987; *Minnesota Daily* (University of Minnesota), May 15, 1984, 6; Papritz and Tremayne, *Reagancomics*, 9.

10. *Minneapolis Star–Tribune*, January 25, 1987, June 5, 1987, July 3, 1987, October 2, 1987, July 3, 1988, October 17, 1988, December 16, 1991, January 1, 1992, and January 13, 1992.

11. *Puck*, June 4, 1879, 194, 208.

12. See Keller, *Art and Politics of Nast*, 52–55, 57, 60, 62–63, 66, 90, 145, 202, 208, 286–87, 335, 340.

13. Leonard, *Power of the Press*, 125; Keller, *Art and Politics of Nast*, 70, 85–86, 96–97, 131, 149, 163, 184, 250, 336–37.

14. See Hess and Kaplan, *The Ungentlemanly Art*, 78–79.

15. For representative examples, see *Puck*, January 6, 1886, 304, and September 28, 1887, 65; and *Judge*, December 18, 1886, 1; June 18, 1887, 8–9; May 26, 1888, 101; December 15, 1888, 166; July 13, 1889, 225; October 26, 1889, 42–43.

16. *Puck*, May 9, 1883, 152–53; September 26, 1883, 49; October 24, 1883, 120–21; January 23, 1884, 328–29; *Judge*, May 7, 1887, 8–9; April 7, 1888, 1.

17. *Puck*, March 17, 1880, 32; July 5, 1882, 284–85; July 19, 1882, 316–17; April 2, 1884, 65; July 2, 1884, 288; April 25, 1888, 137; *Judge*, November 1, 1884, 16; April 2, 1887, 8–9; January 14, 1888, 8–9; September 22, 1888, 379; March 30, 1889, 416; August 30, 1890, 336–37. For Senate responses to Wales' "15–14–13," see Hess and Kaplan, *The Ungentlemanly Art*, 104–05.

18. *Puck*, March 26, 1879, 40–41; June 2, 1880, 219; November 22, 1882, 184–85; May 23, 1883, 177; August 27, 1884, 416; January 21, 1885, 321; November 2, 1887, 156–57; *Judge*, March 26, 1887, 1; December 10, 1887, 8–9; August 25, 1888, 322–23; February 16, 1889, 304–05; November 9, 1889, 67; November 30, 1889, 124–25.

19. *Puck*, October 23, 1878, 16; February 4, 1880, 782–83; September 5, 1883, 8–9; April 16, 1884, 104–05; November 5, 1884, 160; March 31, 1886, 72–73; September 29, 1886, 72–73; August 31, 1887, 8–9; April 10, 1889, 104–05; *Judge*, January 8, 1887, 8–9; October 8, 1887, 8–9; October 22, 1887, 8–9; October 29, 1887, 8–9; December 3, 1887, 1; July 28, 1888, 264; November 24, 1888, 108–09; November 23, 1889, 116. For an informative account of the tattooed man series, see Samuel J. Thomas, "The Tattooed Man Caricatures and the Presidential Campaign of 1884," *Journal of American Culture*, X (Winter 1987), 1–20.

20. *Puck*, November 7, 1877, 1; April 11, 1883, 88–89; May 6, 1885, 152–53; February 1, 1888, 368; October 24, 1888, 131; *Judge*, November 22, 1884, 16; April 30, 1887, 8–9; August 27, 1887, 1; November 12, 1887, 8–9; August 10, 1889, 281.

21. *Puck*, May 2, 1877, 8–9; October 16, 1878, 16; November 12, 1879, 588; September 1, 1880, 456–57; August 19, 1885, 400; July 21, 1886, 336; November 30, 1887, 232; February 29, 1888, 1; April 11, 1888, 112–13; July 10, 1889, 328–29; October 9, 1889, 106–07; June 4, 1891, 232–33; *Judge*, April 2, 1887, 1; April 9, 1887, 1; May 26, 1888, 108–09; September 7, 1889, 345.

22. *Puck*, March 28, 1877, 8–9; April 21, 1880, 112–13; June 30, 1880, 306–07; August 18, 1880, 424–25; September 15, 1880, 24–25; September 22, 1880, 40–41; November 10, 1880, 168; December 29, 1880, 290; January 5, 1881, 300–01; August 31, 1881, 436–37; March 18, 1885, 40–41; *Judge*, April 26, 1884, 8–9; July 5, 1884, 1; August 10, 1887, 8–9.

23. *Puck*, September 4, 1878, 8–9; September 18, 1878, 8–9; February 11, 1879, 1; November 30, 1881, 200–01; January 4, 1882, 284–85; May 10, 1882, 154–55; October 11, 1882, 88–89; October 18, 1882, 112; November 29, 1882, 200–01; September 19, 1883, 33; March 5, 1884, 8–9; May 14, 1884, 161; November 16, 1887, 190–91; November 21, 1888, 193; *Judge*, August 2, 1884, 16; September 6, 1884, 8–9; November 8, 1884, 8–9; November 29, 1884, 8–9; July 9, 1887, 8–9; September 24, 1887, 1; December 3, 1887, 16; January 7, 1888, 8–9; April 21, 1888, 24–25; October 6, 1888, 426; December 14, 1889, 168.

24. *Puck*, May 17, 1882, 163, August 30, 1882, 412–13, May 14, 1884, 176, February 18, 1885, 392–93; July 15, 1885, 320, November 26, 1885, 208; December 2, 1885, 216–17; March 7, 1888, 26–27; *Judge*, February 4, 1888, 8–9; June 19, 1895, 280–81.

25. *Puck*, August 22, 1877, 1; January 23, 1878, 8–9; July 17, 1878, 16; August 7, 1878, 1; April 2, 1879, 64; December 1, 1880, 203; April 9, 1884, 81; September 17, 1884,

48; October 8, 1884, 88–89; November 26, 1890, 209; December 10, 1890, 269; *Judge*, April 14, 1888, 1.

26. *Puck*, April 18, 1877, 1; May 23, 1877, 8–9; May 30, 1877, 16; June 13, 1877, 8–9; October 3, 1877, 8–9; October 31, 1877, 8–9; January 14, 1880, 727; August 25, 1880, 448; May 18, 1881, 179; October 5, 1881, 72–73; October 19, 1881, 112; September 27, 1882, 49; February 6, 1884, 353; November 12, 1884, 168–169; January 7, 1885, 296–97; June 17, 1885, 248–49; October 20, 1886, 122–23; December 28, 1887, 276–77; March 27, 1889, 72–73; January 8, 1890, 350; February 26, 1890, 8–9; August 27, 1890, 1, 8–9; *Judge*, March 12, 1887, 12–13; June 25, 1887, 1; December 10, 1887, 1; January 21, 1888, 8–9; February 18, 1888, 8–9; September 22, 1888, 386–87; October 27, 1888, 40–41; February 2, 1889, 272–73; May 14, 1892, 328–29.

27. *Puck*, June 4, 1884, 216–17; March 4, 1885, 8–9; July 8, 1885, 296–97; December 2, 1885, 216–17; *Judge*, November 12, 1887, 8–9; August 14, 1889, 320–21; November 23, 1889, 108–09; December 14, 1889, 160–61; January 18, 1890, 236, 244–45.

28. *Puck*, June 4, 1879, 194.

CHAPTER VII: LIBERTY

A previous version of this chapter appeared as "Oddity, Icon, Challenge: The Statue of Liberty in American Cartoon Art, 1879–1986" in the *Journal of American Culture*, IX:4 (Winter 1986), 63–81, and is reprinted with permission of the American Culture Association.

1. A splendid survey of Liberty cartoons by foreign as well as American artists is Dani Aguila, ed., *Taking Liberty With the Lady* (Nashville, Tenn., 1986). Excellent on Liberty as iconography, art, and a manifestation of French Republican politics is Marvin Trachtenberg, *The Statue of Liberty* (New York, 1976). Also informative and generally reliable is Hertha Pauli and E.B. Ashton, *I Lift My Lamp: The Way of a Symbol* (New York, 1948), a study especially valuable for its analysis of Bartholdi's promotion of the project in the United States and on American involvement in general. Despite its irreverent, uncritical tenor, Andre Gschaedler, *True Light on the Statue of Liberty and its Creator* (Narbeth, Pa., 1966) provides useful information on Bartholdi and his formidable mother. Informative articles on Liberty's genesis, history, and recent renovation include John Russell, "A Face that Really Launched 1,000 Ships—and Many More," *Smithsonian*, XV:4 (June 1984), 46–55, and Frederick Allen, "Saving the Statue," *American Heritage*, XXXV:4 (June–July 1986), 97–109.

2. *New York Times*, September 29, 1876; *Puck*, October 27, 1886, 135; Trachtenberg, *Statue of Liberty*, 181–83; Pauli and Ashton, *I Lift My Lamp*, 166–67, 221.

3. *Puck*, May 28, 1879, 116, January 12, 1881, 316, and May 10, 1882, 270. The latter cartoon is pictured in *Smithsonian*, XV:4 (June 1984), 55, but efforts to ascertain the identities of artist, publisher, and provenance from the editorial staff of that journal have been unsuccessful.

4. *Puck*, August 29, 1883, 406; April 1, 1885, 80; April 15, 1885, 98; April 22, 1885, 118; *Harper's Weekly*, May 2, 1885, 279.

5. *Puck*, June 10, 1885, 230; October 22, 1884, 115.

6. *Harper's Weekly*, April 2, 1881, 216–17.

7. Currier & Ives also issued this cartoon with the title "Brer Thuldy's Statue," according

to Frederick A. Conningham, comp., *Currier & Ives Prints: An Illustrated Checklist*, 2d. ed. (New York, 1983), 23–24, 36. Worth was well known for his "Darkeytown" cartoons published by *Judge* as back cover illustrations, like this Liberty creation some of the most racist cartoon art ever published in the United States.

8. *Judge*, May 23, 1885, 2, 16; September 4, 1886.

9. *Puck*, December 12, 1882, 232–33; October 29, 1884, 130; *Judge*, February 20, 1886, 8–9.

10. *Harper's Weekly*, June 6, 1885, 367; October 3, 1885, 655; *Judge*, July 4, 1886, 1; October 30, 1886, 8–9; *Puck*, October 27, 1886, 138–39. The latter cartoon is reprinted in Aguila, *Taking Liberty*, 14, incorrectly entitled "Our Freedom Goddess— She Stands Fast and True."

11. *Judge*, November 26, 1886, 3; March 19, 1887, 8–9; December 7, 1889, 142–43; August 10, 1895, 84–85; November 27, 1897, 337; *Puck*, November 23, 1887, 201; Aguila, Taking Liberty, 20–21, 99.

12. *Stars and Stripes*, January 24, 1919, reprinted in Aguila, *Taking Liberty*, 68.

13. See Brooks, *Best Editorial Cartoons, 1974*, 69; Brooks, *Best Editorial Cartoons, 1980*, 46; and Aguila, *Taking Liberty*, 26, 36, 49, 62–65, 70, 85, 157, 168, 169, 226.

14. Aguila, *Taking Liberty*, 77, 164. See also Brooks, *Best Editorial Cartoons, 1974*, 4, for Louis Goodwin's 1973 *Columbus Dispatch* Watergate cartoon "Differing Viewpoints."

15. Brooks, *Best Editorial Cartoons, 1974*, 70, 71; Aguila, *Taking Liberty*, 11, 43, 48, 84, 156.

16. Press, *The Political Cartoon*, 23; Brooks, *Best Editorial Cartoons, 1972*, 72; Brooks, *Best Editorial Cartoons, 1974*, 16, 33; Brooks, *Best Editorial Cartoons, 1976*, 75, 112; Aguila, *Taking Liberty*, 27, 89, 97, 153, 156, 190, 193; *Minneapolis Star–Tribune*, July 2, 1986, 17A.

17. Press, *The Political Cartoon*, 210–17.

18. Aguila, *Taking Liberty*, 96, 177–79.

19. Aguila, *Taking Liberty*, 29, 38, 171, 178, 192, 210.

20. Aguila, *Taking Liberty*, 42, 126, 129, 130, 144, 149; Brooks, *Best Editorial Cartoons, 1982*, 18.

21. Draper Hill, *Political Asylum: Editorial Cartoons by Draper Hill* (Windsor, Ont., 1985), 48–49; Aguila, *Taking Liberty*, 91, 102, 119, 141, 149, 227.

22. Pat Oliphant, *The Year of Living Dangerously: More Cartoons by Pat Oliphant* (Fairway, Kansas, 1984), 113; Carew Papritz and Russ Tremayne, eds., *Reagancomics: A Cornucopia of Cartoons on Ronald Reagan* (Auburn, Wash., 1984), 93; Aguila, *Taking Liberty*, 32, 110, 136, 201; Brooks, *Best Editorial Cartoons, 1980*, 62, 116; *Time*, March 17, 1986, 36; *Minneapolis Star–Tribune*, March 2, 1990.

23. Aguila, *Taking Liberty*, 30, 35–52; Paul Szep, *The Harder They Fall* (Boston, 1975), 53; Doug Marlette, *"It's a Dirty Job . . . But Somebody Has to Do It"* (Charlotte, N.C., 1984), 90; *Minneapolis Star–Tribune*, May 29, 1992.

24. Herbert Block, *Herblock Special Report* (New York, 1974), 15; Press, *The Political Cartoon*, 23; Aguila, *Taking Liberty*, 25, 28, 86–88, 104, 113, 115–20, 158, 164, 173, 175; Westin, *Getting Angry*, 110; Hy Rosen, *"Do They Tell You What to Draw?"* (Albany, N.Y., 1980), 80; Ben Sargent, *Big Brother Blues: The Editorial Cartoons of Ben Sargent* (Austin, Texas, 1984), 103.

25. Herbert Block, *Herblock Through the Looking Glass: The Reagan Years in Words and*

Pictures (New York, 1984), 22; Aguila, *Taking Liberty*, 135; *Minneapolis Star–Tribune*, December 13, 1989, December 29, 1989.

CHAPTER VIII: THE "MONUMENTAL LINCOLN"

This chapter was published originally in *Inks: Cartoon and Comic Art Studies*, II:1 (February 1995), and is reprinted with the permission of the Ohio State University Press.

1. *Chicago Sun-Times*, November 23, 1963; *Newsweek*, July 20, 1964, 5A–5B. Mauldin's original was requested by Jacqueline Kennedy and now graces the John F. Kennedy Library at Harvard. Interestingly, Mauldin was a fan of neither Kennedy nor this cartoon. He thought the drawing a failure because he had botched the Lincoln hairline. On JFK, he later confided to an interviewer for *Rolling Stone* in 1976: "You know, I never was one of those Kennedy suckers. . . . I went to Berlin with Kennedy in 1963. That was when he stood in the square and said 'Ich bin ein Berliner.' I puked. Soured on Kennedy right after that speech. . . . The fucker was inciting them and he knew it." See *Rolling Stone*, November 4, 1976, 58.

2. Raymond B. Rajski, ed., *A Nation Grieved: The Kennedy Assassination in Editorial Cartoons* (Rutland, Vt., 1967), 37–41, 107.

3. For a succinct history of the Lincoln Memorial and its place in the American popular imagination, see Merrill D. Peterson, *Lincoln in American Memory* (New York, 1994), 214–17, 277–78.

4. Stephen Hess and Milton Kaplan, *The Ungentlemanly Art: A History of American Political Cartoons* (New York, 1968), 85–91; Albert Shaw, *Abraham Lincoln* (New York, 1930), 37–270; and Alton Ketchum, *Uncle Sam: The Man and the Legend* (New York, 1959), 80–86. I find Ketchum's hypothesis improbable. Uncle Sam's predecessor Brother Jonathan had been portrayed bearded in *Punch* cartoons long before Lincoln sprouted chin whiskers. Moreover, the caricatured Lincoln was much less fair of feature than the quintessential Yankee trader Uncle Sam and, in *Punch* and other anti-Lincoln British publications, much less worthy of humane virtue than characterizations befitting a generic representation of the American nation.

5. David Donald, *Lincoln Reconsidered: Essays on the Civil War Era*, rev. ed. (New York, 1961), 60.

6. *Harper's Weekly*, November 7, 1868. For a cogent analysis, see Mark E. Neely, Jr., "Wilkes Booth the Second," *Lincoln Lore* (Louis A. Warren Lincoln Library and Museum, Fort Wayne, Ind.), 1752 (February 1984), 1–2. Ironically, Nast had not always been an admirer of the living Lincoln, drawing him on occasion as more simian than human before victory was nearly inevitable, and Lincoln had stroked the ego of the young *Harper's* artist by proclaiming him the Union's premier recruiting sergeant!

7. Donald, *Lincoln Reconsidered*, 144–66; Harold Holzer, Gabor S. Boritt, and Mark E. Neely, Jr., *The Lincoln Image: Abraham Lincoln and the Popular Print* (New York, 1984), 149–216; Peterson, *Lincoln in American Memory*, 3–35.

8. Lawrence J. Friedman, *Inventors of the Promised Land* (New York, 1975), 44–78; John Kingston, *The Life of General George Washington* (Baltimore, Md., 1813), 147; *Richmond Enquirer*, July 23, 1822.

9. Donald, *Lincoln Reconsidered*, 14.

10. *Puck*, June 22, 1881, 267; July 9, 1884, 296–97; *Judge*, December 21, 1889, 169; June 28, 1884, 16.

11. *Judge*, May 30, 1885, 16; July 2, 1887, 8–9.

12. *Judge*, October 5, 1889, 410; May 31, 1890, 122–23; July 19, 1890, 236–37; October 11, 1890, 8–9; September 19, 1896, 184–85; *Puck*, October 28, 1896, 8–9.

13. *Puck*, October 23, 1895, 152–53; *Judge*, October 3, 1895, 8–9; April 2, 1898, 211; January 14, 1899, 17.

14. David Donald, "Getting Right With Lincoln," *Harper's Magazine*, CII (April 1951), 74–80; reprinted in *Lincoln Reconsidered*, 3–18.

15. *Puck*, October 28, 1885, 136–37; July 20, 1887, 340–41; October 19, 1887, 124–25; January 14, 1891, 356–57.

16. *Judge*, January 28, 1888, 1; October 27, 1888, 50; October 3, 1896, 216–17; September 22, 1900, 1.

17. Art Young, *The Best of Art Young* (New York, 1936), 154.

18. *Collier's Weekly*, February 12, 1921, 17, and February 10, 1923, 17; Franklin Meine, ed., *John McCutcheon's Book* (Chicago, 1948), 239, 267; Hess and Kaplan, *Ungentlemanly Art*, 133.

19. Daniel R. Fitzpatrick, *As I Saw It* (New York, 1953), 4–5, 90; *Baltimore Sun*, February 10, 1949; February 13, 1951.

20. *Baltimore Sun*, June 20, 1964 and July 2, 1964; *Washington Post*, July 14, 1964; Brooks, ed., *Best Editorial Cartoons, 1975*, 17, 24.

21. Press, *The Political Cartoon*, 210–12.

22. Reprinted in *Duluth News-Tribune*, April 18, 1990.

23. *Providence Evening Bulletin*, September 10, 1980; Pat Oliphant, *Ban This Book!* (Kansas City, 1982), 102; *Rocky Mountain News* (Denver), July 8, 1986; Steve Benson, *Fencin' with Benson* (Phoenix, Ariz., 1984), 68; *Portland Oregonian*, February 24, 1985; Brooks, ed., *Best Editorial Cartoons 1989*, 48; *Duluth News-Tribune*, November 3, 1990.

24. (New York) *Newsday*, May 4, 1991; Gannett Westchester Newspapers, April 3, 1991; *Portland Oregonian*, September 5, 1991; *Providence Journal–Bulletin*, September 12, 1992; *Dallas Morning News*, February 20, 1993.

25. This cartoon was drawn June 20, 1993, but never published because more pressing events decreed a substitute.

CHAPTER IX: THE LUCIFER LEGACY

An early version of this chapter appeared as "The Lucifer Legacy: Boss Tweed and Richard Nixon as Generic Sleaze Symbols in Cartoon Art," *Journal of American Culture*, 13:2 (Summer 1990), 1–19, and is reprinted with permission of the American Culture Association.

1. Hess and Kaplan, *The Ungentlemanly Art*, 51, 56, 206.

2. Keller, *Art and Politics of Nast*, 66, 96–97, 131, 261, 267; *Judge*, September 26, 1896, 200–01; October 17, 1896, 241; July 7, 1900, 8–9; July 14, 1900, 8–9; September 15, 1900, 1.

3. For good examples, see *Puck*, August 22, 1877, 1; May 17, 1882, 163; September 17, 1884, 48; December 2, 1885, 216–17; March 7, 1888, 26–27; and *Judge*, November 1, 1890, 64; June 19, 1895, 280–81.

4. For an informative study of the tattooed-man series, see Samuel J. Thomas, "The Tattooed Man Caricatures and the Presidential Campaign of 1884," *Journal of American*

Culture, 10 (Winter 1987), 1–20. A fine analysis of Blaine's character and reputation may be found in Morgan, *From Hayes to McKinley*, 65–70.

5. Keller, *Art and Politics of Nast*, 177–215; Leonard, *Power of the Press*, 97–131, 240–44; Hershkowitz, *Tweed's New York*, xii–xix, 149–163, 167–346.

6. *Judge*, July 12, 1884, 8–9; October 11, 1884, 16.

7. *Judge*, December 10, 1881, 1; March 15, 1884, 8–9; *Puck*, January 30, 1884, 337.

8. *Judge*, April 1, 1882, 8–9; April 8, 1882, 8–9; September 28, 1889, 408; *Puck*, August 18, 1886, 392–93; August 25, 1886, 416.

9. *Judge*, September 4, 1886, 16; December 19, 1891, 635.

10. *New York Journal and Advertiser*, April 22, 1897; April 25, 1897; Conrad, *Pro and Conrad*, 42; *Detroit News*, February 17, 1987; January 21, 1993.

11. *Duluth News–Tribune*, April 28, 1994.

12. *Newsweek*, October 13, 1980, 83; *Detroit News*, April 25, 1994. An indication of the inspired quality in Nixon cartooning may be deduced from two superb anthologies, Peters, *The Nixon Chronicles*, and Herbert Block, *Nixon Special Report* (New York, 1974).

13. Ed Stein to author, September 13, 1988; *St. Paul Dispatch*, May 29, 1980; *Minneapolis Star & Tribune*, August 9, 1984; Oliphant, *Ban This Book*, 168.

14. *Minneapolis Star–Tribune*, April 9, 1984; October 18, 1985; November 19, 1985; April 12, 1990; July 22, 1990; March 15, 1992, June 21, 1992; November 22, 1992; *Detroit News*, July 23, 1990; *Duluth News–Tribune*, March 21, 1992.

15. *St. Paul Dispatch*, January 30, 1975; Brooks, *Best Editorial Cartoons, 1981* 39; Pat Oliphant, *The Jellybean Society* (Kansas City, MO, 1981), 60, 64; *Minneapolis Star–Tribune*, December 18, 1987; *Newsweek*, December 28, 1987.

16. Marlette, *Drawing Blood*, 73; Oliphant, *Jellybean Society*, 20; *Duluth News–Tribune & Herald*, July 19, 1983; *Minneapolis Star–Tribune*, February 27, 1985.

17. *Newsweek*, March 9, 1987; *Duluth News–Tribune & Herald*, May 23, 1987; *Minneapolis Star–Tribune*, February 5, 1987; Doug Marlette, *Shred This Book!: The Scandalous Cartoons of Doug Marlette* (Atlanta, 1988), 158.

18. *Detroit News*, September 18, 1988; *Minneapolis Star–Tribune*, November 6, 1989; June 3, 1991; March 10, 1993; *Duluth News–Tribune*, May 23, 1992; January 18, 1994.

19. *Newsweek*, March 27, 1988; February 14, 1994, 17; March 21, 1994, 27; *Detroit News*, June 13, 1988; August 3, 1988; *Duluth News–Tribune & Herald*, October 29, 1988; March 22, 1990; *Heterodoxy*, March, 1994, 3.

20. *Newsweek*, May 2, 1994, 19; May 9, 1994, 15; *Detroit News*, April 27, 1994.

Essay on Sources

An exploration of American political cartooning should begin with three sources rich in primary thought. Thomas C. Leonard, *The Power of the Press: The Birth of American Political Reporting* (New York: Oxford University Press, 1986)—in particular his fourth chapter, "Visual Thinking: The Tammany Tiger Loose"—superbly establishes a context for the medium as journalism and political propaganda. Charles Press, *The Political Cartoon* (Rutherford, N.J.: Fairleigh Dickinson University Press, 1981) is a difficult read and often argumentative, but intellectually impressive in analysis and generally persuasive. *Target: The Political Cartoon Quarterly*, 1–24 (1981–86) consistently provided its readers with cogent insights into the medium from scholars and leading cartoonists. Back issues may be obtained from Richard S. West, 151 Crescent Street, Northampton, Mass. 01060.

A sprightly and informative but somewhat superficial historical overview is Stephen Hess and Milton Kaplan, *The Ungentlemanly Art: A History of American Political Cartoons* (New York: Macmillan, 1968). Alan Westin, ed., *Getting Angry Six Times a Week: A Portfolio of Political Cartoonists* (Boston: The Beacon Press, 1979) is an informative and entertaining collection of interview essays on such artists as Paul Conrad, Hugh Haynie, and Doug Marlette. Gerald W. Johnson, *The Lines Are Drawn: American Life Since the First World War as Reflected in the Pulitzer Prize Cartoons* (Philadelphia: J.B. Lippincott, 1958) features cogent commentary on the medium.

Biography should comprise the basis of rewarding reading on so personal a profession, but incisive biographies of eminent American political cartoonists are rare. Richard S. West, *The Political Cartoons of Joseph Keppler* (Urbana, Ill.: University of Illinois Press, 1988) is superb in every respect save Gilded Age political analysis. The immortal Nast has not fared so well, although Morton Keller, *The Art and Politics of Thomas Nast* (New York: Oxford University Press, 1968) combines a representative portfolio of Nast's more memorable *Harper's Weekly* work with generally perceptive commentary. Useful primarily for its excellent illustrations is J. Chal Vinson, *Thomas Nast: Political Cartoonist* (Athens, Ga.: University of Georgia Press, 1967). Albert Bigelow Paine, *Thomas Nast, His Period and His Pictures* (New York: Macmillan, 1904), informed by lengthy conversations between the elderly artist and his naive young biographer, is useful mainly for Nast's crowning invention, himself. Draper Hill's pending biography of Nast is crucial to the history of the medium and its pioneer genius. Anthologies in print, usually strong on art and weak on biography and analytical criticism, exist for such eminent cartoonists as John McCutcheon, Jay N. "Ding" Darling, Daniel Fitzpatrick, Herbert Block, Bill Mauldin, Paul Conrad, Pat Oliphant, Don Wright, Mike Peters, Doug Marlette, Paul Szep, and Steve Benson. Especially insightful are the myriad Herblock volumes, which feature commentary on artistic and political intent as well as the cartoons inspired.

Worthy topical studies of American political cartooning are more numerous. Albert Shaw, *A Cartoon History of Roosevelt's Career* (New York: Macmillan, 1910) and *Abraham Lincoln: His Path to the Presidency* (New York: Review of Reviews, 1930) usefully blend historical narrative and cartoon art on our two greatest Republican presidents, as does James N. Giglio and Greg G. Thielen, *Truman in Cartoon and Caricature* (Ames, Iowa: Uowa State University Press, 1984). Harold Holzer, Gabor S. Boritt, and Mark E. Neely, Jr., *The Lincoln Image: Abraham Lincoln and the Popular Print* (New York: Oxford University Press, 1983) offers informative insights on Lincoln cartoons within a larger graphic context. Merrill D. Peterson, *Lincoln in American Memory* (New York: Oxford University Press, 1994) provides a cogent context essential to understanding the mythic Lincoln in posthumous cartoons. For other symbols central to American political cartooning, see Alton Ketchum, *Uncle Sam: The Man and the Legend* (New York: Hill and Wang, 1959) and Dani Aguila, comp., *Taking Liberty with the Lady* (Nashville: Eaglenest Publishing Co., 1986).

On persecuted minorities, Gary L. Bunker and Davis Bitton, *The*

Mormon Graphic Image, 1834–1914 (Salt Lake City: University of Utah Press, 1983) is stellar, as is L. Perry Curtis, Jr., *Apes and Angels: The Irishman in Victorian Caricature* (Washington: The Smithsonian Institution Press, 1971). John J. Appel, "From Shanties to Lace Curtains: The Irish Image in Puck, 1876–1910," *Comparative Studies in Sociology and History*, 13:4 (October 1971), suffocates in smug condescension. Appel, "Jews in American Caricature, 1820–1914," *American Jewish History*, 71 (September 1981) and Rudolf Glanz, *The Jew in Early American Wit and Graphic Humor* (New York: KTAV Publishing House, 1973) are both informative but ethically ambivalent on the intent and effect of anti-Semitic cartooning. A recommended corrective is Michael N. Dobkowski, *The Tarnished Dream: The Basis of American Anti-Semitism* (Westport, Conn: Greenwood Press, 1979), as judicious in analysis as it is intolerant of intolerance. No comparable studies exist on the cartooning of blacks and American Indians, although solid foundations are established in such broader studies as Joseph Boskin, *Sambo: The Rise and Demise of an American Jester* (New York: Oxford University Press, 1986), and Robert F. Berkhofer, Jr., *The White Man's Indian: Images of the American Indian from Columbus to the Present* (New York: A. A. Knopf, 1978).

Index

Due to the overwhelming number of newspapers that are mentioned in the text, they have not been included in this index.